THE INFORMAL ECONOMY IN FRANCE

To Colin

The Informal Economy in France

JAN WINDEBANK
University of Sheffield

Avebury

Aldershot · Brookfield USA · Hong Kong · Singapore · Sydney

Published by
Avebury
The Academic Publishing Group
Gower House
Croft Road
Aldershot
Hants GU11 3HR
England

Gower Publishing Company
Old Post Road
Brookfield
Vermont 05036
USA

A CIP catalogue record for this book is available from the British Library.

ISBN 1 85628 191 4

Contents

PART 3: LESSONS TO BE LEARNT FROM THE FRENCH DEBATES

Tables

1 Introduction: Definitions and modes of analysis

The 'informal economy', encompassing such diverse activities as women's domestic labour, D.I.Y., voluntary work and black market work, has been attracting the attention of academics, intellectuals and politicians in France for the past twenty years. Portrayed simultaneously as the enemy of women's emancipation, a rival to the formal economy, a saviour of the unemployed or indeed a model for a new socialist organization of work, the informal economy has been all things to all people. Marxists, feminists, ecologists, neoclassicicists and right wing intellectuals have all put forward their hypotheses, critiques and predictions concerning this 'hidden' sphere of economic life. Furthermore, a number of sociologists, economists and anthropologists have empirically investigated informal economic activity. What all these theorists have in common, however, is that their analyses and propositions swim against the tide, which flows through academic literature and political discourse alike, of defining economic activity as purely that which directly contributes to the G.D.P. and 'work' as purely employment.

This book aims to discover not only the characteristics of the informal economy as it exists in France but also the nature of the informal economy debates as they have been played out in the cultural context of the French language. French ideas and research findings on the informal economy which have not as yet been available to an English-speaking readership will be presented. Furthermore, those studies which have been available in English will be situated in their wider context. Nonetheless, the fact of studying the 'French' debates on the informal economy should not lead one to look solely for their specificity. France shares cultural, economic, political and social characteristics with other Western countries which surpass national boundaries. Thus, the French debates on the informal economy can and indeed must also be viewed as an example of those debates which have taken and are taking place more generally.

These explorations are structured according to the three principal tasks which the book sets itself. These are: first, to discover what led to the concept of the 'informal economy' taking shape in the early 'Seventies in France; second, to identify what is known about this most elusive of economic sectors and to illuminate the major issues at stake between the protagonists in the French debates; and finally, to explore the impact exerted by the concept of the 'informal economy' on traditional definitions of 'work' which equate it solely with employment. In this Introduction, the ground will be laid for these discussions, first by developing a working definition of the informal economy and its constituent parts and second, by outlining the mode of analysis employed in the study.

Defining the 'informal economy'

What exactly is the 'informal economy'? This question by no means invites a straightforward answer. Indeed, as the discussion of the various approaches to the informal economy in France unfolds, it will become evident that its definition depends very much on one's theoretical convictions. Consequently, it will only be possible to develop a working definition of the informal economy at this stage. First and foremost, it must be noted that the informal economy cannot under any circumstances be defined in terms of a simple list of tasks. It is the social relations under which activities are carried out which differentiate those belonging to the informal economy from other categories of activity. This concurs with Brown's method for defining 'work', for example. Brown (1984, p. 262) observes that 'work cannot be defined solely in terms of the activities to which it refers, but must also include reference to the purposes for which and the context within which such activities are performed'. To clarify this point, let us take the example of the observable task of looking after a baby. By describing it in these words, one gives the impression that the task is part of the domestic economy: in other words, that it is unpaid work carried out within the household. However, this same activity expressed as child minding becomes a form of employment: it is paid and recognized by the State. When expressed as baby-sitting, the nature of the activity changes again, implying either some kind of casual, undeclared paid work, or a reciprocal arrangement of exchange of services between friends.

What, then, are the social relations in which an activity must be performed in order to be designated as part of the informal economy? First, it must be stressed that the informal economy is normally defined in terms of what it is not rather than what it is. More specifically, it is usually described with reference to its divergence from the norms of the 'formal' economy. The first stage in this process of definition must therefore be to describe the social relations which pertain to formal economic activity. Simply put, and for our present purposes, the formal economy can be defined as the sum of all the activities which are recognized and regulated by the State and contractual law for tax and social security purposes. Consequently, if the 'formal' economy embraces those activities which are recognized and regulated by the State, then the 'informal' economy encompasses those 'productive' or 'work' activities which are hidden from, or ignored by the State. Indeed, the social relationship of the status of an activity vis à vis State institutions is the only criterion which differentiates all types of informal economic activities from those of the formal economy. This working definition of informal economic activity agrees with those given by a number of French researchers. For example, Sachs (1983, p. 1) describes his 'économie cachée' (hidden economy) as 'all that the national accounts do not include, either for conceptual reasons, or because the figures are hidden from them'.

This method of defining the informal in contrast to the formal economy is perhaps in some ways arbitrary. However, it has the advantage as a working definition of being objective in the sense that it is not open to excessive interpretation: an activity is either registered by the State or it is not. Nonetheless, such a definition does nothing to illuminate the distinction between informal economic activity and leisure. As will be seen, this difference cannot be taken for granted. Indeed, making the distinction between informal work and leisure is one of the principal conceptual problems faced by those studying the subject. That said, I will not attempt to overcome this dilemma here and now since one of the central themes of the book is to discuss the ways in which individual theorists have dealt with this problem in their definitions of 'work'.

The criterion of recognition by or visibility to the State is the general boundary which delimits the scope of the informal economy (on its frontier with formal production at least). However, within the category of the 'informal economy', there are further sub-sets of activity which differ radically from one another. These are: first, black market work; second, domestic and community work; third, voluntary work; and finally, autonomous work. These categories reflect both the preoccupations of those who study the informal economy in France and the objective differences between these various kinds of work. These differences rest on the following criteria: namely, first, whether or not the activity entails a mediated relationship between producer and consumer; second, whether or not it gives rise to exchange values or State transfers; and lastly, whether or not it is performed within hierarchical and functional specialisms.

First, I will examine the question of black market work. The official French government definition of 'le travail noir' (black market work), according to the law of 11th July 1972 (Klatzmann, 1979, p. 46), is the following:

> the undertaking for payment of an activity of production, transformation, repair or service provision, subject to inclusion in the trades registry, by persons who are not included in the above mentioned registry and who have not satisfied the fiscal and social obligations related to that activity.

Thus, black market work is an activity which is paid and which should be declared to the State for social security and tax purposes, but is not. It is legal, however, in every other way which differentiates it from criminal activities per se. As Barthelemy (1982, p. 25) points out, such work should be differentiated from the more all embracing term 'l'économie souterraine' (underground economy) which includes illegal activities, such as drug trafficking, which are not usually included in discussions of the informal economy.

However, one must further distinguish between two types of black market work which differ from formal employment to varying degrees. In the words of the 'Conseil Economique et Social' (1983), there is a significant difference between, on the one hand, undeclared market exchanges between individuals and on the other, undeclared employment instituted by companies. For the most part, this second type of black market work only differs from formal employment on the grounds of it being undeclared since the worker is still selling time for a wage, has no control of the work process, is locked in a system of hierarchical and functional specialism and is involved in an anonymous and mediated relationship with the consumer. It is the first type of black market work which varies most from formal employment. The 'Conseil Economique et Social' (1983, p. 13) says of it

> This activity stands at the crossroads of two sectors: one represented by market employment, declared for tax and social security purposes, the other by non market productive work destined for immediate consumption which includes self help, domestic work, D.I.Y. or occassional paid work for individuals.

It is clear, therefore, that this type of black market work radically diverges from formal employment on the grounds that the producer has power over the work process and that it is not hierarchically organized despite being perhaps functionally specialized. Such black market work can either resemble 'artisanal' work (that is, when it is for a clientele of strangers) or it can be casual work performed for friends and relatives. This kind of black market work is obviously carried out for financial gain. However, the importance of this aspect of the activity to the black market worker him or herself is a point which is hotly debated between theorists.

The second category of activity which goes to make up the informal economy is that of domestic and community work, these being very similar on a number of counts as will be seen. Domestic work is the unpaid work carried out by household members for themselves and each other. This is referred to, for example, by Gaudin & Schiray (1982, p. 3) as 'l'économie domestique' (the domestic economy) which 'covers the totality of economic activities undertaken outside the market within households'. Other terms for such work include 'la production domestique' (domestic production), 'le travail domestique' (domestic work), 'le travail ménager' (housework) or 'les activités ménagères' (housework activities) as well as 'l'autoproduction' (self provisioning). The concepts of 'housework' or 'domestic work' and 'domestic production' are usually taken in the literature to be synonymous with the routine chores associated with women's work. However, one term - 'self provisioning' - always embraces all unpaid domestic work, including D.I.Y., gardening, car repairs and the like. In contrast to 'domestic work', for example, the concept of 'self provisioning' carries with it distinctly positive connotations.

In similarity to domestic work, community work is unpaid, but in contrast, it is performed for people other than household members but who nevertheless belong to a well defined social network. This network could be based on the extended family (including friends), the neighbourhood, on cultural, local or regional identities, on religious affinity or on professional relationships. Furthermore, it is work undertaken outside the realms of an organization (in contrast to voluntary work). As Gaudin & Schiray (1982, p. 3-4) explain, 'the community economy is the production of goods and services and the circuit of generally non monetary exchanges between groups of individuals integrated in different social and community networks which are not institutionalized'. Returning to the example of looking after children, baby-sitting circles between friends could be termed community work as could shopping, or maybe carrying out household repairs for elderly neighbours.

The similarities between domestic and community work are manifest. Neither engender monetary rewards, so neither is recognized by the State for tax or social security purposes. Both occur 'spontaneously', that is, outside the realms of any kind of organization. The consumers of such work always have a non utilitarian relationship to its producers and since neither form of work creates visible exchange values, neither is part of the market (although that does not mean that the domestic and community economies necessarily operate independently of it). Taken together, they can be compared with Yona Friedman's (1982, p. 89) 'secteur quaternaire' (quaternary sector) which encompasses 'that part of the population designated as 'inactive' but which produces socially useful goods which are not taken into account in calculations of the G.D.P. and which are indispensible despite not giving rise to any monetary income'.

It must be stressed that the criterion which distinguishes these two types of work from one another is that of whether or not the beneficiary of the activity is a household member. This is not the same as asking whether or not the work is carried out within the geographical space of the 'home'. Domestic work is unpaid and carried out for family members - it could therefore take place outside the bricks and mortar structure of the 'house'. Shopping for the family would be the most obvious illustration of this point. Conversely, work can be carried out within the physical space of the home which is not for household members. It could be community, voluntary or black market work, or even employment. It should be noted in this context that the term 'le travail à domicile' is used to mean employment performed within the home - homeworking, or outworking in English.

Third, there is voluntary work. The definition of voluntary work which has been established by the 'Centre d'études et d'information sur le volontariat' (1985, p. 9) lays down five conditions which set voluntary work apart from other types of activity: that 'the volunteer commits him or herself; of his or her own free will; without seeking reward; in an organized action; in the service of the community'. Therefore, this is work carried out within the realms of an organization, usually for anonymous recipients. In similarity to the categories of domestic and community work, voluntary work is neither paid, nor gives rise to exchange values, so it is not recognized by the State for tax purposes. However, often being performed within large organizations, voluntary work is liable to be constrained by hierarchical and functional specialisms. Furthermore, the relationship between producer and consumer is not necessarily closer within the realms of the voluntary sector than within the social relations of employment. The relative importance of voluntary work in terms of the attention it receives as a phenomenon in its own right is minimal in comparison with the former two categories of black market and domestic and community work. However, on any logical criteria, it cannot be left aside when discussing the informal economy.

Unlike the previous three categories, the last, that of autonomous work, does not refer to a type of activity which actually exists at present. In other words, it is not an empirically observable category of activity. Rather, it is a conceptual category which is bound up with utopian visions of the possibilities for work in the future. However, the theorists who discuss this concept are central to the debates surrounding the informal economy, particularly in France. Although no strict definition of autonomous work can be made, it is possible to say that it covers visions of a type of work in the future over which the producer will have a large degree of control, which will take place within the family or community, and in which creativity and conviviality will be the driving forces. One must include here the 'travail autonome' (autonomous work) of Gorz (1985); the 'travail libre' (liberated work) of ADRET (1977); and the 'secteur convivial' (convivial sector) of Amado & Stoffaes (1980), to name but a few examples.

With this working definition of the informal economy in hand, I will now discuss the analytical procedure which will be employed in order to understand both the nature of the informal economy and the issues at stake in this field of inquiry in France.

Modes of analysis

To recap briefly, the principal aims of this study are first, to explain the rise of interest in the informal economy over the last twenty years in France; second, to map and explore the multiplicity of approaches to and theories of the informal economy which have been produced by French researchers and intellectuals; and finally, to discuss the impact exerted on traditional conceptions of work by the informal economy debates. Before launching into the discussion of these questions, however, it is necessary to outline the analytical procedures to be employed in order to fulfil these objectives, beginning with the explanation of why interest in the informal economy developed in France in the 'Seventies.

Over time, the 'pool' of phenomena which are accepted as worthy of academic and intellectual interest and the concepts which are used to describe and categorize them change according to social, economic, political and ideological circumstances. In other words, this socio-economic and politico-ideological 'environment' sets limits on the range of subjects which it is permissible to study and the gamut of explanations of reality which are held to be acceptable at any given moment. Since this environment evolves continuously, gradual and constant shifts take place in the range of options available to theorists both in terms of what to study and how to study it. Working on this assumption, I will examine how the social, economic, political and ideological environment has developed over the past twenty years in France to allow activities which we previously considered to lie outside the realms of the 'economy' to be included in it under the umbrella of the informal sector.

Furthermore, it must be stressed that this environment evolves not least as a consequence of the impact of intellectual production itself. The development of debates on a subject must therefore been seen not as a one way street in which theorists' choices are determined by their surroundings, but as a complex and interactive process between the researcher and the wider society. Theorists are not islands: they are influenced by, and influence not only their subject matter, but also the political spectrum of a given time or place as well as the attitudes to be found amongst the wider public. In the conclusions to this book, I will therefore be addressing the question of the extent to which these debates on the informal economy have had an effect on political and public attitudes towards 'work' in France.

The second task which the book sets itself is to chart in a systematic and clear manner the numerous and competing approaches to the study of the informal economy which are to be found in France. The first stage in this process consists of identifying and clustering together groups of like minded theorists. The criteria applied in creating these groupings are the following: first, the specific question which a theorist chooses to study within the broad area of the informal economy is taken into account (in other words, his or her choice of focus); second, the method of study which a theorist adopts is considered (that is, his or her choice of method); and finally, the theoretical explanations which a theorist offers for the situations which he or she observes are examined (that is, his or her choice of explanation).

First, then, let us consider the criterion of 'choice of focus'. All the theorists to be included in this study have made a similar choice in the sense that they all examine the informal economy. There are nonetheless differences between them in that each focuses more particularly on one of two topics. These are first, 'the household division of labour' and second, 'the role of the informal economy in the future of work'. Those who focus on the 'household division of labour' analyse both the gender divisions which result from men working in the market and women in the home as well as the sharing out of domestic tasks between household members. Those who focus on the second topic of the 'role of the informal economy in the future of work' discuss whether the pattern of full time, lifelong employment can survive in the wake of the cultural, economic and social crises which crystallized in the late 'Sixties and early 'Seventies. Subsequently, they examine what part the informal economy could play in the relief of related problems such as unemployment, or indeed, in developing more convivial ways of working. It will be seen that the choice of focus on one or other of these topics correlates to some extent with the way in which theorists choose to explain the mechanisms at work in the social world. As Brown (1984, p. 263) explains, the definition of what is problematic and in need of explanation is often linked to assumptions concerning causation.

The second criterion used to differentiate approaches from one another is that of 'choice of method'. In making this choice, theorists are presented with two general options. The first is to analyse social phenomena by the application of universal theories whilst the second option is to approach one's research subject in a more empirical and inductivist fashion. Those theorists choosing the first option tend, therefore, to work within a general theory of how society operates. This furnishes them with a universal framework into which they may fit particular activities, issues, relationships or problems - in this case, those pertaining to the informal economy. Specific cases are thus analysed in terms of the way in which the are weaved into the wider social and economic canvas.

Researchers who choose the second empirical and inductivist option tend either to concentrate on revealing the correlations which exist between certain, specific variables or to content themselves with a simple description - statistical or qualitative - of a given situation. In the case of the informal economy, researchers who follow this empirical path favour either the examination of the everyday practices of people engaging in informal work, or the evaluation of the amount of such work which is carried out by various groups. It is true to say that these empirical and inductivist theorists avoid the deeper questions concerning the underlying causes of social and economic phenomena addressed by those who favour a more universalist and theoretical approach. Nonetheless, they are of no less value or interest for that. Indeed, as we shall see, it is only by assessing the universalist theories against these empirical studies and vice versa that we can gain a balanced picture of the place of informal economic activities in society and the economy.

After choosing a focus and a method, the next problem, especially for universalist theorists (but also, to a lesser extent, for empirical theorists), is to choose between competing explanations of how society is organized, of individuals' behaviour and actions and ultimately, of the relationship between society and the individual. These competing explanations spring ultimately from the debate between individualism and structuralism as frameworks for understanding the underlying mechanisms at work in society. At one extreme, individualist theorists view society as the outcome of the interaction of individuals who are engaged in making a series of rational choices under certain constraints. At the other extreme, structuralist theorists envisage society in terms of conflicting social groups, the existence and relative power of which rests on and characterizes a particular social structure. Furthermore, within many structuralist theories, oppression is a determining force in the nature of society. Oppression stems from power exercised by men over women, classes over one another, the State and technocrats over civil society, Humankind over Nature, or a combination of all or some of these.

When these three criteria of choice of focus, method and explanation are applied to the field of study of the informal economy in France, six clusters of theorists emerge. Those who study the 'household division of labour' are divided into three clusters: the Empiricists; the Microeconomists (who adopt a universalist and individualist approach); and the Feminists (who take a universalist and structuralist stance). Amongst those who focus on the 'role of the informal economy in the future of work', there are also three clusters of approaches: the Empiricists, once again; the Free Market Dualists (who are universalist and individualist in orientation); and the Radicals (who analyse the informal economy from a universalist and structuralist point of view).

After having presented the arguments and findings of these various clusters of theorists, it will be necessary to evaluate their respective contributions to our understanding of the informal economy. The means adopted in order to undertake this evaluation rest on the following methodological and theoretical premises. It is argued here that all interpretations of reality pass through a screen or filter of values, political and ideological affiliations and theoretical convictions. These can be termed 'perspectives'. This is a concept developed by Lukes (1982, p. 301) who describes a 'perspective' as a more or less closely related set of beliefs, attitudes and assumptions about social reality, the possibilities and responsibilities of living in society as well as the relationship between the individual and society. Thus, it can be said that the conclusions reached on the informal economy by theorists are the result of the interaction of their individual 'perspectives' with the reality which they have been charged to examine. Hence, this book argues that 'knowledge' of the informal economy can exist in diverse forms without one theory or set of results necessarily being right and the others wrong. Consequently, in evaluating the contribution to our knowledge of the informal economy made by these French studies, the aim will not be to single out the most appropriate or truthful. Rather, it will be to compare and contrast the assumptions, theoretical premises and empirical findings of these six clusters of theorists to one another. In this way, the issues over which consensus has developed as well as those around which ideological conflict continues to rage will be unravelled.

The third and final strand of analysis which goes to make

up the present study concerns the extent to which the development of the concept of the 'informal economy' has challenged the traditional conception of work which equates it with formal employment only, using the French debates as an example. This is an important question since the concept of what can be deemed 'work' is central to social and economic theory and to political ideologies alike: 'work' is said to be the activity which determines our social consciousness and which produces wealth. Furthermore, 'work' is a major source of conflict between politicians and intellectuals alike who argue about its form, content, organization and the distribution of its fruits. The very fact of studying the informal economy undermines the centrality of formal employment both to social, economic and political theory and in our everyday lives. I will be exploring this question in detail, examining the particular aspects of the traditional concept of work which certain groups of theorists challenge in their deliberations over the informal economy.

There are three major aspects of this traditional concept of work which come under fire. First, there is the question of what constitutes 'economic' or 'productive' activity. In both neoclassical and Marxist terminology, activity which is sold for a wage is 'productive', and as such can be deemed 'work' as opposed to consumption or leisure. What, then, is the status of unpaid work? Or black market work? How do the theorists of the informal economy challenge the notion of what is 'economic activity'? Second, the traditional concept of work as employment fits easily with the notion that work is an activity for deferred gratification, or, in other words, an effort which one would prefer someone else do but which reaps benefits in terms of the wage which it provides. The question needs to be asked of how the introduction of 'informal work' disrupts this conception, if indeed it does. Third, having a job, for most people, means going out to work. That is, work is assumed to be an activity which is carried out in the public domain which carries more social, economic and political weight than its private counterparts. But much informal economic activity is carried out in the private sphere. Is it thus really important and can it be equated with employment? Or, perhaps, does the revelation that 'work' is carried out in the private sphere have ramifications for the relative importance of the public and the private?

These, therefore, are the objectives of the study, the methodological suppositions on which it is based and the practical method that will be applied in order to fulfil these objectives. Part 1 will discuss 'the growth of the informal economy'. Not only will the circumstances which encouraged interest in the subject be discussed, but as a preface to this, the extent to which the volume of informal economic activity in France has undergone any dramatic rise in real terms over this period will be evaluated. Part 2 goes on to discuss the 'approaches to the study of the informal economy in France', presenting in detail the various approaches, their contributions, their assumptions and their definitions of 'work'. Part 3 will ask what are 'the lessons to be learnt from the French debates'. This section will draw together the threads of the previous discussions, concluding what we 'know' about the informal economy both 'in' France and 'from' France and asking whether the study of the informal economy has been the birthplace of a new concept of work.

PART 1
THE GROWTH OF THE INFORMAL ECONOMY IN FRANCE

2 The size of the informal economy in France: some statistical clues

Introduction

It is the responsibility of this chapter to provide some statistical clues concerning the volume of the various sorts of informal economic activity carried out in France. It is only possible to provide clues and not hard and fast answers simply because sufficient data for a detailed statistical assessment of the activities involved are not available. If one were investigating a branch of the formal labour market, for instance, one would have a full range of government statistics at one's fingertips with which to paint a complete picture of the object of study. Alas, this is not possible in the case of the informal economy since the very criterion which distinguishes informal from formal economic activity is its invisibility to the State and thus to national statistical indicators.

This means that the only source of statistical information on the informal economy available is a number of relatively isolated case studies and a series of macroeconomic 'guestimates'. Furthermore, as we have seen in developing a working definition of the informal economy, it is not a homogenous entity, but an umbrella concept covering a number of disparate types of activity. Consequently, it is not possible to give figures for the volume of informal activity carried out as a whole. Rather, black market work, domestic and community work and voluntary work have to be dealt with separately. Figures cannot be given for 'autonomous' work because this is a conceptual and not an empirical entity. I will begin with 'black market work'.

Black market work

The most important characteristic of black market work to bear in mind is that, unlike domestic and community work, it has an exchange value, even though this is hidden from the State. For that reason, most estimates of the amount of black market work carried out in Western economies are expressed in terms of percentage of Gross National Product (G.N.P.). This entails methods of calculation which are generally 'indirect' and involve pinpointing disparities in economic and especially financial indicators in order to track down those monetary transactions which are eluding the State. Consequently, the results of such calculations produce figures for the size of the underground economy in its entirety rather than for the amount of black market work in particular being performed. [1]

Amongst the most reliable figures of this type to have been produced are the following: Gutmann (1977) estimated that in the United States in 1976, the underground economy was worth 10.6 per cent of G.N.P.. Also in the US, Feige (1982) has asserted that in the same year, 1976, the underground economy was equivalent to between 13.2 and 21.7 per cent of G.N.P. and in 1978, between 25.5 and 33.1 per cent. Tanzi (1982), however, assessed its value in 1976 to be between 5.1 and 11.7 per cent of the G.N.P. of the countries of the Organization of European Cooperation and Development (O.E.C.D.). Thus, even taking the lowest figures into account, it is apparent that the underground economy is a significant economic phenomenon. That said, however, the considerable discrepancies between these figures, ranging as they do from one twentieth to one third of G.N.P., must not be overlooked since these discrepancies throw doubt on the validity of all these figures. Furthermore, the actual value of black market work remains an unknown quantity since it constitutes a hidden percentage of the activities of the underground economy as a whole.

These studies are widely quoted in France as indicative of the size of the French underground econony. However, in addition, a number of studies of black market work and the underground economy have been undertaken within France using both indirect methods, such as those above, and survey techniques. Once again, these paint a picture which is more confusing than enlightening because of the immense differences in their results. Working chronologically, in 1963 an 'Institut français de l'opinion publique' (IFOP) opinion poll estimated that twenty five per cent of the French population were taking part in black market work. In 1970, the 'Confédération de l'artisanat et des petites entreprises du bâtiment' (CAPEB) assessed the turnover of the black economy to be between five and seven billion francs. This represented a loss of 880 million francs in V.A.T. and a further loss of 1.8 billion francs in social security contributions. In 1971, the 'Conseil Economique et Social' estimated that salaries derived from black market work were equal to three per cent of the total mass of salaries. In Vitek's 1977 report for the 'Bureau International du Travail' (BIT), it was indicated that the number of black market workers in France could represent between three and five per cent of the total workforce. Some of the latest figures come from the 'Centre de documentation et de l'information de l'assurance' (CDIA) and are valid for 1985. This assessment estimates that some 800,000 people took part in an some kind of clandestine work during that year and received ten billion francs, cash-in-hand, in return without paying tax, V.A.T. or social security contributions.

The only conclusion which it is possible to draw from these disparate figures is that no one really knows how much black market work is being carried out in France, or elsewhere for that matter. Consequently, one cannot say whether the volume of black market work has increased or decreased over the past twenty years. This lack of precise knowledge only serves to increase the intensity of fear and suspicion of black market workers. As long as no hard and fast evidence exists, wild exaggerations of the amount of such work being performed and its growth rate retain the possibility of being taken seriously.

Domestic and community work

In contrast to black market work, neither domestic nor community work, being unpaid, has an exchange value. Accordingly, the amount of such work performed is usually expressed in terms of the hours it occupies, although Chadeau & Fouquet (1981) have attempted to set a monetary value on domestic work (see Chapter 9 for a full discussion of their method).

The perfect tool for such measurement is the time-budget study.[2] Such studies have generated comprehensive figures on the amount of hours spent on domestic work in particular. However, since time-budget studies and their results are to be fully analysed elsewhere (see Chapter 6), I will only use the results gleaned from the 1974/5 'Institut national des statistiques et des études économiques' (INSEE) time-budget study as presented by Chadeau & Fouquet (1981) at this point. These will give an indication of the size of the phenomenon with which we are dealing.

Chadeau & Fouquet (1981) estimate that an economically active woman spends on average twenty eight hours a week on domestic labour and thirty four hours a week on employment. A woman who is not economically active spends forty three hours on domestic work. That is one hour more on average than an employed man spends on his job. Employed men spend an average of ten hours on domestic labour whilst economically inactive men spend only eighteen hours per week on such work. (see Table 2.1).

Table 2.1
Paid and unpaid work time

	For all men	For all women	Total
Time spent (hours per week)			
In professional work	27.9	13.3	41.2
In unpaid domestic work	11.1	50.3	89.3
Total	39.0	50.3	89.3

Source: Adapted from Chadeau & Fouquet (1981, p. 32).

This culminates in 48.1 billion hours a year being spent in total by the French population on domestic work and only 41.2 billion hours on professional work: that is, the majority of time devoted to 'work' by the French population in this year was devoted to 'domestic work', as opposed to employment. One can therefore see from a glance at these figures that the amount of work carried out in the domestic sphere is vast and worthy of the attention that it has received. Indeed, it could be suggested that domestic work constitutes the bulk of the activity in the informal economy.

Indicators other than those provided by time-budget

studies may be, and indeed, have been used to estimate the amount of domestic work being performed in France. For example, in the case of D.I.Y., one can measure the amount of D.I.Y. material purchased. For example, the authors of the 'Commissariat Général du Plan' (1983, p. 69) report Comment vivrons-nous demain? note that the real value of D.I.Y. goods sold rose by 11 per cent between 1968 and 1974, and nearly 8 per cent between 1974 and 1980. That represents a growth rate of more than double that of the G.N.P. for the same periods. This, therefore, suggests a relative rise in the level of D.I.Y. activity among the population during that time.

In the case of gardening, Dubost (1981) has examined the development of the number of gardens in France and the proportion of this land which is given over to food production. He (1991, p. 396) asserts that in the ten years from 1968 to 1977, 240,000 gardens per year were created. By 1977, 11,500,000 households enjoyed the use of a garden. He adds that in the period from 1975 to 1979, between 40 and 46 per cent of garden area was used for vegetable production. More interesting still, Dubost asserts that 30 per cent of national vegetable production is assured by private individuals in their own gardens.

Turning now to the question of 'community' work, we can see that it has been far less thoroughly documented. The analyses of Héran (1987) represent one of the few sources available which give any clues whatsoever as to the amount of this type of work which is conducted in France. One part of Hérans' study of 'le voisinage' (relations within the neighbourhood) concerns the services which neighbours render for each other. He (1987, p. 43) asserts that 43 per cent of French households have rendered a service to their neighbours or received a service from them which could be termed 'community work'. The extent of this exchange of services is very variable - ranging from the occasional favour to more general help on major projects. Taking participation in 'l'entraide pour les grands travaux' (mutual help in major tasks) as a principal indicator, 28 per cent of Héran's research participants had taken part in such work. However, there is no evidence to confirm or deny that a continued and stable network of exchange of services between neighbours is a common social phenomenon in France.

Thus, out of the three types of informal economic activity reviewed this far - that is, black market work, domestic work and community work - the only one about which one can draw a firm conclusion is domestic work, thanks to the INSEE time-budget surveys. Unfortunately, no such conclusions can be drawn about the incidence of community work, not because of the existence of a plethora of confusing and varied statistics - as is the case with black market work - but because of a simple lack of information concerning the phenomenon. This is the same problem which is encountered when considering the volume of voluntary work undertaken in France.

Voluntary work

In similarity to domestic and community work, voluntary work is unpaid by definition and as such, cannot be measured directly in monetary units. However, in contrast to domestic, community and black market work, it takes place within the realms of official and legally registered organizations. For that reason, one would hope that it may be easier to evaluate. This, unfortunately, is not the case. Statistics indicating the amount of voluntary work which is performed in France are very hard to find. There are no reliable statistics either on the number of volunteers, the time that they devote to their voluntary work commitments, or the duration of their engagement. Le Net & Werquin (1985, p. 125), in their analysis of voluntary work in France for the Commissariat Général du Plan, note that 'the voluntary sector is not well enough known in France: an effort to clarify the situation is necessary'.

Figures abound on the number of 'associations' in existence in France. However, although associations are one of the major benefactors of voluntary work, they not only use volunteer helpers, but also employ workers. Furthermore, many of their members are consumers and recipients of services. Therefore, there is no way to calculate the amount of voluntary help received on average by associations from which one could deduce the incidence of voluntary work in France in general. The only indication of the proportion of volunteer workers helping in the running of associations has been produced by the 'Centre National du Volontariat'. In its 1980 study of fourteen associations active in the health and social service sectors, it found that there were 191,490 volunteers to 18,287 employees, serving 2,472,220 members (of variable status). Thus, in very approximate terms, on the basis of this study, one can say that there is one volunteer for every twelve members of associations, and one employee for every ten volunteer workers.

There are some further clues to the amount of voluntary work performed in France. Marcou (1983) estimates that there are between one and four million volunteer workers in France of which 600,000 to 800,000 work for sports associations,

100,000 for the Red Cross, 50,000 for 'associations familiales rurales' (rural family associations) and several tens of thousands for other family associations, 'Maisons des Jeunes et de la Culture' (youth and community centres) and pensioners' clubs.

But how many hours are devoted to voluntary work? Horaist (1983) has carried out a pilot study on 215 associations in order to discover their role in the economy. He discovered that these 215 associations benefitted from the labour of 3,000 volunteer workers, each of whom provided an average of two hours of work per week. Related to the amount of paid work performed within associations, there was one hour of voluntary labour to every two hours of paid employment. Furthermore, the figures provided by the 'Centre de volontariat' in Paris suggest that in 1981, 8 per cent of volunteers worked five days a week; 25-30 per cent worked two or three half days a week; and 30 per cent worked half a day a week. On the basis of such figures, Archambault (1985) estimates that the amount of voluntary work performed in France is equivalent to 200,000 full time jobs. In other words, it is equivalent to the amount of work performed by 1 per cent of the economically active population of France in their employment. Archambault arrives at this figure by multiplying the average figure of two hours weekly devoted to their work by volunteers - estimated by Horaist (1983) - with the highest estimate of the number of volunteers working in France - that is, four million.

In comparison with domestic work (or even the estimates of black market work), this does not represent a very large amount of activity. Nevertheless, 1 per cent of all the time devoted to employment performed in France represents a large pool of effort from which society draws in order to satify need.

Conclusions

From the preceding discussion, it thus becomes clear why only clues to the size of the informal economy in France can be offered at present. First and foremost, the quality of the statistics relevant to this field of inquiry is variable to say the least. In some areas, they are very full: for example, on domestic labour, one has evidence from a national survey. Nonetheless, in other areas, information is sketchy and vague and one can only speculate on the basis of the data available. The measurement of black market work is hampered by the controversy surrounding it and the fact that is illegal, whilst the stumbling block in evaluating the amount of community and voluntary work which takes place is purely and simply lack of research.

Nonetheless, there is ample evidence to suggest that much productive and useful activity is being performed outside the realms of the formal labour market. There is little if any evidence, however, to suggest a growth in the size of the informal economy in France in the last twenty years which could explain the rise of interest in it over this period. In fact, one must look elsewhere for explanations for the relatively recent curiosity about this 'hidden' sector of the economy. This is the task which Chapter 3 sets out to fulfill.

Notes

1. The term 'black market work' covers activities which should be declared to the State for social security and tax purposes but which are not. However, they are legal in every other way. The 'underground economy' embraces more generally criminal activities. See Chapter 1.
2. A time-budget study is a method of detailing all the daily activities minute by minute of a set of research subjects. For a more detailed discussion, see Chapter 6.

3 Contextualizing the development of the informal economy in France: socio-economic, political and ideological factors

Introduction

It is the function of this chapter to supply possible explanations for the evolution of the field of study of the informal economy in France over the past twenty years. From the conclusions drawn from the previous chapter, it is plain that this interest cannot be explained by a dramatic - and catalogued - increase in the amount of such economic activity undertaken. Consequently, it is necessary to cast one's gaze further afield in the search for possible explanations. Indeed, it is to the changes in the social, economic, political and ideological environment in which theorizing and research on the informal economy has taken place that one must turn in this quest.

Examining the role of such factors is not tantamount to suggesting that intellectual production is determined by this environment. It is rather that this environment sets the limits of what is possible and acceptable for a theorist to study. Furthermore, as Offe (1985, p. 842) contends, changing circumstances can give salience to a hitherto unrecognized problem or situation, bestowing upon it the status of an 'issue' worthy of attention in the academic and intellectual domain. Moreover, an analysis of the factors influencing the development of the debates on the informal economy does not deny the theorists any role in advancing and extending the range of choices of what to study and how to study it. Theorists, for example, have been very much in the forefront of the ideological developments which I will discuss here. There exists an iterative process between intellectual production and political and social realities. Intellectual creativity may push back the boundaries of what are accepted as probable explanations and practical solutions to problems as well as give expression, at a propositional level, to what is happening in society at large. It is important to remember, as Brown (1984, p. 268) contends, that 'the relationship between change in society and change in what social scientists are encouraged, allowed or want to investigate is far from straightforward'.

The social and economic factors which have encouraged interest in the informal economy in France will be discussed in a first section, the political and ideological factors being discussed in a second. Although separated here for the sake of clarity, it should be stressed that these two kinds of factors are inextricably linked. Not only is it the case that changing social and economic circumstances induce different ways of viewing the world, but these very changes can themselves only be understood by means of intervening, or mediating mechanisms of a more ideological (or subjective) nature. For these reasons, the following discussions will attempt to make links between the two types of variables wherever possible. I will begin with the question of the socio-economic environment.

The socio-economic environment

The socio-economic developments which have influenced interest in the question of the informal economy are of two basic types. On the one hand, there are those which pertain to changes in patterns of employment. On the other hand, one must take into account the changes in lifestyles and aspirations which have been observed over the last twenty years in France which have affected attitudes to 'work'. I will begin with the question of patterns of employment.

Patterns of employment

The way in which patterns of employment have developed over the last two to three decades in France have affected men and women entirely differently. There have been three general trends. First, for women, the period since the 'Sixties has been characterized by a massive increase in their participation in the labour market. This has aroused interest in informal economic activity principally in terms of the question of the household division of labour (see Chapters 4, 5 and 6). Second, men have experienced a decrease in the number of hours which they spend in a day, a week or a year in their full time jobs. Third, the crisis of unemployment has rendered the world of work increasingly unstable and precarious for men. These latter two developments have encouraged interest, for the most part, in the role that the informal economy could play in the future of work (see Chapters 7, 8 and 9). I will begin with the first question, namely, that of women and employment.

Women and employment. From the early 'Sixties onwards, one has witnessed an increasing percentage of the female population of France, both married and single, with or without dependent children, seeking employment on the labour market. Of all French women over the age of fifteen in 1962 [1], 36.2 per cent were economically active [2], a figure which rose to 38.7 per cent by 1975. Taking only the twenty-two to fifty-five year old age bracket into account, the rise over the same period was even more dramatic, from 42.3 per cent to 53.0 per cent. [3] In the ensuing nine years to 1984, the percentage of economically active women of fifteen years and upwards soared from 38.7 per cent to 68.0 per cent. Hidden within these statistics is an even more pronounced increase in the number not of economically active women - which can include women who participate in running a family farm or business - but of employed women. In 1962, of all economically active women, only 68.5 per cent were employed; by 1975, this figure had jumped to 83.2 per cent.

Furthermore, French women are not as likely to leave their employment on marriage or the arrival of children as they once were. In 1973, of women aged between twenty-five and thirty-nine, 8.4 per cent left their employment on marriage whereas only 6.3 per cent did so in 1980. Additionally, a recent study in Nancy on 2,000 women found that amongst women of the thirty-five to thirty-nine age group, the average length of their career break for raising children was seven years and four months whereas amongst thirty to thirty-four year old women, the average break was reduced to four years and seven months. [4]

Such socio-economic changes have led progressively to the adoption of a new division of labour between husband and wife. Courson & Saboulin (1985) report that the 1982 census showed for the first time that families with two wage earners had become the dominant form of family in France. In 1982, 45 per cent of couples (legally married or not) were composed of two 'economically active' partners. Of these couples, 70 per cent had children.

These developments have had a major impact on the way in which the family has been viewed in academic study over the past twenty or so years. First, the entry of women into the labour force, and the fact that married women and mothers were remaining there for longer and longer periods, raised concerns about the survival of the family. Since the family is the prime institution for the rearing of children, women 'abandoning' their familial duties summoned up fears of demographic decline - France is a country concerned to the point of obsession with demographic trends. Such concerns underlined the necessity of the work accomplished by women in the household which had been taken for granted for so long and opened the door to the measurement of the amount of domestic labour being performed.

Moreover, this trend laid the foundations for building theories of women's responsibility for domestic work which viewed it in terms of a gendered division of labour with an economic basis as opposed to an aspect of sex role or a result of psychological suitability. Whilst women fulfilled the functions of childminder and homemaker silently and without question, this remained a natural part of what it was to be a woman. By seeking employment, women themselves were questioning the 'naturalness' of this role and demanding a more sophisticated explanation of their responsibility for domestic labour.

Viewed in this light, the entry of women into the labour market could not help but raise questions of practical, political and academic significance. However, it was not this socio-economic change alone which raised the question of the 'economic' character of domestic work. An ideological and political input was also required, namely, the rise of the 'Mouvement pour la Libération des Femmes' (women's liberation movement) which put the spotlight on women's specific oppression as a gender group. The role of the 'MLF' will be discussed in more detail later.

Reduction in working hours. There is no doubt that working hours have decreased in the last two decades. The average employee in France now enjoys a shorter working week and longer holidays than did his or her parents. Providing a general impression of the scale of the reduction with which we are dealing, Grossin (1984) explains that on average, the overall work time of blue collar workers has decreased by 20 per cent (this figure rises to 30 per cent in some industrial sectors) in the past two decades in France. Fourastie (1979) furnishes more detailed statistics on work time. He notes that between 1946 and 1975, the number of hours worked per person per year fell from 2,100 to 1,850; hours per day from 8.8 to 8.4; days per week from 5.1 to 5; and weeks per year from 50 to 48. Up-dating these statistics to 1980, the Eurostat (1984) report on working time asserts that the average working week in France for a manual worker was 41.0 hours and for a white collar worker, it was 39.9 hours. In comparison with Fourastie's figures for 1975, this represents a further drop in the working week of 1 hour and 2.1 hours respectively.[5]

However, such averages must be contextualized in the light of the massive increase in hours spent in employment by women as a group. This means that the very notion of falling hours of employment is only valid in the case of men. Curiously, the entry of women into the labour force actually contributes to the reduction of these average working times because women often work on a part time or flexible basis. Indeed, 21 per cent of women in employment in 1984 (that is, 1,850,000 women) had part-time jobs (See Table 3.1 below).

Table 3.1
Part time employees as percentage of total workforce

	1978	1979	1980	1981	1982	1983
Men	1.7	1.8	1.8	1.7	1.7	1.6
Women	7.4	8.7	8.7	8.8	9.2	9.6
Total	4.1	4.7	4.7	4.5	4.7	4.8
%Women	75.7	77.4	77.4	77.4	78.1	79.4

Source: Llehmann, (1985, p. 51, Table 4).

The apparent reduction in the amount of time taken up by employment as a result of the reduced working hours of individuals has contributed to the rise of the issue of the informal economy. This is because it encourages theorists and researchers to examine life outside the realms of employment more seriously. The question arises of what people do with this time, especially if more free time does not entail a reduction in income.

However, it is not only reductions in working hours which liberate time for other activities. Another 'liberator' of time has been 'unemployment'. As the authors of the

Commissariat Général du Plan report (1983, p. 92) assert

> The social volume of free time has ... continued to increase, but in an unbalanced way, concentrated amongst certain sectors of the population (the unemployed and those having taken early retirement) instead of being spread evenly across the whole active population.

Nevertheless, since unemployment is a sign of impoverishment, whereas increased leisure is taken as a sign of wealth, the implications of these two types of changes are very different and I will thus deal with them separately.

The crisis of unemployment. Since the 1973 oil crisis, the combination of low growth, fierce foreign competition and continued rises in productivity in both the manufacturing and service sectors has meant that mass unemployment has seemingly become a permanent feature of the economy in some regions of France. In the past two decades, unemployment has risen inexorably (see Table 3.2 below). By 1976, it had tipped the million mark, continuing to rise in the years 1975 to 1980 by 631,000. The situation worsened considerably in the early 'Eighties. In 1981, 7.3 per cent of the working population were unemployed, a figure which rose to 10.3 per cent by 1985. Unemployment continued its progress to a peak in November 1986 of 2,673,400 people being registered at the 'Agence nationale pour l'emploi' (ANPE) (National Employment Agency) as seeking full time employment. After this time, unemployment began to fall back slightly. Nonetheless, by the summer of 1990, the unemployed total still stood at around 10 per cent of the active population.

Whatever the future holds, there is no denying that in the period with which this book deals, unemployment has been a major social and economic concern. The spectre of unemployment has raised interest in the informal economy not only because of the time it frees - as is the case with the reduction in working hours - but also because of the decrease in income which it provokes for the individual or the household concerned. Thus, theorists in France have become interested in black market work and domestic production in particular as sources of income generation or of saving on expenditure. In fact, interest in the informal economy has gone hand in hand with a certain pessimism vis à vis employment.

Furthermore, unemployment affects the division of labour between men and women because even in the post '73 period of

Table 3.2
Rate of unemployment (BIT definition)

Date	% Active population
31. 12 72	2.7
31. 12. 74	3.4
31. 12. 79	6.1
31. 12. 81	7.9
31. 12. 82	8.2
31. 12. 83	9.0
31. 12. 84	10.2
31. 12. 85	10.2
31. 12. 86	10.5
31. 12. 87	10.4

Source: Collections de l'INSEE D123, (1988, p. 56, Table 4.2).

unemployment, women's participation in the labour force in France has continued to grow. As Bouillaguet-Bernard & Gauvin (1988, p. 49) note

> ... despite rising unemployment, the growth of women's participation in the labour force has continued unabated. Between 1975 and 1982, participation rates for adult women increased at a higher rate than for the period 1968-1975. In March 1982, 63.5 per cent of women aged between 25 and 55 were economically active, compared with 53.1 per cent in March 1975 and 44.6 per cent in March 1968.

Thus, the relative numbers of male and female wage earners has changed. In March 1984, 41 per cent of wage earners were women, compared with 38 per cent in March 1975 and 35 per cent in March 1968. This has much to do with the continued creation of jobs in the service sector. Bouillaguet-Bernard

& Gauvin (1988, p. 63) point out that

> For the first time, it is no longer women, but men, both young and adult, who have been the first to suffer the effects of the recession that were first felt at the end of 1974 and that until the beginning of the 1980's amplified fluctuations in unemployment levels, both upwards and downwards.

Consequently, as the strict 'natural' division between 'man the breadwinner' and 'woman the homemaker' has broken down, it is not surprising that the question of what constitutes work and how it is organized and remunerated has been reactivated.

From this discussion, it is clear that the informal economy has become a subject of inquiry for two starkly different reasons as far as patterns of employment are concerned. On the one hand, the fact of women ceasing to devote all their time to domestic work has resulted in this form of activity being taken seriously. This means that the division of roles between spouses has been treated as a division of labour. On the other hand, the reduction in the number of hours taken up by employment in the lives of men has raised questions concerning how they use their newly acquired free time. More importantly, the fact that unemployment results in people not only having more free time, but greatly reduced earnings as well, has led theorists to wonder whether people can compensate for this loss through black market or domestic activities. In sum, wherever time is vacated by employment, the possibility arises that it will be filled by 'informal work'.

However, patterns of employment alone are not the whole story as far as socio-economic developments are concerned. Especially in the early to mid 'Seventies, the notion abounded that lifestyles and aspirations were changing in such a way as to favour kinds of activity other than employment.

Lifestyles and aspirations

There has been a general idea over the last two decades that lifesyles [6] are undergoing a radical transformation, or at least, that there is now a greater variety of lifestyles in France which have neither the Protestant work ethic, nor an unambiguous consumption ethic at their core. This has paved the way for some theorists to suggest that informal ways of working may be more suited to these new aspirations than the old patterns of full time employment for life. Such 'new' lifestyles and aspirations have been dubbed, for example, 'post bourgeois' or 'post materialist'. Rose (1985, p. 139) defines 'post bourgeois' values as being 'imperative self-actualisation', 'Hedonism', 'entitlementalism', and 'anti-authoritarianism'. De Jouvenel (1980, p. 11) adds that one must also take into account the new demands which have been put forward in this period for a better 'quality of life', improved working conditions and for wider democratic participation. 'Interfuturs' (1979, p. 111), in a study carried out between 1970 and 1978, found that there was a net contrast in the values of different generations, with younger people tending towards 'post materialist' values. These were protection of nature, a society in which ideas count more than money, which is less impersonal and in which there is more participation in work and politics. The development of such values and aspirations can be related to the crises of consumer society and the awakening to the environmental crises which were crystallizing in this period.

Furthermore, Forsé (1984) claims that one of the most important changes in aspirations to have come about over the last two decades is the desire of people to belong to, and work in more human scale social groupings. He contends that it is against the backdrop of this change that one can understand the interest generated by informal work activities in the late 'Seventies and early 'Eighties. There are two signs of this which he pinpoints: they are, first, deunionization and second, the rise in membership of associations. Citing Landier (1981), Forsé (1984, pp. 106-107) notes that France's two largest unions began to lose members in the late 'Seventies. The 'Confédération française démocratique du travail' (CFDT) lost 2.7 per cent of its members in 1978 and 3 per cent in 1979, whilst the membership of the 'Confédération générale du travail' (CGT) dropped by 3 per cent between 1975 and 1979. This represents, according to Forsé, a disenchantment on the part of the population with mass, highly structured and centralized organizations based on the workplace. In contrast, membership of associations has boomed, these being often, although not necessarily, small scale, local organizations which offer the possibility of activity in a 'human scale' grouping. In 1977, 30,000 associations were created and in 1982, 40,000 emerged (this is in comparison with the creation of only several thousand a year in the 'Fifties). In total, in 1982, membership of associations stood at around twenty million.

More specifically, one must consider the question of attitudes to employment amongst the population at large. Although from the indicators at hand, one cannot draw hard and fast conclusions about the general attitudes of the French to their employment, a general notion abounded, at least until recent years, that people did not perceive employment as the prime source of satisfaction in their lives. In a much cited opinion survey carried out by the 'Société française d'enquêtes par sondage' (SOFRES) and published in 1980 entitled 'The economy and the perception of work time', it was discovered that 33 per cent of blue collar workers, 52 per cent of clerical workers and 59 per cent of middle managers would choose a reduction in working hours in preference to a rise in pay. Scardigli (1981, p. 19), basing his judgements on a survey carried out by Rabier (1978), concurs with this finding, affirming that today's workers, having satisfied the majority of their material needs, prefer to liberate their time rather than increase their income.

Such findings can be interpreted to mean that people, at least in the 'Seventies, wanted freedom from the constraints of employment in order to participate in more 'convivial' activities. However, the two studies cited were carried out before the massive rise in unemployment which France has experienced over the past ten years took place. It is not improbable that this crisis has meant that people now place more value on their jobs. That said, no recent studies examining attitudes to employment have been produced with which to test this hypothesis.

In sum, the changes in lifestyles and aspirations which have been observed, especially during the 'Seventies, seem to suggest that some people were, and maybe still are searching for new, more convivial ways of living. This prompted a number of French intellectuals to devise visions of the future which would respond to these desires. One central theme of these visions has been the notion of working 'autonomously' (see Chapter 1).

Conclusion

The informal economy therefore emerged as an issue amongst French theorists against a backdrop of an increased number of women entering employment; shorter working hours; increased unemployment; and signs that some parts of the population were aspiring to more convivial modes of living and even more time free of their employment. Although such developments undoubtedly provided some of the sparks which led theorists to examine the informal economy, these factors alone are not sufficient to explain the rise in interest in the subject which has occured in intellectual and academic circles. It is necessary to consider political and ideological changes in order to complete the picture.

The political and ideological environment

In this second section, changes in the French political and ideological environment which have encouraged interest in the informal economy will be discussed. These developments are of two distinct types. First, there are those which have taken place on the political Left. There has been a multiplication of 'radical' groups and theories on this side of the ideological spectrum over the past twenty years which have sprung up in the wake of the events of May '68. These have challenged the orthodox Marxist/socialist preoccupation with, and commitment to the factory, industrial labour and the primacy of the State. As a consequence of these challenges, new areas of life have been opened up for public debate, including various aspects of the informal economy. Second, the development occuring on the political Right which is of interest here is the reaffirmation of neoclassical (or liberal) economic principles. Such a reaffirmation goes hand in hand with an increased faith in the power of the market, as opposed to the State, to regulate human interaction. In consequence, activities, such as those of the informal economy, which escape the regulation of the State have been given serious consideration by certain French intellectuals interested in resolving the problem of unemployment, for example. Equally, the notion that the 'market' is a forceful analogy, applicable to all aspects of human existence, means that activities such as housework - hitherto relegated to the 'social' world - have been brought into the economic realm.

It is quite evident that the theorists who take a universalist and structuralist approach to the study of the informal economy- that is, the Feminists and the Radicals - have been influenced by the developments which have taken place on the Left, whilst those of a more 'individualist' bent - the Microeconomists and the Free Market Dualists - are related to the evolution of thought on the Right (see Chapter 1). Furthermore, it should not be forgotten that the ideological environment influences the choice of subject (or problem) of even the most empirically-based researchers, setting limits on their options of what to study and how to study it. I will begin the discussion with the developments which have affected the Left.

Developments on the Left

Until the late 'Sixites, the Left in France, as elsewhere in the world, took little interest in what we have described here as the informal economy. Most Marxists [7] had made the factory and industrial labour the focus of their theories. Indeed, a Marxist approach based on the socialist model of the USSR succeeded in developing into an orthodoxy in France through the medium of the 'Parti Communiste' (Pc) (Communist Party). This orthodoxy takes up the deterministic and the productivist strands of Marx's writings. It is from these strands that the concentration of orthodox Marxists on industrial labour flows.

The orthodox Marxist approach is deterministic in that it proposes that society evolves in accordance with certain immutable laws which supercede human will. Accordingly, the assumption is made that history has a meaning independent of the consiousness of individuals. Indeed, history realizes itself, whatever individuals may think, in their actions. This determinism, in which matter becomes a separate category, an absolute of which consciousness is only the reflection, turned quite easily, in the evolution of Marxist thought into an economic determinism. This determinism is based on the assumption that Humankind will progress to greater and greater technological mastery, of which the precondition is greater and greater industrialization of the production process.

Related to this economic determinism is the 'productivism' of the orthodox theory. Within this approach, the technology developed by capitalism is accepted as a tool kit which is appropriate to socialism. This is because the orthodox vision of socialist society is productivist in the sense that socialist society shares with capitalism the ultimate aim of increasing material production, even though a socialist state would distribute the fruits of this production in a different manner. Consequently, the organization and division of labour which goes hand in hand with industrial technology is accepted by orthodox Marxists. Hence, given these assertions, it is not surprising that orthodox Marxism has largely ignored the work which goes on outside the factory gates.

It was not until the post '68 era that challenges were mounted from within the Left to this vision of socialism and analysis of the mechanisms at work in society. These challenges came both from within the socialist movement - the so called 'New Left' whose roots are to be found in the French 'autogestionnaire' (self management) tradition - as well as from the New Social Movements of political ecology and feminism. Indeed, it will become clear that the 'New Left' was heavily influenced during the 'Seventies by the social critiques put forth by the New Social Movements.

Touraine (1987, p. 209) describes the characteristics of the New Social Movements so:

> They reject the major cultural issues of industrial society ... even, in the case of the ecologists, rejecting the whole of the concept of technological progress; they no longer believe that all forms of domination are the result of capitalism, and they are based on kinds of awareness which look to new utopias as well as new forms of organization.

This concurs with the view of Offe (1985, p. 826) who underlines the fact that the New Social Movements concern themselves with the non political and non economic spheres of life. Offe posits that they represent a 'new paradigm' of politics. This new paradigm claims a type of issue which is neither 'private' (in the sense of being of no legitimate concern to others) nor 'public' (in the sense of being recognized as the legitimate object of official political institutions and actors) but which has collectively 'relevant' implications. This 'new paradigm' is characterized by issues and concerns which have a common root, Offe explains, in the values of 'autonomy' and 'identity' (meaning, in this instance, decentralization, self government, self help). It is within this 'new' radical political paradigm that the question of informal economic activity, and particularly visions of a new type of 'autonomous' work - as neither a 'public' nor a 'private' phenomenon - has emerged as an issue which is worthy of academic and political consideration.

To examine this question in more detail, I will take 'feminism', 'the political ecology movement' and the 'New Left' as separate subjects for discussion. Indeed, feminism has contributed mainly to the issue of domestic work being brought to the fore in the context of the debates on the 'household division of labour'. Meanwhile, the raising of the more general question of the role which the informal economy could play in the future of work owes much to the political ecology movement and to the changes of the 'New Left'. I will begin with the question of feminism.

Feminism. Many anthologies of French feminist thought, all with full discussions of the rise of the 'MLF' in France, have already been published in English and I have no wish to summarize their analyses here. [8] Instead, I wish to explore in particular the way in which the posing of women's oppression as a political issue by the 'MLF' in the late 'Sixties enabled the routine domestic activities performed by women in the home to be taken seriously as a form of labour. Furthermore, this movement provided a new way of conceptualizing the oppressive relationships existing in society.

It was in the wake of May '68 that 'feminist' groups began to spring up in France, this being the result of radical women's frustration with the far from enlightened practices of their revolutionary 'brothers'. In the face of this disillusionment with male revolutionary politics, these women sought both autonomous and alternative forms of political organization and new interpretations of society which would more fully take into account women's experiences. The existence of the 'MLF' as a political force gave validity to discussing 'female' issues with the gravity usually afforded to questions relating to areas of life dominated by men. The feminist movement provided a fresh perspective and a changed climate, especially for intellectual women.

This new 'radical' feminism of the post '68 period aimed at developing a new theory of sexist society. Until then, 'oppression' in political ideology had mainly been applied to the proletariat. The feminist movement introduced a new kind of oppressive relationship to the political scene, that of women by men, or women by capital. The feminist movement led researchers, especially women, to look again at what they had been taught and to ask why their respective disciplines had ignored the specificity of women's position. Fougeyrollas [9], for example, explained that

> I would not have asked why economics didn't examine the question of the gender division of labour in the same way if it had not been for feminism, or if I had not been active in the feminist movement.

Combes [10] notes also that if the feminist movement is at the root of her analyses of women's work, and those of others like her, it is because it has fed the fires of theoretical reflection and given women researchers the energy to confront dominant sociological and economic traditions which marginalized, and still to some extent today, marginalize their work. The climate created by the 'MLF' also obliged some male socialists to take women's experiences seriously in political and ideological debate. However, as Geoghegan (1987, p. 138) notes, 'When the [women's] movement ... didn't go away, the Left was forced to rejig its theory - but it never quite worked. The new elements were rather uncomfortably tacked on'.

In sum, feminism emerged as a challenge to the ingrained notions of Marxists that the major battle in society is fought between capitalists and proletarians and that the principal battleground is the factory. Feminists raised the possibility that the most fundamental conflict which divides society could be that which exists between women and men and that the site of the conflict could be the household. Even if the battle is indeed with capital, perhaps that too takes place in the household as well as in the factory. It was therefore against this political background, and the practical changes taking place in women's lives which we have already discussed, that domestic work became a phenomenon of social, and more importantly, of economic interest in the 'Seventies.

Political ecology. It may seem curious to link the rise of political ecology with an awakening of interest in informal work amongst French theorists. Indeed, it is true to say that the issues usually associated with the ecology movement in France concern society's use of energy and resources (see Conti, 1978) with particular attention being paid to the question of nuclear power (see Duverger, 1980). However, within the political ecology movement, these questions are embedded in an all embracing critique of industrial society (as opposed to capitalist society), including its aims, its technology, and especially its relationship to Nature. It is as a result of this universal critique of the organization of society that the question of how to organize 'work' arose for participants in this movement. Indeed, it is suggested, for example, by some ecologists (see Chapter 8) that informal, or 'autonomous' ways of working, can provide an ecologically sound alternative to industrial wage labour.

The critical stance of the ecology movement to industrial society stems from the assertion that the environment cannot sustain continued economic growth since economic growth inexorably results in environmental destruction. Environmental destruction is not a phenomenon specific to the last two decades. However, in the 'Seventies, the various aspects of this problem were formally recorded for the first time. Relevant 'facts' were collated and published in the Club of Rome report Limits to Growth (Meadows, et al, 1972) which brought the ecological crisis out onto the world stage. These crises concerned population, resource scarcity, industrial activity, agricultural production and pollution. This catalogue of disaster was one of the spurs which awakened people to the idea that industrial society could not continue along its projected path of either capitalist or socialist growth.

As Rosanvallon (1977, p. 76) explains 'basically, ecology is disturbing' because it 'muddies the waters of political conflict by creating new divisions'. Indeed, by raising the fundamental question of the relationship of Humankind with its environment, the ecology movement has sollicited doubt in the minds of some that it is possibile to build a truly socialist society upon the foundations of industrial capitalism. One could go so far as to say that the political ecology movement has introduced the idea that all classes are guilty of the exploitation of Nature. In sum, then, the political ecology movement has influenced the direction in which some currents of socialist thought, at least, have developed.

Conversely, the teachings of the 'autogestionnaire' socialist movement have helped to mould the political identities of many ecologists. The need to protect the planet could have led ecologists to propose draconian and totalitarian measures designed to restrict people's 'freedom' to destroy the environment. However, the influence of the libertarian Left has so far prevented such a current of thought from coming to dominate. Lebreton (1978) reminds us of the closeness of ecologist thought to that of the nineteenth century utopian socialists. Hence, the political ecology movement and the New Left cannot be completely separated since it is true to say that they have had a reciprocal influence on one another. Together, their principal success has been to disrupt the Left-Right consensus which favours growth, the centrality of industry and the continuation of a pattern of work based on employment. I will now proceed, therefore, to a discussion of the 'New Left'.

The New Left. The currents of thought which can be subsumed under the heading 'the New Left' have in common a critical attitude to industrial and technocratic society, and especially to the organization of labour by which this society is characterized, namely, full time formal employment. This set of ideas is described as 'new' in the sense of having evolved in contrast to the orthodox Marxist approach outlined above. However, such ideas are not novel in any absolute sense since the New Left in France owes much to the pre Marxist socialist and anarchist traditions of the nineteenth century. In particular, the attitude adopted by these nineteenth century socialists to 'work' has been a major influence on contemporary New Left thinking.

Let us take, in this connection, the example of the Fourier. Fourier (Contre la civilisation, 1835, discussed in Debout, 1978) declares that 'work' should be a source of immediate fulfilment, not something to be suffered for a mediated reward. Moreover, he proposes that joy will result from work when communities are organized in such a way as to allow 'man the butterfly' to exercise both his manual and intellectual skills on a variety of tasks. Fourier warned (in Debout, 1978, p. 68)that

> Civilized industry can only create the elements for happiness, but not happiness itself. On the contrary, it will be seen that an excess of industry will lead civilization to great unhappiness if the real means to social progress cannot be discovered.

Proudhon [11], too, was of the opinion that the greatest evil of capitalism was the relationship that it engendered between the worker and his or her work. In difference to Fourier, Proudhon was an advocate of the specialist craft ethos, believing that capitalism undermined the dignity of the craftsman and denied workers any opportunity to express their creativity. Indeed, this, according to Proudhon, was the principal source of alienation within capitalism.

Although not totally ignored, the question of alienation from one's labour and the need for creativity in work was marginalized for many years in the French socialist movement. It was overshadowed by struggles concerning pay, hours and conditions. Nonetheless, in the 'Sixties and 'Seventies, these questions were again taken up, this time, by the 'New Left'. Some socialists began to question the objectivity of work organization in industry and in the service sector as it had been modelled by Taylorism and Fordism: deskilling, automation and the most minute functional and hierarchical division of labour had combined to render work repetitive and the worker's tasks meaningless. Against the backdrop of rising living standards during this period, the New Left was free to consider issues of the 'quality of life', such as the dehumanizing effect of much employment. Furthermore, the experiences of nationalized industries at home, and the example presented by the USSR abroad, suggested to some that simple State ownership of the industrial structure created by capitalism was not enough to bring about fundamental changes in the everyday experience of the worker.

Friedman (1966) was one of the first French socialists of the modern period to question whether factory labour could ever again be humanized. He concluded that it could not. This led him to advocate increased automation of the production process in order to provide more leisure time for the workforce. His proposition was that workers could use this time for creative 'leisure' activities which would compensate for the lack of creative outlets in their jobs. Friedman (1966, p. 147) explains that 'leisure is essentially about choice, freedom. Leisure corresponds to individual predispositions and tastes, to the complex mixture of preferences which go to make up the personality'. Although the vocabulary is different, Friedman's idea of 'leisure' here is highly compatible with the modern notion of 'autonomous' work (see Chapter 1). He stresses the need for people to take control of their leisure time. He warns against this time being wasted on commercially prepared and controlled leisure which is as stifling as the factory labour which he criticizes.

Friedman can be seen as a forerunner of the 'Modernist Left' [12], this being one of the central strands of the New Left in France. The protagonists of this ideological stance, including such figures as Serge Mallet, Alain Touraine, Michel Rocard, Jacques Delors and André Gorz [13], criticized the industrial and technocratic complex as a whole, as opposed to merely its capitalist manifestation. Indeed, they suggested that the power of the property owning class had been usurped by technocrats and therefore the nature of the class struggle had changed. Consequently, wholesale nationalization would only serve to concentrate power in the hands of this new, 'technocratic' ruling elite. The old working class, it was argued by the Modernists, was incapable of combatting this new seat of power. Only the new skilled workers could challenge technocracy. The conclusion was that the Left should organize the 'salariat' (skilled workers) against the technocrats. Thus, the theory of the 'New Working Class' was born.

Mallet (1969), for example, put forward the hypothesis that Fordism had robbed workers of their consciousness as producers by narrowly controlling their actions and denying them the power of decision making. However, the more fully automated production processes which were coming into being at the end of the 'Sixties, he asserted, would increasingly require a workforce of skilled technicians. This new type of worker would constitute the 'New Working Class', as he termed them. They would regain some of their autonomy as producers thanks to their education. Indeed, their technical expertise would make management dependent on them, thus giving them a degree of control over the production process. The strength of the New Working Class would dissolve the power wielded by employers and management over the workforce which was the principal characteristic of the capitalist market economy. This relationship of mutual dependence between workers and employers would allow socialism to be built within a 'natural market economy'. Thus, the real progress made by the Modernist Left, on the basis of the 'New Working Class' theory, was to suggest that social and economic change could come about without the need for massive State intervention.

As time went on, the 'New Working Class' lost its specificity as the technical aspects of the theory became less relevant. Nonetheless, the notion that socialism could exist in a 'natural market' sowed the seeds from which one could see grow, from 1968 onwards, an anti-Statist and pluralist notion of social change with revolution being replaced by social experimentation. This more decentralist notion of social change is what allowed the informal economy and autonomous work to emerge in the mid 'Seventies as both part of a socialist solution to the alienating aspects of industrial labour and as a method of bringing about such social change amongst certain New Left intellectuals (see Chapter 8).

Interest in the informal economy was given a new boost in the early 'Eighties with the election of the first left wing French government of the Fifth Republic. During its period in opposition, the 'Parti socialiste' (Ps) (Socialist Party) had been permeated with much New Left thinking. For example, the party had adopted the concept of 'l'autogestion' in 1975. Thus, when the Socialists won power in 1981, hopes for radical social change of the decentralist and self management type and a new organization of work including informal activities, were aroused. Stankiewicz [14] is of the opinion that the coming to power of the Socialists in 1981 encouraged researchers to examine the informal economy, explaining that this radical change of government

> encouraged reflections on alternative ways of living. which in turn explains all the deliberations on the convivial econony, the informal economy and so on ... Some works, such as those of Gorz, owe much to this political climate.

In sum, if, for 'traditional' socialism, the factory, and thus employment, were at the heart of society, new forms of socialist ideology have grown up which treat industrial labour as an ill to be overcome. Furthermore, these socialists are much more wary of reinforcing the power of the State and bureaucracy than their more 'orthodox' counterparts. It is this current of socialism that has sparked interest in the informal economy and its possibilities.

To conclude the discussion of the changes in the left wing ideological and political environment which have encouraged the study of the informal economy, one can say that challenges to an 'orthodox' Marxism by the New Social Movements as well as from within the Left itself, have opened up new areas of life for discussion. Feminism, in particular, has criticized the fact that women's specific contributions to society have been ignored and the particular forms of oppression suffered by women have been marginalized by traditional socialist analyses. Thus, feminist researchers have taken a fresh look at the gender division of labour in society, and in particular, at domestic work. To a large extent, the political ecology movement and the New Left have enjoyed a somewhat symbiotic relationship in France. Both have encouraged interest in autonomous, creative and decentralized forms of work on the basis of their critiques of industrialism and technocracy. Next, I will discuss the developments on the Right in France which have contributed to the evolution of this subject.

Developments on the Right

The developments on the Right which have contributed to the informal economy becoming a subject for discussion amongst French theorists will be outlined here. Essentially, these concern a renewed faith in the capacity of the market, not only to regulate economic life (which carries with it an implicit critique of State intervention), but also as an analogy with which to explain all social action.

The first part of this discussion will deal with the extension of the analogy of the market to explain the division of gender roles, or, in other words, the 'household division of labour'. The examination of women's domestic work as an economic activity has not only come about thanks to the theoretical inputs of the feminist movement. This has also been the result of neoclassical (or micro-) economists extending the analogy of the market and hypotheses of economic rationality to determine women's relationship to housework. It was the American 'Chicago School of Economics' which first extended the neoclassical approach in this way. Therefore, the origins of the Chicago School as well as the factors which influenced the introduction of its theories into French academic circles will be discussed.

In the second part of this section, I will turn my attention to those political and ideological developments which encouraged right wing theorists to consider the informal economy as a possible solution to the crisis of unemployment. Of relevance here is the general rehabilitation amongst academics and politicians of the market as the best suited mechanism for regulating economic activity. Part of this development has been the emergence of market orientated visions of post industrial society. These underline the necessity of curing unemployment whilst retaining and enhancing the free play of the market. I will begin, therefore, with a discussion of the origins of 'Chicago School Economics' and its introduction in France.

The rise of the Chicago School of Economics in France.

Analysing domestic work and the household division of labour in terms of microeconomics is not a French invention. It is, in fact, an American import from the Chicago School theorists (known affectionately in France as 'les Chicagoboys') which occurred approximately from the mid to late 'Seventies onwards. This development is essentially academic, being a reworking and extension of the field of application of neoclassical economic hypotheses. However, the degree to which the approach has been adopted in France as an acceptable model for explaining social reality has much to do with the nature of the political and ideological climate in general.

The leader of the Chicago School, G.S. Becker [15], began his pioneering work in the 'Sixties. Becker (1981, p. 3) explains that two social and economic changes taking place at that time rendered a reworking of neoclassical hypotheses necessary. The first was the growing number of married women entering the labour market. This meant that the neoclassical theory of the 'determination of the offer of labour' had to be modified. Hitherto, this theory had been based on the notion that the worker had to choose between work (income) and leisure. However, this theory could not explain the marked increase in the rate of employment of married women. In order to provide an economic explanation for this increase, the factor of 'domestic work' had to be included in the range of choices available to women alongside employment and leisure (see Chapter 4).

The second, and parallel change concerns the steady increase in hourly wage rates occurring at the time. Becker (1981, p. 4) argues that until the 'Sixties, the low hourly wage rates received by individuals (the expression of their low productivity and the low value of their human capital) meant that people had to work long hours in employment in order to improve their income and standard of living. They did not enjoy much free time. However, higher wage rates meant that people could spend more time in the household without loss of earnings. In other words, in the 'Sixties, people had increasing amounts of money and increasing amounts of spare time. As a consequence, microeconomists were obliged to introduce 'non work' time as a determining element in the theory of 'consumer choice'. It was, therefore, in response to these two changes that many of the activities performed in the household came to be described as factors in a production process (as opposed to merely factors of consumption) within the neoclassical theory.

However, the degree of acceptance of this approach in France was not purely the result of rational responses to observed social and economic change. The Chicago School economists argue that all phenomena are liable to be analysed with the tools of neoclassical economics and the analogy of the market. They profess faith in the abilities of the mechanisms of the market to explain, and also to regulate social action. This is clearly an ideological, and ultimately, political stance. It is this 'political' side of the School which explains the time lapse which separates its appearance in America to the moment in the late 'Seventies when it started to take a hold in France. Sofer [16] explained that in the 'Seventies, there was a rejection by the French economic profession of microeconomic theory. Not only was this a rejection most obviously by Marxists, who were very well represented in the discipline at the time, but also by traditionalist macroeconomic, Keynsian professors who were suspicious of the far reaching extensions of the theory proposed by the 'Chicagoboys'. Only slowly, over the past ten years, has the political and academic climate surrounding French economics evolved to the point where microeconomic analysis of this type became acceptable. Interest in microeconomic analysis has gone hand in hand both with a strengthening of belief in the mechanism of the market to regulate society, as well as with an interest in 'individuals' as opposed to 'structures' in explaining social and economic phenomena. Thus, this trend concerns a shift of the centre of intellectual gravity from structuralism to individualism. Such an evolution has not only been witnessed in economics in France, but also in history, sociology and political science. Nonetheless, Lemmenicier [17] expressed the opinion that as a consequence of macroeconomic dominance in France, the (neoclassical) economic analysis of the family (and therefore, domestic production) has been somewhat neglected, even to this day.

The 'free market' answer to the recession. We have seen above how the political climate which favours the 'free market' has encouraged the growth of microeconomics in France. Here, I will explain how this same climate has enabled certain types of informal activity - particularly black market work - to be put forward as a possible solution to the unemployment crisis. In the face of the post '79 recession, the political and economic centre ground of the

Western countries has shifted to the Right. There has been a move away from reliance on Keynsian regulation which has appeared incapable of resolving modern economic problems. Furthermore, the notion of the mixed economy has given way to an ideology which favours the disengagement of the State from economic life.

In terms of electoral victories for right wing parties, France has been a belated follower of this trend.[18] Nevertheless, regardless of which party has been in power, it seems that the centre of consensus in France has moved to the Right, with politicians on all sides of the political divide expounding the need to work with market forces as opposed to attempting to contradict or supplant them. Even the Socialist government, elected in 1981 on a far reaching nationalization programme, had been forced, by 1983, into a complete U-turn which involved gearing their economic policies to the strictures of the market.

This political and ideological climate has led to interest in the informal economy in some quarters in three related ways. First, in a political environment imbued with Keynsianism, only those activities which are part of the formal, State regulated domain are of interest. This is because Keynsianism relies on the State to fulfil the role of principal planner of economic activity. Conversely, when a political climate reigns which favours the free market, theorists are more likely to take interest in productive activities which escape the gaze of the State, the prime example of this being black market work.

Second, in the days of Keynsian consensus, visions of post industrial society tended to be based on extrapolations of the technocratic management model (for example, that of Daniel Bell, 1973). However, the emphasis of these earlier post industrial ideologies on technocratic management has been replaced, according to Frankel (1987, p. 5), with a common belief in the virtues of free entreprise and high technology. That is to say, they have been modified to make room for current demands concerning the deregulation of the market. In consequence, some 'post industrial' theorists have looked to the informal economy to provide new patterns of 'deregulated' post industrial living.

Third, this political climate has affected the propositions made by some to deal with the unemployment crisis. In the free market environment, the suggestion of bringing back full employment by protectionism or State led reflationary means becomes increasingly unacceptable. Furthermore, calls to reduce the costs of unemployment borne by the State become louder. Consequently, various theorists have developed the idea that informal work could ease the plight of the unemployed without burdening the State with the cost of increasing social benefit payments. However, not all interest in the informal economy from right wing quarters has been positive and encouraging: that is, some 'traditional' interests in France (principally to be found in the construction industry) have been vehemently opposed to black market work. Nonetheless, in their own way, these critics have played their part in the kindling of interest in the informal economy in general.

Conclusions

From the preceding discussions, we can see that the discovery, or rediscovery, of a world of work outside employment has been influenced by a range of socio-economic, ideological and political factors. The socio-economic factors include the changing role of women, the reduction in work time and the rise in unemployment, not to mention changes in people's aspirations vis à vis their work life. Ideological and political factors such as the rise of feminism, the political ecology movement, and the New Left have all had their part to play in creating an environment in which the debates on the informal economy could grow. Furthermore, the reemergence of neoclassical economic ideologies in their modern 'Chicago-School' form have changed conceptions about what constitutes production, whilst the new found faith in the market on the political Right has been a factor in theorists taking interest in activities which escape the grasp of the State. Additionally, it has been shown that such developments have not encouraged interest in the informal economy per se, but as an aspect of two specific issues, these being, on the one hand, the household division of labour, and on the other, the future of work. It is around these two issues that the discussions in Part 2 will be structured.

Notes

1. Source: <u>Enquêtes annuelles sur l'emploi</u>, for 1962, 1975 and 1984.
2. Defined as employed, self-employed or registered unemployed.
3. The difference between the increases for the two age groups is owed, in part, to the rising percentage of fifteen to twenty-two year olds remaining in full-time education.

4. This study was carried out by INSEE (Direction régionale de Nancy).
5. This comparison is arrived at by multiplying the hours per day (8.4) by the days per week (5).
6. Cathelat (1981, p. 49) asserts that the concept of 'lifestyles' embraces value systems, behaviour patterns, ways of making sense of the world and how people give themselves status and a role in society.
7. One must note that the use of the term 'Marxist' in any context raises important and instant problems. It is one of those terms which all social scientists readily understand. Nonetheless, upon embarking on a search for its definitive meaning, they invariably end up in a theoretical cul-de-sac. One of the basic reasons for this is that Marx was writing over a forty year span, his thoughts evolving from a more voluntarist, philosophical emphasis in the early days to the more deterministic political economy approach of the later Capital. This being so, even without complicating the issue by introducing the question of interpretation, no one single definition of the concept of 'Marxist' can be agreed upon.
8. Duchen (1986); Marks & de Courtivron (1980); Moi (1987).
9. Comments collected by an interview which took place in Paris in April 1987.
10. Daniele Combes made these points in a discussion of the book Le sexe du travail (1984) to which she was a contributor at a meeting of the 'Cercle d'études et de recherches Flora Tristan' on 28th April, 1984.
11. As discussed in Oeuvres choisies, presented by Bancal (1967).
12. 'Modernist', as a concept, comes from the anti-orthodox intellectual movement in the Church. The orthodoxy to be challenged here, however, was Marxism.
13. Gorz and Delors are discussed in further detail in Chapter 8..
14. Comments collected during an interview which took place in Lille in April 1988.
15. Becker has published the following works exposing his theory: (1965) 'A theory of allocation of time', Economic Journal, Sept., No. 75, pp.493-517; (1976) The economic approach to human behaviour, Chicago, University of Chicago Press; (1981), A treatise on the family, Cambridge, Mass., Harvard University Press; (1985) 'Human capital, effort and the sexual division of labour', Journal of Labour Economics, 3, 1, (2), pp.333-58.

16. Comments collected during an interview conducted in Orléans in April 1988.
17. Comments collected during an interview conducted in Paris in April 1988.
18. In Britain, we have had an uninterrupted period of radical right-wing government since 1979 which appears, at present at least, to have been 'successful' in economic terms. Over the same period, France has had a right wing government, followed by the first socialist governement in the Fifth republic. In 1986 with the parliamentary victory of Chirac's right-wing 'RPR' (Rassemblement pour la République), it seemed that France was maybe following the British path. However, recent electoral events, namely, the reelection of Mitterrand as President and the return of a minority Socialist governement, do not seem to have corroborated this.

PART 2
APPROACHES TO THE STUDY OF THE INFORMAL ECONOMY IN FRANCE

Having outlined the circumstances under which the informal economy developed as a subject for academic and intellectual debate in France in Part 1, Part 2 examines and evaluates the range of approaches to its study. Chapters 4, 5 and 6 will explore the ways in which theorists have dealt with and attempted to explain the household division of labour between men and women whilst in Chapters 6, 7 and 8 attention turns to the question of the role which the informal economy could play in the future of work. Within each chapter, the basic propositions of each approach will be laid bare; differences between individual theorists will be discussed; the assumptions and premises upon which the approaches rest will be analysed; and finally, the ways in which theorists define 'work' within the context of the informal economy will be explored.

Chapter 4 exposes the views of those Microeconomists who have taken up the question of women's domestic production whilst Chapter 5 delves into the considerable amounts of Feminist literature which has been devoted to domestic labour and women's responsibility for it. Both approaches have in common the fact that they analyse the household division of labour as a part of the wider canvas of their respective general theories of society. In other words, they adopt a 'universalist' methodology (see Chapter 1). Chapter 6 discusses the Empirical approaches to the household division of labour. These studies employ either time-budget research or qualitative interview methods to discover in detail the characteristics of the division of labour which exists between household members. The contributions of these Empirical approaches will be assessed not only in terms of their own inherent worth but also in terms of the extent to which their results confirm or contradict the premises upon which are built the theories of the Microeconomists and Feminists.

The future of work is the principal preoccupation for the theorists discussed in the following three chapters. Chapter 7 describes and assesses the work of the Free Market Dualists whilst Chapter 8 analyses the approach of the Radicals. These two sets of theorists concern themselves with the informal economy primarily in terms of how it could fit into the general scenarios for the future of work which they propose. On the one hand, the Free Market Dualists are interested first and foremost in unemployment and in the role that the informal economy could play in cushioning its most harmful social and economic effects. On the other hand, the Radicals are not only concerned with unemployment, but with the alienation produced by most jobs and the environmental unsustainability of the industrial system.

Indeed, they believe that the informal economy could open the door to a new 'autonomous' organization of work for everyone. In contrast to the predictions and prescriptions of the Free Market Dualists and the Radicals, the Empirical approaches to the informal economy and the future of work, discussed in Chapter 9, concern themselves with informal economic activities as they exist at present, examining such questions as the relationship of the unemployed to black market and domestic work; the role of the informal economy in small communities; the motivations of those who participate in black market work; and the overall contribution of informal work in macroeconomic terms. In so doing, they put to the test some of the hypotheses and predictions on which the analyses of the Radicals and Free Market Dualists are based. Thus, the foundations laid in these chapters will allow us to move on, in Part 3, to answer the questions of what we 'know' about the informal economy in France and whether or not this area of study has been the birthplace of a 'new' concept of work.

4 The Microeconomists

Introduction

The Microeconomists approach the question of the household division of labour in both an 'individualist' and a 'universalist' manner. Their approach is 'individualist' in that it is an interpretation of society which concerns itself with exchange between individuals rather than with social structures. It is 'universalist' in that these theorists apply the general theory of microeconomics to explain individuals' behaviour. Indeed, Microeconomists have become interested in domestic work as a factor in the decisions which couples make regarding how to use their time in the most rational way possible.

Only two French Microeconomists have concerned themselves specifically with the question of the household division of labour in the way proposed by Becker and the 'Chicago School of the New Home Economics'. These are first, Bertrand Lemmenicier and second, Cathérine Sofer. I will begin the discussion by outlining the bases of this approach as it has been established by Becker. Having completed this introduction, I will pass on to the ways in which Lemmenicier and Sofer have applied this theory.

The foundations of the Microeconomic approach

The general innovative hypothesis upon which Lemmenicier and Sofer's work is based is Becker's assertion that the family is not purely a unit of consumption, or a black box into which commodities disappear and from which utility is produced as if by magic. Instead, they understand that it has a productive function and an internal organization just like a company. Becker (1976, p. 92) contends that market goods are not direct sources of 'utility' (the economic term for the satisfaction of need). To be rendered ready for consumption, market goods require the input of the time of household members. Consequently, market goods and household time are the two primary factors in the process of 'domestic production'.

The direct sources of 'utility' created by domestic production are called 'household commodities'. Such commodities are produced by the household itself by combining market goods and services with some of its own time. This means that all market goods are inputs into the production process of the non market sector. Becker (1981) asserts that the main utilities produced in the household concern the procreation and rearing of children. This, therefore, is the principal aim of domestic work. As Lemmenicier (1988, p. 19) contends

> The family is an enterprise or a community of interests which offers to its members benefits of all kinds which it is difficult to procure at a reasonable price on the market. ... These benefits are produced by family members combining the purchase of goods and services with the use of their own time and skills.

The comparison of market with domestic production is rendered possible in this model by the use of the common denominator of 'time'. The variable of money cannot be used since domestic production has no direct market value. By applying the microeconomic hypothesis of opportunity cost[1] to the element of an individual's time, the unitary value of this 'time' can be calculated. In this way, domestic production can be given a 'shadow price' dependent on the market value of the individual carrying it out. On this basis, the economist can explain when and why more 'utility' can be gained from devoting one's time to domestic as opposed to market production or vice versa.

Bertrand Lemmenicier uses the above model for several purposes. First, in his 1980 paper, he examines the costs and benefits of marriage and divorce, arguing that the more specialized the wife is in domestic production, and the husband is in market production, the more economically rational it is for the couple to stay together. Second, he has explored the choice that married women face between 'autarky' (domestic production) and the market (with Levy-Garboua, 1981). Furthermore, on the basis of this analysis, he has suggested various reasons for the recent increase in participation in the labour market by married women. This is all brought together in his latest work 'Le marché du mariage et de la famille' (1988) (The market of marriage and the family) in which he uses the basic ideas illustrated above in order to explain the existence of the family and the changes occuring within its organization. Additionally, his views were further illuminated for the purposes of this book by two interviews which I conducted with him in 1987 and 1988.

Lemmencier's work on the household division of labour is inspired by the Ricardian theory of the exchanges which take place between nations. For example, he (1981, p. 31) explains that 'the economic analysis of conjugal roles can find inspiration from the tools of the theory of international commerce'. According to his theory, family members specialize in certain skills and forms of production, the results of which they exchange with one another. In this way, the combined family unit can produce more than if the individuals which go to make it up produced all their needs independently. Indeed, this is the economic rationale behind the formation of families. Lemmenicier (1980, p. 35) explains that 'solely from the economic point of view, the differentiation of roles has an important function'. It leads to an 'efficient allocation of resources within the family as a whole', meaning that they can 'produce more goods without having to work harder.' Furthermore, he (1981, p. 68) suggests that

> marriage ... resembles an employment contract through which spouses agree to pool their resources and to cooperate in family production in the hope of producing more together than they could separately. The 'production supplement' which results from this union constitutes, by definition, the benefit of marriage.

The important assumption behind Lemmencier's vision of the household division of labour is that the family has a collective utility function. In other words, he argues that spouses exchange skills and use their specific expertise to the common good of the family unit. From this assertion, the hypothesis is put forward that families attempt to maximize their utility through mobilising their forces in market and domestic production in the most efficient way possible. This entails differing divisions of labour between spouses according to differing circumstances. Consequently, Lemmenicier's model is flexible enough to explain changes in the patterns of the household division of labour, taking into account the fact that households modify their organization in response to changes in prices, in the relative productivity of different activities, in the relative shadow prices of commodities and in their real incomes. As Lemmenicier (1980, p. 36) maintains, 'men and women change their behaviour because the relative prices of non market goods and the opportunity costs of time change'.

Lemmencier (1980) bases his analysis of the gains of marriage and the prospect of divorce on the above model. He attempts to explain why in some families there is a high degree of specialization by husband and wife in market and domestic production respectively, whilst in others, an interchangeability of roles exists. He concludes that a high degree of specialization occurs when the husband can earn more on the market than his wife and when the wife cannot cover the costs of running a home with her potential income. Furthermore, Lemmenicier argues that the higher the degree of specialization, the higher the gains of marriage for both partners. The lower the degree of specialization, the less the marriage has an economically rational basis. This renders the marriage unstable. In consequence, divorce is most likely to occur between relatively 'unspecialized' marriage partners.

Lemmenicier (1981) also sets out a procedure for interpreting, in a microeconomic way, the offer of labour and allocation of time of married women. He explains the participation (or equally, non participation) of married women in the labour market in terms of whether or not it is more efficient for them to deploy their productive capacities in the home or in employment. Therefore, according to Lemmenicier, the level of the female labour supply is dependent on the respective costs and benefits of domestic as opposed to market production (or, as Lemmenicier terms it, between 'l'autarcie et le marché', autarky or the market). Thus, married women 'specialize' in domestic work when their opportunity costs of working in the market are too great: that is, when the cost of paying for market substitutes for their domestic production, such as the cost of prepared meals and of childcare, is not adequately covered by their potential salary.

There are two major sets of circumstantial factors which have contributed to the rise in the offer of female labour according to Lemmenicier (1981). First, there is the 'effet-richesse': this is the effect of the increasing wealth of households. The development of market production, through advances in technology, economies of scale and the division of labour, has delivered considerable gains in productivity. These are translated, in the long term, by continued and marked rises in the real salaries offered to women. Since women will enter the market if the salary rate offered reaches the marginal productivity of their domestic production, these generally rising wage rates mean that this condition is fulfilled for an increasing number of women. Furthermore, the education of women has increased their market productivity, but it has not improved their domestic productivity.

Second, there is the 'effet-prix': this is the effect of falling prices of some market substitutes to domestic production. This has come about thanks to technological progress which makes market goods and services available to households which are cheap and efficient. As a consequence, an expansion of market production to the detriment of traditional forms of production takes place. In this context, one must also mention the increased provision of affordable childcare provided by the French State in the post war period. The above are factors which reduce the degree to which women specialize in domestic work. However, Lemmenicier (1981) maintains that there are also counter-forces which mitigate against women entering the labour market and thus encourage specialization. These include urbanization; the planning of work time; the risks of career interruption and the responsibilities of having children.

Many of these propositions are echoed by Cathérine Sofer in her work on the theory of the division of labour - professional and domestic - between men and women (1985) and in an interview conducted with her in April 1988. Sofer (1985, p. 118) explains that her basic economic model is that of Lemmenicier (1981). However, there are two points over which differences emerge between the two theorists. The first is essentially a difference of emphasis. Sofer (1985) places great importance - in comparison with Lemmenicier - on the fact that the price of equivalent market substitutes for domestic goods is not identical for all families, but depends on the number of children present. In her opinion, the production of children is the raison d'être of the family and the household division of labour. She (1985, p. 118) asserts that 'domestic work has a fundamental role to play, not directly in terms of the quantity of domestic production achieved, but as an intermediary form of work used in the production of children'.

Thus, Sofer insists that the factor which determines whether or not women specialize in domestic production, or seek employment on the labour market, is the number of children in the family. She argues that the higher the number of dependent children in the family, the higher the saturation level of the consumption of domestic production will be. Simply put, a large family demands more hours of the mother's time being devoted to domestic work than a small one. Sofer (1985, p. 118) explains that

> The price of domestic goods will be that of their market equivalent in a family for which such consumption is of value, but it will be nil if the saturation threshold of such consumption has been crossed; the price of the products of domestic work therefore increases along with the number of people in the family.

The presence of children increases the value of domestic work significantly because the woman's marginal utility in the market has to be extremely high to make it worthwhile for her to go out to work. Furthermore, Sofer stresses that one reason why children constitute this constraint on women entering the labour market is because there are not many affordable and good market substitutes for parental childcare. In sum, Sofer maintains that in Western countries, domestic work only takes on social and economic significance when there are children present in the family. When there are no children in the family, the level of saturation of consumption of domestically produced goods is so low that domestic work does not compete with other time uses.

The most significant difference between Sofer and Lemmenicier concerns the degree to which each asserts that the interests of husbands and wives coincide. On the one hand, Lemmenicier (1981, p. 68) argues that when married, men and women share a common 'utility function', in plain terms, meaning that their interests coincide. On the other hand, Sofer insists that spouses can and do have conflictual interests and that those interests can and must be taken into account by Microeconomic analyses. Husbands and wives, therefore, have different 'utility functions' which must be taken into consideration when explaining the choices they make. Sofer [2] maintains that the assumption of a common utility function between spouses masks the conflicts that exist between them. Furthermore, it hides the disadvantaged and heavily constrained position in which many women find themselves.

These, therefore, are the basic propositions made by Sofer and Lemmenicier. Next, I will discuss in greater detail the assumptions which inform these propositions, paying particular attention to the differences and similarities in political persuasion between Sofer and Lemmenicier and the way in which these influence their respective theoretical positions.

Evaluating the Microeconomic approach

It is to state the obvious to say that for any given social or economic situation, there are competing explanations, the case of the household division of labour being no exception. However, in order to be able eventually to evaluate the relative worth of these competing explanations, we must lay bare some of the assumptions and theoretical and political premises on which they are based. The guiding principle of the Microeconomic explanations proffered by Lemmenicier and Sofer concerning the household division is that of 'individualism'. That is, their explanations assume that 'all social phenomena result from the interactions of individuals' (Lemmencier, 1988, p. 15). Moreover, Lemmenicier and Sofer work on the premise that these interactions result from individuals exercising their ability and freedom to make 'rational choices under constraint'. Thus, first, we will discuss what is meant by 'rationality' within the Microeconomic model before moving on to an examination of the notion of 'choice' and finally to an analysis of the constraints to which women are subject when making choices concerning employment and domestic production.

The notion that individuals behave 'rationally' is the universal logic which informs the Microeconomic explanations of the household division of labour. The ability to compete in a 'rational' or 'intentional' way for scarce resources is the essential characteristic of 'homo microeconomicus'. [3] Thus, it is supposed that individuals are able to evaluate situations, to be inventive and to maximize their utility with the aim of gaining more satisfaction rather than less. For example, Lemmenicier (1988, p. 15) declares that every individual acts with the aim of substituting an unfavourable situation for a more favourable one. Indeed, this is what Microeconomists mean when they talk about individuals making rational choices. It is in this way that Microeconomists explain the decisions arrived at by couples concerning the division of labour which they implement in their households.

Faugère (1980, p. 332) makes the criticism of this approach that 'when one is talking about the division of labour in the household', choices do not depend on an 'explicit economic calculation'. Indeed, in one sense, this criticism is justified since the approach does make sweeping assumptions about people's motivations which do not always ring true with one's personal experience. Moreover, when discussing the Empirical Approaches, we will see that there is much evidence to suggest that individuals do not necessarily rationalize their own actions and decisions in this way.

Nonetheless, it should be remembered that Microeconomists themselves acknowledge the limitations of their approach, stressing that it is a post hoc rationalization and explanation of individuals' behaviour. For example, Lemmenicier [4] has stated that his theory takes a given action and then explains it within a preestablished logic. Indeed, he insisted that he makes no pretensions to see into people's minds and predict what they will do, or to say what constitutes 'more satisfaction as opposed to less' for any particular individual. Sofer (1985, p. 139) too accepts the limitation that her model lacks the ability to describe women's actual reasonings when deciding to have children, or how many to have, for example. Thus, when evaluating the relative contributions of the various approaches to the household division of labour, these self imposed limitations of the explanatory power of the Microeconomists will have to be borne in mind.

The notion of 'rationality' in this model of human behaviour goes hand in hand with the notion of 'choice' since it cannot be said that an individual has behaved rationally and with intention if he or she has not been able to 'choose' his or her actions. According to the Microeconomic model, people have the capacity and opportunity to make choices about how to run their lives within the constraints imposed on them by their own skills and characteristics and by the prevailing scarcity of resources. If it is women who tend to take responsibility for domestic production, it is because, ultimately, they have chosen this option. From the premise that individuals enjoy choice flow three related assumptions.

First, this insistence on the notion of 'choice' means that for Sofer and Lemmenicier, freedom should take precedence over equality in the organization of society. Indeed, the notion of 'freedom' is weaved into the fabric of these Microeconomic analyses. As an example of this attitude, we can take Sofer's assertion that she does not look forward to the day when men and women will be 'equal' in an absolute sense, but when women are 'as free from constraints' upon their choices as men. She (1985, p. 302) explains that a 'good' division of labour between men and women is one which people have freely chosen.'

Second, to perceive society as the outcome of individuals'

choices implies that if inequality exists, it is the product of real differences in the capabilities and preferences of individuals which cannot, or indeed, should not be eradicated.

Third, the assumption that all individuals enjoy choice in their actions means that Microeconomists do not easily accept the notion of 'exploitation'. For example, the primacy of 'choice' in his analyses of the marriage market leads Lemmenicier [5] to conclude that since women are legally free to 'choose' marriage, or not as the case may be, no a priori exploitation exists in the marriage contract. This insistance on women's freedom to choose is what brings the Microeconomic theorists into conflict with the 'structuralist' analyses of the Feminist theorists, as will become clear later.

Finally, we turn our attention to the notion of 'constraint'. Sofer and Lemmenicier cite three basic types of constraints with which women are faced when making choices about whether to devote their energies to domestic or market production: first, there is the constraint of their reproductive function; second, there is the role of their education; and third and finally, there is the factor of employers' attitudes to actual and potential female employees. Sofer and Lemmenicier strike different balances between these various factors in their explanations of women's responsibility for domestic production. Indeed, the weight and significance which they accord to each factor is revealing of their gender politics. First, let us take the example of the relative importance given to biological as opposed to educational factors by Sofer and Lemmenicier.

These two factors cannot be discussed separately since they are the two primary building blocks of a person's 'human capital'. Within the Microeconomist framework, it is argued that the individual possesses a certain amount and type of 'human capital' (skills, abilities, characteristics and the like). It is the quality of one's human capital which makes one suited to specific forms of production and which determines one's market value, this being expressed in differential wage rates. The question emerges, therefore, of whether it is the human capital with which women are born which leads them to specialize in domestic production more frequently than men, or whether it is the subsequent 'investments' which are made in this 'capital' - through education, experience and training - which are determinant. The relative importance accorded to each type of 'constraint' will be revealed to be indicative of the gender politics of the theorists concerned.

For the founding father of the approach - G.S. Becker -

the nature and value of the 'human capital' of men and women is different from birth because of the biological difference which exists between them. He believes that even though education can accentuate or diminish these differences, it cannot eradicate them. Consequently, Becker (1981, p. 22) states that women's greater marginal utility will usually be in the home because of the 'complementarity between bearing and rearing children and producing other household commodities'. In his view, the maternal function is usually incompatible with holding down a job.

The statements on this matter made by both Lemmenicier and Sofer are more equivocal. Lemmenicier (1988) argues that the division of labour between husbands and wives is not rooted in a timeless, essential difference between the sexes and that education does indeed have a part to play. Even though it may appear a tenuous distinction, Lemmenicier does his best to stress that child rearing and domestic production do not constitute women's 'natural' role, but an economically rational one given certain circumstances. Nevertheless, his explanation puts a great deal of weight on the physiological factor of women's childbearing capacities. Lemmenicier explained that [6]

> Once one looks at the marriage market and the labour market as being two comparable or similar things, it is obvious that women, for the present, have the means to produce children. They therefore have a big advantage, a comparative advantage in entering into the job of housewife and mother producing children.

Indeed, within such a logic, one could go so far as to say that women have an absolute advantage in this sphere - at least until a scientific breakthrough drastically alters the human reproduction process.

We have already witnessed how Sofer, by giving husbands and wives separate utility functions, expresses her 'feminist' sensibilities within the Microeconomic framework. This political persuasion leaves traces also in the balance that she strikes between the three types of constraints outlined above. In comparison with Lemmenicier, Sofer puts less emphasis on women's childbearing role, (although she insists that it must be taken into account) and more on their education and particularly on employers' attitudes towards women candidates and employees. Indeed, Sofer argues that if patriarchal elements remain in society, these will be expressed in the form of the biases that male employers hold against women. Economically, these prejudices find voice in the lower market value attached to women.

Lemmenicier's view of employers' attitudes is much less

'feminist' in its orientation. He [7] explains that women are 'worth less' than men in the eyes of employers because they are viewed as being less committed to the labour market, the reason being that they have a 'job', or a potential one, in the marriage market. Lemmenicier accepts this 'job' within the family as being women's first priority. He explains the rise in women seeking other kinds of occupations with reference to the fact that men have become less profitable on the labour market and women have found themselves under employed in the marriage market (the undertone always being that this is first and foremost their natural place).

Additionally, the question of the degree to which change in women's situation vis à vis domestic production is desirable or possible separates Sofer and Lemmenicier, once more along the lines of their gender politics. These differences are a product of whether or not each believes the constraints on women to be 'unfair', and concomitantly, the extent to which each is prepared to accept the need for institutional intervention to change the situation. On the one hand, Lemmenicier reveals his highly 'conservative' views by suggesting that change is not desirable and that the question of 'fairness' is not relevant if one accepts that people are exercising freedom of choice. Asserting that the criteria of buying and selling can be extended to regulate all areas of life, Lemmenicier takes the logical step that people should be free of State control of their lives in order to carry out these explicit and implicit exchanges unhindered. He accepts the differences which others may call inequalities as a fact of life and, as such, a fact of gender specialization.

On the other hand, whilst Sofer accepts that profound change in women's work situation can only be brought about by an agregate of individual changes, she maintains that some circumstantial factors (constraints), such as the availability and price of childcare facilities, are in the hands of political institutions and can therefore be changed by the State. Additional suggestions which she has put forward include making maternity leave more widely available and promoting images of equality in State education. Sofer does not believe that the 'method' of Microeconomic analysis is the sole domain of what one could call liberal, bourgeois or conservative politics. It is also compatible with political views which want to change some of the constraints which come to bear on women. Consequently, Sofer does not take the constraints that she lists for granted, nor preclude planned action to change the environment in which women make their choices. Thus, the 'individualism' of Sofer is tempered by a guarded call for institutional change, a decision which can be understood if one realizes that Sofer has feminist inclinations which she tries to express within the Microeconomic mould.

In conclusion, therefore, it is clear that Lemmenicier and Sofer have opted to see society as a juxtaposition of individuals and, particularly in the case of Lemmenicier, the 'market' as being the best mechanism for regulating human interaction. Furthermore, they have placed the concept of 'choice under constraint' at the heart of their analyses. The implication of these assumptions is that there is no sweeping way to improve 'society' even if that is one's goal because society - however unfair, unjust or unequal it is - is the expression of individuals' abilities and preferences and not the cause of their perversion. Additionally, Sofer and Lemmenicier both adopt a universalist methodology, explaining people's behaviour by means of generalizable, abstract laws. For example, Lemmenicier & Levy-Garboua explain of their model of the female labour supply that they wanted it to be more predictive and less reliant on unexplained value changes than other models. They (1981, p. 43) assert

> ... we will try to give an economic interpretation of the offer of labour and the allocation of time of married women which has a precision, a refutability and a predictive capacity which is superior to those which have gone before.

Indeed, it is the quest to make these laws more and more generalizable which has been at the root of the evolution of the concept of work which underlies the analyses of these theorists. It is this question that I will now explore.

A new concept of work?

It remains for this Chapter to investigate the definition of 'work' which underlies the analyses of Sofer, Lemmenicier and the 'New Home Economists' in general. First, the innovative aspects of their definitions of work and production will be examined in contrast to the more traditional conceptions of this category of activity which have been used by other neoclassical economists. Second, the problems that the Microeconomists have encountered in differentiating domestic production from leisure and consumption will be discussed. Finally, the question of why some Microeconomists were encouraged to broaden the scope of their concept of 'work' will be answered. We will begin, therefore, with a discussion of how the creator of the New

Home Economics School, G.S. Becker, transformed the neoclassical conception of what constitutes work and production.

Before Becker, the household figured in neoclassical analysis as a place of 'consumption'. According to this traditional approach [8], the 'consumer' is faced with two options concerning the way in which he or she may spend his or her time: the first is to 'work' - that is, to participate in an activity for which one gains pecuniary reward. The second is to enjoy 'leisure' (or consumption) [9]. Thus, everything for which one does not receive a wage is deemed 'leisure' as opposed to 'work'. As we have already seen, the novelty of the Beckerian approach has been to suggest that the consumer had not one, but two means of procuring 'utilities' and satifying his or her needs and desires, these being market production and domestic production. Indeed, it was by this means that Becker elevated many of the activities which take place in the household to the status of 'work', theoretically speaking. In this way, domestic work was placed on a par with paid work and the definition of 'work' as opposed to leisure was widened accordingly.

However, the pioneering work of Becker was not without its teething problems since it blurred the traditional rigid dichotomy between production and consumption, and thus work and leisure, which was based on the difference between those activities for which one receives pay and those for which one does not. Indeed, Becker's model implies that all time is an input into the production of human capital and thus <u>all</u> activity is 'work'. It is impossible to identify empirically the output of this production. Consequently, 'work' loses all meaning as a category of activity with a specific identity.

In order to rectify this shortcoming of the Beckerian approach, Gronau (1977) up-dated the original theory to take account of the qualitative differences which do indeed exist between various time uses. In short, Gronau has reintroduced the 'leisure' factor into the Beckerian theory. Lemmenicier and Sofer follow in this wake cut by Gronau. For example, Lemmenicier [10] is insistent that a distinction must be made between work and leisure, without returning to the 'traditional' approach which ignores the contribution to the production of utility made by domestic activities. This he does by defining work as an activity which can be carried out by a second person, but which produces <u>the same effect</u> as if it had been performed by the person whom it is to benefit.

Thus, any activity from which people derive direct

pleasure would not be counted as 'work'. For example, watching television, swimming, reading a book or going for a walk for pleasure would not be 'work' because no one else can do it for you. Thus, it is the dichotomy of pleasurable and unpleasurable activity which Lemmenicier, and others use in order to distinguish between work and leisure. However, the variable of pleasure cannot be included in the Microeconomic analysis as such since it is only individuals themselves who can know whether or not they gain pleasure from an activity. This is a choice which is ultimately expressed, according to the Microeconomists, in individuals' economic preferences.

Finally, we must take a closer look at the reasons why the Microeconomists have treated some household activities as factors in a process of production and consequently defined them as 'work'. It should not be thought that the Microeconomists single out domestic work as a special category of activity (alongside paid work) which is worthy of economic analysis. The Microeconomists do not concern themselves with setting the limits of what is, and what is not part of 'the economy'. This is because their primary objective is to extend their model of rational economic choice to explain all human behaviour and not just that associated with the formal market. As Levy-Garboua [11] notes

> social facts can also benefit from the economic approach, from its hypotheses of rationality and of equilibrium. Or, if one prefers, from methodological individualism. Education, the family, training and the distribution of income as well as social policy can all be included.

Lemmenicier (1980, p. 28) explains that in applying this model to the costs and benefits of marriage and divorce, he was trying to test 'the explanatory powers of economic analysis'. Analysing the family as a place of production is a by-product of this over-all strategy. Thus, one is witnessing the attempt by French Microeconomists to cast themselves in the role of universal social scientists, extending the general explicative power of their brand of economics.

Therefore, the elevation of the status of domestic work in theoretical terms is not the product of an ethical (or political) motivation on the part of the Microeconomists, nor does it mean that they want to bring about practical change in the way society organizes work. Furthermore, they do not want to include the 'value' of domestic work in the G.N.P.. Nor do they want domestic work to be remunerated as paid employment. Their interest is purely in augmenting the theory of individuals' economic behaviour. The byproduct of this is to recognize the contribution of domestic work as a factor in individuals' economic choices.

As we will see repeatedly in the following discussions, when one is exploring the rise of the subject of the informal economy in all its various disguises, one is not dealing with the study of activities previously left outside the academic domain, but activities previously marginalized within economics which have been brought more fully into the realms of the discipline. This new economistic approach to areas traditionally allocated to sociology has provided a new angle from which to study women's housework - rendering it 'domestic production'.

Conclusions

In sum, Lemmencier and Sofer deal with the question of the household division of labour from the angle of consumer choice, their novelty, following in the theoretical footsteps of Becker, being to include the variable of domestic production in the options available to consumers. It is within this theoretical framework that women's relationship to domestic production is explained as an economically rational one which, ultimately, women choose given certain circumstances. Moreover, it is in this way that they elevate the status of household activities to that of 'production' alongside employment, using the common denominator of 'time' to compare the two. This is, however, part of a larger canvas in which Microeconomics attempts to become a general theory of social as well as economic phenomena by applying the universal theory of the 'rational individual' to all situations.

The next cluster of theorists to be analysed - the Feminists - differ from the Microeconomists on many counts. This results mainly from their structuralist, as opposed to individualist leanings. It will become clear that in many areas, but most specifically on the notion of 'choice', these theorists are in direct conflict with the Microeconomists. It is to these theorists that we now turn.

Notes

1. In layman's terms, this means the amount that one could earn on the market if one were not engaged in other activities. It can also mean how much it would cost to enter the market: transport, childcare etc. In other words, it depends on (i) what an individual is worth on

the market and (ii) how much it costs him or her to participate in a particular market.

2. Sofer made this comment in response to a question put to her during a debate on her book (1985) on 21st June, 1986 at the 'Cercles d'études Flora Tristan'.
3. It must be noted that Sofer (interview, Orléans, 1988) argues that 'homo oeconomicus' does not have to be motivated solely by financial gain.
4. Comments collected during an interview conducted in Paris in April 1987.
5. Comments collected during an interview conducted in Paris in April 1988.
6. Comments collected during an interview conducted in Paris in April 1988.
7. Comments collected during an interview conducted in Paris in April 1987.
8. As it is exposed by Fauguère, (1980, p. 316).
9. For example, Lecaillon & Vernières (1974) are of this traditional mould.
10. Comments collected during an interview conducted in Paris in April 1987.
11. 1987 report to the 'Conseil National de Recherche Scientifique' (CNRS) (National Council for Scientific Research) of the 'Laboratoire de Microéconomie Appliquée', p.3.

5 The Feminists

Introduction

The word 'Feminist' has many different connotations and meanings: here it will be applied to theorists who describe the relationship of women to domestic work in terms of their belonging to an oppressed class - this being either a social class, a gender class, or a combination of the two. Adopting a structuralist methodology, Feminists discuss domestic work with a view to exposing its relationship to women's oppression. In fact, many deem domestic work to be the 'material' base of women's exploitation. That said, it must be stressed that 'Feminist' is used here as an umbrella category. It shelters diverging and often conflictual explanations both of women's responsibility for domestic work and of the function of domestic work in determining the structure of society (this structure being either 'capitalist' or 'patriarchal'). Furthermore, some, especially male theorists brought under this umbrella would not recognize themselves as 'feminists'. Nonetheless, their work on women as a social group which suffers a specific form of oppression under capitalism means that they are most conveniently subsumed under this heading.

Four groups of Feminist theorists will be discussed: first, there are the Marxist Feminists whose basic hypothesis is that it is capitalism which oppresses women and which benefits from their domestic labour. In sum, they argue that domestic work is 'functional' to capital. However, this is a category of theorists which embraces two sub-groups, these being, on the one hand, the unproductive functionalists - Jean-Louis Moynot (1978), Claude Meillassoux (1981), and Jean-François Godchau (1970) - and on the other hand, the productive functionalists - the 'Insoumise' collective (1977) and Danièle Drevet (1977). The former sub-group argues that domestic work cannot be described, in strict Marxist terminology, as 'productive' labour in the same way as one can describe wage labour. The latter sub-group, howoever, is adamant that domestic work is 'productive' in the Marxist sense of the word.

Second, there are the Feminist Marxists - Claude Alzon (1973), the 'Elles Voient Rouge' collective (1981), and Alain Testard (1982) - who contend that women are oppressed by men and by capital; that domestic labour has remained the mode of reproduction in capitalism because of the existence of patriarchy; and that the structure of society results from the combination of the structures of patriarchy and capitalism.

Third, there are the Radical Feminists - Christine Delphy (1984) and Colette Guillaumin (1978) - who assert that women are oppressed by men; that patriarchy and capitalism have their own distinct modes of production; and that domestic labour constitutes the patriarchal mode of production.

Lastly, there is the Rapports Sociaux group, including Danièle Chabaud, Dominique Fougeyrollas, Monique Haicault, Andrée Kartchevsky, Françoise Bourgeois and Anne-Marie Daune-Richard [1] who propose that society is characterized by relations of both patriarchy and capitalism and that domestic labour is part of the sphere of social reproduction, a position which is not too dissimilar from that of the Feminist Marxists. However, the novelty of the 'Rapports sociaux' group in comparison with the other groups of Feminists is based, first, on the more empirical nature of their approach and second, on their treatment of domestic labour as a 'social' phenomenon influenced by the social relations of both patriarchy and capitalism.

Presentation of the Feminist approaches

None of the Feminist theorists included here would disagree with the following statements when taken at their face value: namely, that women are disadvantaged persons in society; that one aspect of this disadvantage is that they are on the whole responsible for household work, whether employed or not; that this household work is not remunerated by a wage in any normal sense of the term; and that the amount of housework performed globally is significant both in terms of its results and the time which it occupies. Nonetheless, beneath this outward unity reside deep rooted divisions. When one wishes to move further to a causal explanation of why the picture of women's oppression is as it is, or to a more detailed account of the mechanisms which hold the that picture together, disagreement arises because such an act of evaluation involves choices between the competing frameworks of interpretation described above. I will begin with the Marxist Feminist theorists.

The Marxist Feminists

The theorists to be discussed under this banner are the following: Jean-Louis Moynot (1978) who in the late 'Seventies was a leading member of the Communist trade union, the 'CGT' and of the Communist Party as well as being an economist working with the 'Centre d'études et de recherches marxistes' for whom he produced an analysis of the gender division of labour. Second is Claude Meillassoux (1981), an anthropologist, who provides new insights into the reproduction process in capitalism. Third is Jean-François Godchau (1970) who was one of the first socialists to reply to the more 'Radical' feminist analyses of domestic labour in an early feminist review entitled Partisans. These three theorists constitute the 'unproductive functionalist' sub-group of Marxist Feminists. As for the 'productive functionalist' sub-group, the theorists involved are the French speaking Swiss feminist collective 'Insoumise' (1977), and Danièle Drevet (1977).

Socialists had not completely ignored the 'economic' aspect of the domestic sphere until the rise of the women's movement in the early 'Seventies. Although Marx had nothing to say directly on the topic of women's oppression and the place of domestic work in political economy, Engels produced an analysis of women's position in capitalism. Indeed, it is Engels' propositions which must be taken into account if one is to understand the thinking of present day Marxist Feminists. Engels[2] proposed that women were the first form of private property and the first victims of class oppression. Monogamous marriage resulted from considerable wealth being concentrated in the hands of a single individual. Since this individual was male, his only means of guaranteeing the paternity of his children to whom he would bequeath his wealth was the confinement of a woman in monogamous marriage.

In this way, the rise of private property engendered the rise of the 'nuclear' family (woman and children dependent on a man). Women were confined in the home, in other words, in the private sphere, and their socially necessary labour was transformed into a 'private' service for the nuclear family. Prior to this, women's domestic work had been performed within the context of the clan (in which public and private were not separate in space or time). The nuclear family thus became the basic economic unit of society. Engels (1972, p. 137) declares that 'with the single, monogamous family, ... household management lost its public character' and 'became a private service.' This resulted in women's effective exclusion from public production as their private duties in the service of their families held them back. Engels (1972, p. 137) explains that 'the modern individual family is founded on the open or concealed domestic slavery of the wife and modern society is a mass composed of these individual families as its molecules'.

Engels argued that women remained chained in the private sphere because the family continued to be the basic economic unit of society. This situation would only be resolved with the establishment of common ownership. He (1972, p. 139) concludes that 'with the transfer of the means of production into common ownership, the single family ceases to be the economic unit of society' and thus 'private housekeeping is transformed into a social industry'. Nonetheless, according to Engels, the proletarian family, having virtually no inheritance, was marginal to the survival of capitalism; it was part of the social superstructure and as such, possessed no material justification.

In the early 'Seventies, however, socialists were obliged to look again at Engels' assertions that domestic labour was part of the private domain, a backward sphere relatively sheltered from the social relations of capitalism. This explanation of the existence of the family, domestic labour and women's relationship to it was not enough to satisfy the aspirations of socialist women tired of the gender blindness of Marxist analysis. Neither was it an adequate theory with which male socialists, faced with the challenge of the post '68 feminist explosion could defend themselves. The Marxist Feminist analyses constitute an attempt to surpass Engels' dismissal of women's domestic work in the proletarian family as an anachronism. The basis of the Marxist Feminist argument is that modern capitalism is at least conditionally dependent on the preservation of women's unpaid domestic labour for its survival. Consequently, capitalism exploits women through their domestic labour.

What, however, are the exact mechanisms by which

capitalism exploits women's domestic labour, according to the Marxist Feminists? Furthermore, what is the relationship between capitalists' profits, the extorsion of surplus value and the production of use values at home by women? All the Marxist Feminists would agree on the following assessment of the situation: that all capitalist economies rely on the domestic economy for the production of that most essential ingredient in the production process - labour power. Not only is the family the place for the biological reproduction of the future generation of workers, but women prepare these future workers for the day when they will enter the employment of capital. Moreover, women maintain the labour power of the current generation of workers. This they do by raising the value of the market goods consumed by the family by the value of their own labour in the home. Furthermore, women's unpaid domestic services, it is argued, are a very cost effective method of reproduction, and without women's contribution, capital would not be able to appropriate as much surplus value as it does at present. All in all, the Marxist Feminists contend that capitalism uses women's unpaid domestic work, 'to extract maximum profit from waged labour' (Moynot, 1978, p. 140).

Beyond this limited exposition of the relationship between capitalism, domestic labour and women's oppression, however, the consensus between the three male members of this group - Moynot, Meillassoux and Godchau - on the one hand, and the female members - Drevet and the 'Insoumise' collective - on the other hand, ends. The former group will be termed the 'unproductive functionalists' since they argue that wage labour is 'productive' in contrast to domestic labour which is 'unproductive', thus stopping short of according domestic labour the same status as wage labour. The latter group will be labelled the 'productive functionalists' because they do not accept this unequal evaluation of paid and unpaid work.

To be 'productive' in the original Marxist sense, an activity must fulfil both of two criteria. In the first instance, to be 'productive', labour must be exchanged on the market against a wage and second, it must work directly with capital's means of production. As such, it produces commodities which have a calculable value. The value of a commodity is equal to the labour time socially necessary for its production. Surplus value is extracted from 'productive labour' when the wage against which it is exchanged is not equal to the value of the work time contained in the commodities produced. Thus, 'productive labour' is the only sort of labour to be directly exploited by capital.

It is obvious that a strict interpretation of Marx's theory must lead one to conclude that domestic labour is 'unproductive' since it fails to fulfil either of the above criteria. It is not wage labour as it is not exchanged on the market. Since it does not enter the market, it does not work directly for capital, or produce commodities, value and thus surplus value. However, Drevet and the 'Insoumise' collective were not slow to realize that labelling domestic work 'unproductive' relegated it to a place of secondary importance behind wage labour. Consequently, they set out to argue that domestic work was productive. I will begin, however, with a discussion of the 'traditional' approach of the 'unproductive functionalists'.

The unproductive functionalists. The crux of the 'unproductive functionalist' argument is that domestic work does not play the same kind of role in the capitalist mode of production as industrial labour, nor does it function according to the same rules. The 'unproductive functionalists' argue that capital annexed the patriarchal family in order to use women's unpaid domestic labour to reproduce the workforce. This means that housewives produce not saleable commodities but labour power itself, principally in the form of their employed husband, but also of their children. Moynot (1978, p. 147-8) asserts that this domestic work 'is not the object of private consumption' and only serves to produce 'labour power', which is a 'special commodity'. For these reasons, Moynot, Godchau and Meillassoux put forward the proposition that domestic labour makes an indirect economic contribution to capital, the corollary of which is the indirect exploitation of housewives by capital. The intermediary between capital and housewives is the labour power which they reproduce, the 'surplus value' of women's domestic work being appropriated when capital buys the labour power of their husbands and children.

Meillassoux (1981) argues that it is precisely the fact that domestic labour functions under different rules to capitalist industrial production - and thus remains relatively autonomous from that production - that makes it so vital to the survival of capitalism. Meillassoux agrees that domestic labour is not analagous to capitalist wage labour because the labour power of the husband and children cannot be sold for a profit by their producer, namely, the mother/wife. However, the very fact that the labour power cannot be sold in this way means that capital is free to exploit it at no cost. Additionally, this method of reproduction retains the image of the free labourer, that is, a labourer free to exchange his or her labour power on the market for a wage. If reproduction were collectivized through the State, and thereby controlled more directly by capital, the notion of the free labourer would collapse, the labourer becoming a slave, totally appropriated by capital. Consequently, the self justification of the capitalist mode of production would find itself on rocky ground in that 'liberalism' would have given way to 'totalitarianism'.

In sum, then, according to these three theorists, it is the very difference between domestic and wage work which makes domestic labour so indispensable to capitalism. From this follows the conclusion that women's role in 'reproduction' is the root of their oppression in capitalism.

The productive functionalists. The second group of Marxist Feminists has its roots in Italy with Maria-Rosa Dalla Costa (& James, 1972) and the 'wages for housework' campaign. It has had only limited influence in France, with Drevet (1977), for example, and in the French speaking academic and intellectual community with the Swiss 'Insoumise' collective (1977). Dalla Costa (1972) dedicated herself to showing that the family in the capitalist system is a centre of production and that the commodities produced by domestic labour (those being, first and foremost, labour power and the use values which contribute to that production, for example, the provision of cooked meals, clean clothes, warmth and comfort) are no different in nature from those commodities produced by wage labour. In other words, domestic labour is as 'productive' as any other personal service performed in the market. Despite the fact of being performed within the family and thus of being invisible, the 'productive functionalists' argue that domestic labour is a form of social production on which capitalism imposes its norms. Accordingly, women performing domestic tasks are exploited by capital to the same degree as their employed husbands. Drevet (1977, p. 18) explains that

> Capitalist society has been able to model the family according to its needs. Instead of examining the age old oppression of the female sex, it is necessary to understand the way in which capitalism ... has structured this specific form of oppression, subjugates it and uses it to its own ends.

Dalla Costa (1972) agrees with the argument of the unproductive functionalist school that the main product of domestic labour is the human being whose labour power is exchanged on the market. Thus, one can say that it is not the description of the mechanism which links domestic labour and women's oppression to capital which divides the two groups, but its evaluation. It is the fact that one group wishes to call the function of domestic labour 'unproductive' and the other to call it 'productive' which divides them. The choice of the one evaluation as opposed to the other is a consequence of the attitude of the various theorists to the future of domestic labour. In particular, the issue which divides them is that of whether 'wages for housework' should be paid to women for their domestic labour services. Indeed, the choice of the term 'productive' is political in the widest sense of the term.

On the one hand, the 'unproductive functionalists', claiming that domestic labour does not conform to the rules of the capitalist market, assert that it cannot be remunerated in the same way as wage labour. Moynot (1978, p. 145) goes further and argues that because domestic labour is in the last analysis an under socialized anachronism, it should not be encouraged with a 'domestic wage', but dispensed with as quickly as possible. To pay such a wage explains Moynot (1978, p. 167) would be to 'maintain, and therefore, give credence to the survival of an outdated phenomon which constitutes a major obstacle to the socialization of the feminine personality'. Thus, in Moynot's opinion, employment within the capitalist labour market remains women's only source of liberation.

On the other hand, Dalla Costa (1972), the 'Insoumise' collective (1977) and Drevet (1977) are of the opposite opinion that a wage for housework is desirable. Therefore, they wish to show that domestic labour is deserving of one. In short, they argue that it is 'productive' labour. Additionally, they believe that the fight for wages for housework on the part of women would enhance the class struggle because the State would have to take reproduction on board financially. Thereby, it would be incurred as a direct cost to capital. Moreover, the concerted withdrawal of domestic services by women in the home would disrupt capitalism in the same way as would an industrial strike. The assumption, therefore, is that domestic labour is absolutely and not conditionally necessary to capitalism - it is on a par with, and not secondary to industrial production. Drevet (1977, p. 24), in the Revue d'en face, replying to their editorial criticism of the demand for wages for housework, contends that 'we must fight not only so that women no longer suffer the consequences of unemployment and of capitalist reconstruction, but also so that their work in the house be recognized as real work'.

Furthermore, the 'Insoumise' collective (1977, p. 5) are in favour of wages for housework because they do not believe that employment is the real solution for women. They assert that

> As an alternative to housework, we do not propose 'outside employment' because these are only two sides of the same coin of forced labour which we are obliged to carry out solely because of the fact that we need money to live.

They explain that women need money, not work. They propose that a domestic wage would enable women to 'establish a relationship of power with capital'. Thus, they call for wages for housework as a means to power in the struggle for collective facilities, for example, creches and laundries.

However, these arguments have failed to convince many French Feminists that in practical terms, such a policy could avoid encouraging women back into the home. This is an unsurprising reaction from women brought up in a country which is obsessed by the birth rate; which already pays bonuses in the form of enhanced child benefit for the production of the 'third' child; and the most right wing political forces of which in the 1988 presidential elections proposed just such a payment to mothers staying at home to look after children.[3]

Despite their differences, all the Marxist Feminists concentrate on the responsibility of capitalism for women's relationship to domestic labour and their generally disadvantaged position in society. However, this is not a universally accepted notion, as has been pointed out earlier Certain socialist women argue that domestic labour is not first and foremost functional to capitalism. These are the 'Feminist Marxists'.

The Feminist Marxists

The theorists of this sub-group attempt to explain the oppression of women, their responsibility for domestic labour and thus the household division of labour in terms of the interaction between the structures of patriarchy and capitalism. The prinicipal exponent of this position in France is the 'Elles Voient Rouge' collective (1981) which split from the Communist Party because its position concerning women was too conservative for their taste. Their analysis is shared by Alain Testard (1982), whilst, as far as the class status of women is concerned, the Feminist Marxist position is also expounded by Claude Alzon (1973).

According to the exponents of this brand of feminism, women's unpaid domestic labour is not only functional to capitalism, but to men as a class as well. As Testard (1982,

p. 1158) asserts

> when a woman works in the home, it is the husband who is the owner of the only property which belongs to the working class family, namely, labour power, which, through its sale, provides them with the means of subsistence. This is the economic foundation of the patriarchal form of the modern family.

The product of a housewife's work escapes her control, not merely because it is ultimately sold to capital in the form of labour power, but because it is, in the first instance, the sole possession of her husband. The wife is exploited by her husband because the labour power which she produces is inseparable from him. Indeed, the 'Elles Voient Rouge' collective (1981, p. 33) contend that 'if capital profits from the domestic work of women, then men profit from it even more' in terms of the sexual and psychological power which women's economic dependency represents for men. They believe that men's labour power is liberated by their wives' domestic labour for their own use as much as for capital's gain, suggesting that if men did not receive this free service, it would be they who would suffer first, and not capital.

Nevertheless, the Feminist Marxists agree that it is capital which shores up the domination of women in the home by paying the major part of the familial salary to the man. The very notion of the 'family wage', coupled with legislation limiting the use of female labour, contributes to the continuation of women's confinement to the domestic sphere. The Marxist Feminsts argue that this is easily explained because capital needs the domestic services provided by women. In contrast, the Feminists Marxists understand this situation to be a contradiction in the development of capitalism.

The Feminist Marxists hold the view that taken to its logical extension, capitalism would have freed women from their domestic slavery in the home in order to put their labour power into competition with that of men. The fact that this did not happen, and that women were not granted the freedom to sell their labour on the market, is proof that capitalism had to mould itself to the social organization which predated it, namely, patriarchy. Testard (1982, p. 1147) notes that in the birth place of the Industrial Revolution, namely England, the proletarian family, at the time of Marx's writing, appeared to have been dissolved. Women and children worked in the factories. Canteens and dormitories were often provided by employers for their workforce. The precapitalist domestic sphere seemed to have broken down and reproduction was being taken into the market sphere. Testard stresses the importance of the fact that this trend reversed. In his opinion, this reversal suggests that a different social structure - that of patriarchy - was at work to halt capitalism's natural progress. In sum, the Feminist Marxists argue that capitalism did not supercede patriarchal structures. Rather, it was obliged to accommodate to them.

The Feminist Marxist analysis of the role and purpose of domestic labour cannot be separated from the 'political' persuasions of those who espouse it. For example, the 'Elles Voient Rouge' collective (1981, p. 26) propose that women must be freed of their ties to family, domestic labour and reproduction if they are to be liberated. The wages for housework of the 'productive functionalists' is thus derided because it would bind women even more tightly to the home and family. The 'Elles Voient Rouge' collective (1981) maintain that domestic labour imprisons women so that they may be better controlled by men and capital. To pay for these domestic services directly, that is, by giving a salary to wives and mothers at home, would be to crystalize this imprisonment and reinforce the idea that domestic labour is specifically a woman's duty.

Furthermore, the 'Elles Voient Rouge' collective (1981, p. 134) arguing as they do that domestic labour benefits 'men' and is a prime manifestation of the existence of patriarchy, believe that women will not automatically be freed from domestic slavery with the downfall of capitalism, although this is a precondition of their eventual liberation. The political corollary of this is that the women's movement must be at least partially autonomous vis à vis the proletarian struggle. Not only capitalism, but patriarchy too must be challenged in all its economic, social, political and ideological dimensions as they are institutionalized within the family. Indeed, they contend that the gender division of labour structures the class struggle. Since the appropriation of women by men was the first manifestation of private property, it is the liberation of women from their domestic slavery which is the condition for the abolition of that private property.

The principal question which arises from these assertions is: do women owe allegiance first and foremost to a social (capitalist) class, or do they belong to a class of women all similarly oppressed and exploited? It is in the response to this question that the Feminist Marxists stop short of the Radical Feminist point of view in that they assert that women belong to various capitalist classes and that no homogeneous class of women exists. Alzon (1973), in his famous collection of papers La femme potiche et la femme bonniche is one of the major protagonists of this point of view (although it must be noted that he has been criticized by many feminists for his portrayal of bourgeois women). He rejects the Radical Feminist claim that all women are exploited (economically) and dominated (psychologically) in the same fashion. He argues that only working class men appropriate their wives' domestic services (interpreted as concrete activities, such as cleaning, washing, and cooking: he excludes such duties as producing children or status enhancing activities such as entertaining) and exploit them. The bourgeois wife, however, provides no such domestic services and consequently, her husband cannot exploit her economically, even if he can, and does, dominate her psychologically. Although in general agreement, the 'Elles Voient Rouge' collective (1981) prefer to take a less dogmatic stance on this question. They do not wish to separate social and gender class, but to expose the way in which the two are interrelated in order to link the feminist to the proletarian struggles without supporting one at the expense of the other.

In sum, the Feminist Marxist approach proposes that domestic labour is functional to men as well as to capitalism and that capitalism was obliged to take on board certain aspects of patriarchy. However, they disagree that women form a homogeneous class, asserting that bourgeois and working class women do indeed suffer in different ways, especially vis à vis domestic labour, and thus have diverging interests. For that reason, women owe allegiance to differing social classes. It is this assertion which separates the Feminist Marxists from the Radical Feminists. It is the Radical Feminists who will be the subject of discussion of the next section.

The Radical Feminists

This group has one dominating figure: Christine Delphy. She has played a major part in the debate on women's domestic work since the early 'Seventies when her article (1970) (written under the name of Dupont) 'L'ennemi principal' appeared in the feminist review Partisans. This title, as we shall see, sums up the direction of her approach. Colette Guillaumin (1978) is also of this Radical Feminist mould and we shall be considering her work here also.

In agreement with the 'unproductive functionalist' sub-group of Marxist Feminists, and indeed with the Feminist Marxists, Delphy insists that domestic labour is not analogous to capitalist wage labour. However, she stresses that this assertion must lead one not to dismiss the importance of this form of work (which is the danger inherent in the 'unproductive functionalist' approach), but rather to explore the relationship of domestic labour to patriarchy.

Indeed, the novelty of Delphy's approach is to posit the existence of two modes of production. She argues that if domestic labour cannot be explained in terms of the Capitalist Mode of Production, this is not because it has only a reproductive function, but because it belongs to a different mode of production altogether - the Domestic Mode of Production. Delphy (1978, p. 50) explains

> Our hypothesis is that the reason why housework is not considered to be productive and not included in the national accounts is that it is carried out for free within the household ... This is not because of the particular nature of the services of which this work is composed, ... nor because of the characteristics of the persons who provide them, ... but because of the specific nature of the contract which links the worker - that is, the wife - to the household and to her boss.

In her original studies of inheritance in peasant farming families, Delphy (1984, p. 80) explains that she found that inheritance practices led to possessors and non possessors of the means of production within the family itself. 'The family' as such did not own anything; it was the inheriting brothers who owned the property. Women and younger siblings owned nothing, but 'worked for' the principal inheritors. In non property owning families, the same effect is produced by the systematic discrimination women face in the labour market. Their lack of opportunity to provide for themselves through a wage (being akin to lack of land) obliges them to enter the 'domestic relations of production' by marrying.

Indeed, the Domestic Mode of Production is embodied in the social institution of marriage since it is through the marriage contract that the domestic labour of women is appropriated by men. The link between marriage and the 'Domestic Mode of Production' is also that which gives domestic labour its specific characteristics in contrast to capitalist wage labour. Delphy maintains that the relationship between marriage partners is entirely different from that which exists between employer and employee because the time of the wife is appropriated as a whole by her husband. She is not given a set sum per hour for the work she accomplishes. In return for her domestic services, the wife is 'kept' according to the income and generosity of her spouse. Delphy (Dupont, 1970, p. 159) explains that 'the only obligation on the part of the husband - which is obviously in his own interests - is to maintain his wife's labour power'. Guillaumin (1978, p. 168) goes so far as to say that 'the free provision of services within the framework of an all embracing and personal relationship (marriage) constitutes a 'relationship of slavery'.

According to the Radical Feminists, it is their common position within marriage which gives 'women' an identity as a homogeneous class. Even unmarried women are affected because, being expected to take their place in the Domestic Mode of Production, they are not treated as permanent features in the labour market. This explains their low wages and scant career prospects. Thus, in the opinion of these theorists, the division between men and women is a class division akin to that which exists between the bourgeoisie and the proletariat. Delphy (1984, p. 25-27) explains that she employs the concept of class in this context in order to stress that gender difference is social and not natural, and is based on the economic exploitation and social domination characteristic of the Domestic Mode of Production. Furthermore, Guillaumin (1978, p. 7) speaks of a 'power relationship' in which women as a class are appropriated by men as a class and of which marriage is only the facade.

In similarity to the Marxist Feminists and Feminist Marxists, the theoretical position of the Radical Feminists cannot be divorced from their political perspective which seeks to cast women's struggle as an autonomous one essentially against patriarchy in a way which the Marxist Feminists and Feminist Marxists find too extreme. In other words, for Delphy and Guillaumin, to posit the existence of a Domestic Mode of Production is to put women's oppression on a direct par with that of the proletariat.

The debates and disagreements characteristic of the last three groups of Feminist theorists have tended to be highly theoretical in nature, concerning the relationship of domestic work to established structuralist categories. The latest development in the 'structuralist' analysis in France of women's domestic work, as we will see in the following section, attempts to break free of the theoretical arguments which we have witnessed thus far. Indeed, it adds a sociological and empirical (as well as a new theoretical) dimension to the question of the gender division of labour. This is the contribution of the 'Rapports Sociaux' (social relations) group.

The 'Rapports sociaux' group

The most recent developments in the study of domestic labour within a Feminist perspective in France have come from a broad and varied group of Marxist inspired sociologists and economists who participate in the seminar group 'Atelier Production/Reproduction' (APRE) (Production/Reproduction workshop).[4] We shall call them the 'Rapports Sociaux' (Social Relations) group here. Bourgeois, Brener, Chabaud, Cot, Fougeyrollas, Haicault and Kartchevsky (1978) laid the foundations of the approach by criticizing the attempts to fit domestic labour as an 'economic' category into the schema of Marx's Capital. They argue that it should be discussed in terms of the social relations in which it is embedded, hence the title of the group. This criticism is informed by the four basic characteristics which differentiate the theorists of this group from the other Feminists: first, they are non economistic in their approach; second, they understand the relationship between production and reproduction to be a question of social relations; third, they are more explicitly empirical than the other Feminists; and finally, they are more interested in the interaction of domestic and professional work in the lives of women than in domestic labour per se.

First, then, theirs is essentially a non economistic approach to the place of domestic labour in capitalism and patriarchy. This is in contrast to the other Feminists discussed in this book who attempt to define women's domestic labour in terms of what economic functions it fulfils within capitalism and/or patriarchy. Indeed, the theorists of the 'Rapports Sociaux' group criticize the attempts to fit domestic work into economic categories which are not suited to its analysis. The editorial collective of Le sexe du travail (1984, p. 8) explain that one should not 'shape domestic labour in order to make it acceptable to the dominant concept of work by seeking to describe it in terms of market production to which it is not suited'. Moreover, Kartchevsky & Bourgeois (1983, p. 579) speak for the group when they assert that the 'attempts to integrate domestic labour into political economy have led to a dead end'. This is because in examining its relationship to production in terms of value, researchers come up against the impossibility of reducing to a common denominator those activities with and those activities without a monetary value. They (1978, p. 23) explain that the 'break with economism' allows them to expose both the 'specific' and 'capitalist' nature of domestic labour and 'opens up the issue of the relationship between production and reproduction'. Thus, as Dominique Fougeyrollas [5] explained, one can posit that domestic labour fulfils a function within capitalism without having to justify its importance in Marxist economic terms.

The relationship of women's domestic labour to capitalism and to patriarchy must, in the opinion of this group of theorists, pass through the intermediary of the family, this being the social institution in which domestic work is embedded. This notion has its roots in the ideas of Lautier (1977, p. 83) who declares that 'the Marxist wing of the feminist movement has committed the error of basing the majority of its analyses on domestic labour itself, rather than on the family'. The theorists of the 'Rapport sociaux' group realize that there are dangers inherent in advocating an approach which places domestic work firmly back in the social sphere of the family in a world in which the 'economic' and 'public' sphere dominates. In order to minimize these dangers, they stress that the 'family' and 'work' should not be researched separately and call for productive systems and familial structures to be analysed simultaneously.

The second characteristic of this group of Feminists is their conviction that all social phenomena - whether they be of production or of reproduction - must be examined in the light of the social relations of both gender and class. Consequently, one can say that in political and theoretical terms, the analysis of the 'Rapports Sociaux' group is very much akin to that of the Feminist Marxists. In their opinion, a given social organization is constituted not only according to the way in which social classes relate to one another, but also according to the relationship which exists between men and women. This means that a given phenomenon is not influenced exclusively by one type of social relations as opposed to the other (this being the difference to Delphy's Radical Feminist analysis). Thus, when specific women in specific situations perform domestic tasks, they are influenced by a mixture of gender and class relationships, and no prior assumptions should be made about which type of relations is most important. This should be decided empirically case by case.

This view is, therefore, related to the third characteristic of these theorists, namely, their methodological approach. Theirs are principally inductive and sociological studies of women's domestic labour as opposed to deductive, theoretical and for a large part, economistic ones. Refusing to chase their theoretical tails as in their opinion many of their Feminist counterparts do, these theorists insist that it is necessary to carry out empirical research in order to decide whether social relations of class or gender are determinant, if indeed either is, in given situations.

These researchers have embarked on a variety of empirical projects to discover women's experience of family and work, and the social relations concerning domestic labour.[6] For example, Combes & Haicault (1984) attempt to provide empirical evidence for the coexistence of both the relations of production and reproduction, or gender and class, in both the domestic and market spheres. Others, for example, Haicault (1984), test the relationship of gender and class by looking at the experience of work by women from specific social classes. Moreover, Fougeyrollas[7] explained that she was drawn to empirical work because of the sheer lack of information on the everyday practices of women in terms of the way in which they organize their work lives, both domestic and professional.

The fourth characteristic common to these theorists is their interest in the interaction of domestic and professional work in the lives of women. This is a product, first, of their interest in the interaction of the social relations of production and reproduction and gender and class. Second, it results from their insistence that 'work' and 'family' are not two separate entities which can be researched independently.

Thus, the theorists involved in the 'APRE' are not all interested primarily in domestic work. Indeed, domestic labour as a specific subject sometimes fades into the background. This is not because it is ignored, however, but because its importance is accepted a priori. It features as a necessary, but not necessarily primary subject in all analyses which concern women's working lives. That is, the equal status of domestic work and employment is taken for granted. Consequently, the aim becomes less and less to analyse domestic labour in its own right and more and more to include it as a salient and important factor in studies from which it was hitherto excluded.

In sum, then, the theorists of the 'Rapports Sociaux' group have tried to provide empirical evidence for the coexistence of both the relations of production and reproduction, or class and gender, in both the domestic and market spheres. They have also tested the relationship of gender and class by examining how women from specific social categories experience domestic work. However, the possibility of obtaining an unequivocal answer to the question of the relative importance of class and gender through empirical research alone seems doubtful. This is because one must consider that the arguments about the supremacy of one as opposed to the other is essentially an argument between conflicting ideological standpoints. Indeed, the importance of the conflicting ideologies which are at work in the Feminist cluster will form the basis of the discussion in the following section.

Evaluating the Feminist approaches

We have seen, therefore, that from the same basic description of women's social and economic position, different explanations of women's oppression and the relationship of domestic work to that oppression are possible. The task of this section is to bring the various Feminist strands together in order to elucidate the choices which these theorists have made in producing their analyses of domestic work. There are three basic choices which divide certain groups of Feminists from certain others. First, Feminist theorists have to choose whether to label domestic labour 'production' or 'reproduction' (or, 'productive' or 'unproductive' labour) and offer reasons for this choice. Second, there is the question of whether women constitute a homogenous 'gender class' or are divided between social classes and of how this affects our understanding of the role of domestic labour. Finally, a decision must be made as to whether the over arching structure of society is best understood in terms of capitalism or patriarchy. [8]

I will begin with the question of whether or not domestic work is considered to constitute 'production' or 'reproduction'. On this point, only 'productive functionalist' Marxist Feminists posit that domestic labour constitutes 'production' within the 'Capitalist Mode of Production', this being their justification for demanding wages for housework. The 'unproductive functionalist' Marxist Feminists, the Feminist Marxists and the Radical Feminists are superficially in agreement that it does not. Nevertheless, their reasons for putting forward this argument vary radically.

On the one hand, the fact that Marxist Feminists of the 'unproductive functionalist' school deem domestic work 'reproduction' results from their accepting that capitalist, industrial production is the central motor of history. For example, Moynot [9] was unequivocal that the sphere of production is the ultimate source of socialization and eventually, social and economic change. By creating and maintaining a hierarchy between production and reproduction, Marxist Feminists succeed in relegating domestic work in importance in comparison with wage labour. By this means, they subjugate the feminist to the proletarian struggle.

On the other hand, although agreeing that domestic work is not a form of 'productive labour' in capitalism, the Feminist Marxists, the Radical Feminists and the 'Rapports Sociaux' group do not draw the conclusion from this that domestic labour is any less important in the structuring of society than capitalist wage labour. Indeed, their conclusion that domestic labour is important constitutes the starting point for their respective critiques of the traditional Marxist analysis of society which reduces the oppression of women to secondary importance. That is to say, they draw the conclusion that this form of labour (which is different from wage labour and in which women have a particular role to play) exists because of the existence of patriarchy.

The second, but closely related, matter is that of whether women belong first and foremost to a 'social class' or to a 'gender class'. This is an issue which divides Marxist Feminists and Feminist Marxists, and to a lesser extent, the 'Rapports Sociaux' group (because of their relative lack of dogmatism on this issue), on the one hand, from the Radical Feminists, on the other. Delphy's (1984, p. 25) 'political' position is that women should join together to fight a common cause because they all labour under a similar oppression in the Domestic Mode of Production. That is, whatever their different social situations, women's oppression as a gender class by men transends them. However, the rest of the Feminists are reluctant to single out the gender variable in this way. For the Marxist Feminists, the struggle against capitalism remains of prime importance whilst for the Feminist Marxists, the fight against patriarchy cannot be distinguished from the fight against capitalism. The underlying premise of the analyses of the 'Rapports Sociaux' group is that one cannot generalize over the domination of class or gender relations: one must decide in a given situation whether class or gender is the determinant variable.

Third comes the question of the relationship between 'capitalism' and 'patriarchy' as social structures and the place of domestic labour within them. Even the Marxist Feminists do not categorically deny the existence of patriarchy in the oppression of women and the shaping of domestic labour. However, they assert that patriarchy has no material base: it is merely part of the social superstructure. If the man remains 'in charge' in the family, it is because capital wishes him to be, and thus, women's situation is attributable to capitalism. The Marxist notion of dialectical materialism allows the Marxist

Feminists to explain what has gone before in terms of what is now. In other words, history should not be considered in an evolutionist manner; on the contrary, one should extrapolate back from the most developed social form in order to explain previous phenomena. It is in this way that these Marxist Feminist theorists attempt to keep intact their analysis of society in terms of capitalism whilst acknowledging the 'fundamental' oppression of women (by men?). However, as Moynot [10] conceded, since the domination of women by men existed before capitalism, the theory of capitalism alone - however hard one tries - cannot explain women's oppression.

The Feminist Marxists - being more willing to accept a larger role for patriarchy in the social structure - view the historical meeting of capitalism and patriarchy somewhat differently. They posit that since patriarchy predated capitalism, capitalism was obliged to take on board the subjugation of women to men. In fact, they argue that capital would have been able to extract more surplus value from the workforce had the labour power of women been put into direct competition with that of men.

For the Radical Feminists, domestic labour is the material basis of patriarchy. Delphy (1984, p. 18), for example, explains that 'patriarchy is the system of subordination of women to men in contemporary industrial socities. This system has an economic base and this base is the domestic mode of production'. Delphy and Guillaumin understand history in terms of patriarchy, that is, in terms of a system of relations between men and women which enables men to dominate women. Patriarchy, argues Delphy, is not an a-historic phenomenon, as some Feminist Marxists seem to suggest, but one which changes in accordance with different historical social forms.

Once again, the 'Rapports Sociaux' group attempt to follow the pragmatic line on this question. Instead of discussing abstract, invariable concepts such as patriarchy or capitalism, they talk of the extent of the influence of the 'social relations of class and gender'. They disagree with Marxist Feminists that one set of relations is more important than another and with Delphy that different modes of production exist. For example, Combes & Haicault assert that a universal reappraisal of social structure has been sparked off by examining domestic work: namely that all phenomena should be studied in terms of their patriarchal relationships as well as in terms of their class relationships. They (1984, p. 165) add that for them, studying the social relations of gender and class is a means of 'overcoming the deficiencies of structural analysis which is incapable of taking into account the dynamics of social relations'.

Thus, from treating domestic labour in its specificity - that is, by not trying to confine it to the rules of industrial labour - these theorists have developed a new angle altogether from which to analyse society. For example, Chabaud, Fougeyrollas & Sonnthonnax (1985, p. 21) explain

> The relative autonomization of production and reproduction within a society based on employment led us to put forward the hypothesis that social relations of reproduction distinct from the relations of production exist and that they are not reducible to the latter.

To recap, therefore, one could list the following relationships between capitalism and patriarchy which these feminist theorists adopt: (i) that patriarchy is a former social structure which has been annexed by capitalism because it efficiently fulfils the reproduction function; (ii) that capitalism had to integrate patriarchy into its social formation because patriarchy was a powerful social structure which predated capitalism; (iii) that patriarchy and capitalism exist side by side at present, each structuring its own distinct mode of production; and (iv) that social relations of class (capitalism) and gender (patriarchy) co-exist, but they are not confined to different and specific spheres of life, but interact with one another. However, what they have in common is that they understand society in terms of social classes and relationships of power, some being more functionalist and universalist than others. The 'Rapports Sociaux' group is the most empiricist and individualist in this respect.

Collin [11] remarks that the first debate that influenced, nourished and also blocked feminism was its ideological (and practical) debate with Marxism. Indeed, it was Marxist analysis in the first place which provided a framework for explaining domestic labour and women's responsibility for it in terms of women's oppression as a social group. Chabaud, Fougeyrollas & Sonnthonnax (1985, p. 145) explain that Feminists have sought to escape from physiological or psychological representations concerning the gender division of labour and of women's oppression as well as from the notion of complementarity of the sexes thanks to their respective specialisms. In so doing, socialist and radical feminists have defined domestic labour as an economic activity in the same way as they would wage labour. In order to do this, they have borrowed from Marxist categories, picking and choosing from the tool kit of Marxist concepts in order to shape and mould their theories. We thus have a situation in which Marxist categories (such as production, reproduction, class and so on) are used in different ways to justify certain theoretical and ideological positions.

However, the act of examining women as a separate social group has undermined the legitimacy of these same Marxist categories as universally applicable. If one maintains that domestic labour is a serious form of work, but on comparing it with categories for defining capitalist wage labour one finds that it does not fit, then one is obliged to take a second look at the analytical framework itself. This is very much what Delphy, the 'Rapports Sociaux' group theorists and the 'Elles Voient Rouge' collective have done.

Thus, we can see that the choices for the Feminists in the field of domestic labour entail how to relate Marxist analyses, terminology and political aspirations to explain women's situation. Domestic labour and women's oppression muddy the waters of a 'traditional', (Marxist) structuralist analysis of society. These Feminist analyses question the centrality of production and industrial labour; of 'class'; and of capitalism. In sum, the choice of analysing domestic work in this way is both a tribute to the staying power of Marxist analysis and its claim to be a truly 'universal' interpretation of society, but also a threat to the class analysis of society in terms of capitalist classes only.

The exploration of 'women' as a social group with their own relationship to work carries with it something profoundly disturbing for the dominance of Marxism over the structuralist analysis of society. French feminists, along with their Anglo-Saxon sisters, have used a new plane along which to cut the crystal of society. This new plane is gender division which represents a new perspective on the exploitative relations existing in the world. These relations cannot be easily reduced to a sub-division of the traditional social classes. So, the raising of the question of domestic labour is linked to a theoretical challenge to the dominance of Marxism as the only critical social and economic theory. Moreover, it questions the centrality of industrial labour as the kingpin of the 'structure' of this society. Consequently, it affects how one defines 'work', this being the question to which I now turn.

A new concept of work?

Simply by studying women, the family and the household under the banner of 'domestic labour', these Feminist theorists are refuting the assumption that the modern industrial family has surrendered all its productive functions.

Moreover, by asserting that 'work' goes on in the private sphere of the family, they bring to light women's hidden contribution to society. These are major contributions to the debate on 'work' in themselves.

However, it should not be forgotten that the word 'travail' in French means both 'work' and 'labour'. In English, there is a subtle distinction between the two: 'work' refers very much to the empirically observable activity whilst 'labour', especially in structuralist analyses, is a conceptual category. In similarity to the Microeconomists, Feminist theorists are interested not in bringing about a change in the 'empirical' category of 'work' but in the conceptual category of 'labour' by including domestic work within its realm of application. In other words, the change in the concept of 'work' which they propose is a theoretical one: that is, they wish to expand the concepts of production, labour and the rest to 'housework' which was previously an activity excluded from them.

Thus, as 'structuralist' theorists, their interest in exploring women's housework as a form of 'labour' (even if it is 'reproductive' labour) has a significance which is deeper than merely stressing that women work hard in the home. These theorists all use women's responsibility for domestic labour to define their relationship to the mode of production - whether this be patriarchal or capitalist. In this way, they hope to enhance the theoretical status of women's oppression in a world in which the ideological Left is imbued with Marxism. Indeed, explaining women's oppression in these economic terms is part of the striving to anchor it in a material base.

For the most part, on a practical level, the Feminist theorists do not wish to see a development of the role played by domestic labour in the economy. In granting 'housework' the lofty value of 'labour', they are not suggesting that it should be expanded. Quite the opposite, in fact. The Marxist Feminists believe that domestic labour will disappear with the advent of socialism. It is doomed to extinction along with capitalism and private property. Women's liberation will come through participation in public industry. For example, Moynot (1978, p. 139) explains that the same development of human and material production forces which is carrying us towards socialism will enable women to participate in the labour force on the same terms as men. Domestic labour is private and thus an obstacle to universal socialization in which the private and the public are once again merged. Despite the contradictions and oppression involved, capitalist employment is a step along the path.

Indeed, all Feminists - with the exception of the 'productive functionalist' Marxist Feminists - perceive a danger in advocating any policy which could be used to prevent women from competing with men on an equal basis in the labour market. Although not all would agree in detail, the principle that women's salvation will come through their participation in employment - if for no other reason than that viable alternatives are not to hand - enjoys a wide consensus.

Thus, despite their insight into the 'value' of domestic labour, the Feminist theorists have no sweeping plan to bring about a change in the way in which work is organized, distributed and remunerated which diverges from the 'masculine' model of full time employment. This can be judged as a wasted opportunity or understandable caution on their part. Any reference to the 'essential' usefulness or contribution of domestic work could be misinterpreted as invoking an 'essential' feminine being which would undermine the whole reason for asserting that domestic labour is the material basis of women's oppression. This position, as we shall see in Chapter 10, brings them into conflict with the Radical theorists.

In conclusion, one can say that if the assumption that work is a synonym of employment is today not as all pervading as perhaps it once was, feminist research into domestic labour must take much of the credit. In order to render domestic labour a subject worthy of sociological, and especially economic analysis, feminist theorists have had to stress that domestic labour is a form of 'work' whose importance could be equated with that of employment. In so doing, they struck at the root of many preconceived notions about the production of wealth and well being in society. The editors of the book Le sexe du travail (1984, p. 8) so rightly point out that 'by denouncing the invisibility of domestic labour in their sociological and economic analyses, feminism has introduced a decisive breakthrough'. However, this 'decisive breakthrough' is essentially theoretical since, when it comes to advocating practical change on the basis of their theoretical assertions, Feminists theorists reinforce the dominance of employment by suggesting that women's liberation passes, on the whole, through the doorway of access to the formal labour market.

Conclusions

In sum, for these Feminist theorists, domestic labour is the socio-economic basis of women's oppression. In fact, only those strands of feminism which define women's oppression in such terms - as opposed to psychoanalytical or essentialist ones - discuss domestic labour at all. These socio-economic strands of French feminism are divided between socialist and radical Feminists. That is, between those who want to ally women's subjugation to the class struggle and those who posit that women form a homogenous separate class whose needs are different from those of the proletariat. These ideological persuasions determine whether domestic labour is interpreted as a mode of production or reproduction in capitalism; or whether it is a mode of production in patriarchy. Some, as we have seen, attempt to combine the two, others to solve the question with empirical research.

No single explanation of the nature of the relationship between domestic labour and women's oppression arises from these studies. Many questions remain, such as whether the gendered division of labour in general is the 'source' or the 'expression' of women's oppression; whether women's role in domestic labour is the source of their devalued social position; or, whether women are assigned to this already devalued role because they are oppressed. Neither is it decided whether the link between women and domestic labour is 'natural' or not. Nor is the matter of whether the oppression of the executors of these tasks devalues the tasks themselves or whether it is capitalism or industrialism which devalued the 'natural' role of women in reproduction. In keeping with the methodological principles of this study, no attempt will be made to answer these questions from a detached standpoint. However, I pose them in order to highlight the impossibilty of describing unequivocally the causal relationship which exists between correlating variables in general, and those which relate to this area of study in particular.

Notes

1. These are a loose group of women sociologists, and to a lesser extent, economists, who, sharing a common theoretical stance on the question of analysing 'social relations' participate in the seminar group 'Atelier Production/Reproduction' (APRE).
2. As found in the 1972 reproduction of <u>The family, private property and the State</u> by Lawrence & Wishart.
3. Chirac and Barre proposed allowing a payment of 3,900F a month net to women (or men) with three or more children who gave up their job to look after them. Le Pen followed suit, offering 5,000F a month to mothers to

stay at home.

4. The following 'cahiers' from this seminar group have been produced so far: Crise et emploi des femmes, no.1, Feb. 1985; Temps sociaux et trajectoires selon le sexe, no.2, May 1985; Production / Reproduction et rapports sociaux de sexe, no.3, September 1985; La famille comme unité de production, no.4, February 1986; Rapports intra-familiaux et rapports sociaux de sexe, no.5, May 1986; Division sexuelle du travail, famille et rapport salarial, no. 6, Sept. 1986.
5. Interview conducted in Paris, April 1987.
6. Le sexe du travail (1984) is a collection of articles setting out the findings of the various projects of this group of theorists.
7. Interview conducted in Paris, April 1987.
8. One important point to remember made by Delphy (in an interview, 1988), is that the 'debate' in France over domestic labour has been subdued rather than open and polemical. Delphy says that this is because one is in a rather small group of people. Interestingly, she says that the only person to have an approach distinctly different from her own was Cathérine Sofer. Thus, perhaps the sharp distinctions which I have drawn between theoretical positions would not be recognizable to the people involved in the debates themselves.
9. Interview conducted in Paris, April 1988.
10. Interview conducted in Paris, April 1988.
12. In Duchen (1986, p. 40).

6 Empirical studies of the household division of labour

Introduction

In addition to the work of the Feminist and Microeconomist theorists, there have been a number of Empirical studies carried out in France concerning the household division of labour and domestic work. These are of two sorts. First, there is a set of analyses which provide estimates of the number of hours devoted to domestic tasks by men and women. These are based on the results of two national time-budget surveys carried out by 'INSEE'. Second, there are three ethnographic, or qualitative analyses of domestic organization which focus on the division of labour between spouses. These adopt an approach based on interviews in which couples describe their various modes of sharing the household work load.

In the case of the time-budget analyses, I will investigate the extent to which the statistics concerning the domestic division of labour uphold the consensus of opinion which exists between the Microeconomists and the Feminists. This states that gender is the determining variable in deciding how much domestic work a person carries out. In the case of the three qualitative studies, I will examine the extent to which the explanations for the division of labour which they glean from couples themselves match either the explanations of the Microeconomist or the

Feminist theorists. I will begin with an analysis of the time-budget studies.

Time-budget studies

Presentation of the findings

Broadly speaking, time-budgeting is a technique for data collection whereby the research participants are invited to complete 'diaries'. These diaries chronicle the number of minutes spent on a certain range of activities. According to its supporters, time-budgeting is a technique especially suited to the discussion of household work and its division of labour because, as Yannick Lemel (1984) [1] points out, time-budget studies provide a panorama of ways of life, permitting the evaluation of the relative importance of different activities in a person's day. Additionally, time-budgets appear, on the surface, to be the perfect 'descriptive' technique. In other words, for some, at least, they are the most apt tool for the neutral observation of everyday life.

The idea of evaluating the amount of time consumed by domestic responsibilities, and especially childcare, is not completely new in France. For example, in 1948, Stoetzel measured the correlation between hours taken up in housework and number of children in order to calculate the social cost of educating a child. In 1959, Girard & Bastide examined the impact of household equipment on the amount of time necessary for women to spend carrying out housework. However, neither of these studies compared the time-budgets of men and women. They took it for granted that housework and childcare were part of the female domain. In 1966, the first national survey of the time-budgets of the French population permitted the comparison of the daily activities of men and women. [2] Nonetheless, it was not used to any great degree to study the household division of labour, nor to compare the time taken up in domestic duties with that devoted to professional work.

The two most recent national time-budget studies produced by 'INSEE' in 1974/5 and 1985/6 have both provided such information. What, then, have been the results of these analyses? First, as far as the gender division of domestic labour [3] is concerned, these last two time-budget studies have uncovered the weight of the domestic burden which falls on women in comparison with that which comes to bear on men. In 1975, in the eighteen to sixty-four age range, employed women spent thirty-two hours fifty-four minutes on average on domestic work per week whereas employed men spent only sixteen hours twenty minutes. Housewives devoted fifty-four hours twenty-nine minutes a week to such activities.

Nonetheless, the 1986 time-budget study reveals that the gap has narrowed a little. Once again, in the eighteen to sixty four age group, the time spent by housewives on domestic work per week decreased by six hours eighteen minutes to forty-eight hours eleven minutes and by twenty-eight minutes to thirty hours twenty-six minutes per week for employed women. Concomitantly, the time spent by employed men rose over this period by two hours forty-seven minutes to eighteen hours forty-seven minutes. However, one should be wary of reading too much into these figures: first, because the difference between the time devoted to domestic work by men and women remains enormous: in the case of employed men as compared with employed women, the disparity is in the region of fourteen hours per week. Second, one must remember that the category of 'domestic work' in this instance takes into account traditionally male activities such as DIY, gardening and the like which account for most of the increase in the time spent on such work by men. An increase in this non routine activity does not necessarily represent a lessening of the everyday burden of routine domestic labour on women.

Second, a comparison of the amount of domestic and professional work performed produces more surprising results. Taking a grand average for the entire adult population for the year 1975, thirty hours two minutes per person per week were spent on domestic labour whilst professional work (including training and travelling time) occupied only twenty-eight hours seven minutes [4] - that is, two hours fifty-five minutes less than domestic work. Adding together these results and applying them on a national level for France, Chadeau & Fouquet (1981) estimate that the total number of hours worked by men and women in 1975 (professional and domestic combined) was 89.3 billion. Of this, the majority of 48.1 billion hours were spent on domestic work, with 41.2 billion on professional work: that is, 6.9 billion hours less. The gap continued to widen in the next decade with domestic work time increasing to occupy thirty-one hours thirty-seven minutes per person per week with the time taken by professional work falling to twenty-four hours forty-four minutes, according to Grimler & Roy (1987).

Third, by combining professional and domestic work time to produce a figure for overall work time, one can compare the total amount of 'work' performed by men and women. On the basis of the figures for the adult population aged between eighteen and sixty-four in 1985, women's contribution to the production of wealth and well-being in the country was more than that of men when this contribution is based on the amount of time they spend on both domestic and professional activities. Grimler & Roy (1987, p. 1) note that in 1985, although employed women spent less time than men on professional work, their overall working time - at fifty-nine hours twenty-one minutes - was longer than that of employed men - at fifty-three hours twenty-six minutes - whilst housewives spent only five hours less on housework - at forty-eight hours eleven minutes - than employed men on all forms of work.

As yet, only a primary analysis of the 1985/6 time-budget study has been completed. However, more detailed analyses of the 1974/5 study have been carried out. These relate to the domestic division of labour first, in different social classes and second, at different stages of the lifecycle. As regards the variable of social class, Chastand (1982) found that in total, housewives with children under fourteen in working class households carried out sixty hours of domestic work per week and women from middle class households carried out fifty-six hours. Employed mothers of children under fourteen from working class households performed thirty-nine hours of domestic work as opposed to thirty-one hours of professional work. Women from middle class households carried out thirty-five hours of domestic work and thirty-five hours of professional work. Roy (1981), in a similar study, corroborated the bases of these results.

Even though it seems that the variable of social class creates a difference of between three and four hours a week in the amount of domestic work performed by middle, as opposed to working class women, differences of such magnitude are as nothing in comparison with those existing between men and women. Thus, social class must be contextualised in relation to other factors. For example, Roy (1981, p. 279) notes that

> time spent in performing household activities is explained essentially by demographic variables. Gender, but also employment status and age play a determining role. It is also necessary to include marital status and above all the presence or absence of young children. Nonetheless, one must not forget that socio-professional category has a not insignificant influence on the time spent on housework because it allows certain women to release themselves a little from the constraints imposed by this work.

On the question of the variable of stage in the lifecycle,

that being determined by age, marital status and presence of children or parents in the household, Rousse & Roy (1981) have found that women always perform more household activities than men, single or married, employed or housewives, irrespective of the number of children they have. Only 12 per cent of young men living in the parental home made any significant contribution to completing household tasks as compared with 18 per cent of young women. In the case of young people living alone, only 58 per cent of young men as compared with 74 per cent of young women took responsibility for the majority of their own housework. Living alone (single or widowed), women take responsibility for their household chores, neither leaving things undone, nor eliciting help (paid or unpaid) from outside as often as single men or widowers. Married women, unsurprisingly, take responsibility for the bulk of domestic chores in their households. Thus, one phenomenon remains constant: once a woman is present in the household, very little work remains undone. It is proposed to replicate these studies on the basis of the 1985/6 time-budget study. However, the results of these analyses are yet to be published.

Relationship to the Microeconomists and Feminists: choices and limitations

There is no doubt that these studies provide the statistical evidence to support the hypothesis that women bear the greater burden of domestic work which, in comparison with professional work, is highly significant in terms of the time which it demands. Thus, the time-budget studies furnish the debates on the household division of labour with solid, quantitative foundations, a 'quantitatif de base' as Roy[5] has put it. Nevertheless, these analyses carry with them their own assumptions and have their own limitations.

At the level of the adoption of the time-budget technique itself, it should be noted that the whole concept of 'budgeting' time is borrowed from the microeconomic model according to which people make choices (whether these be of how to use their money or their time) under the constraint of scarcity. 'Time' is thus assumed to be both quantifiable and in limited supply. Furthermore, thanks to the use of 'time' as a common denominator (this also being used by the Microeconomist theorists), categories of activities may be compared irrespective of their qualitative differences.

This is in sharp contrast to the empirical investigations and theoretical premises of the work of Chabaud, Fougeyrollas & Sonnthonnax (1985) of the 'Rapports Sociaux' group of Feminists, for example. They are of the opinion that the content and social relations of women's domestic work - as distinct from men's domestic and professional work - are irreducible to other categories of activity. Fougeyrollas [6] declared that 'time-budget studies have produced some interesting things' but 'cannot come to grips with the qualitative content of this type of work which is not part of the network of monetary exchange'. Likewise, Chabaud [7] asserts that the same observable task, when performed by a man is different when performed by a woman. Studying the distribution of domestic work in terms of the amount of time spent on it by men and women masks this qualitative difference. When women perform domestic activities, it is in the social relations of 'permanent availability', she contends, which the measuring of hours and minutes cannot capture. Thus, the very choice of the common denominator of time carries with it theoretical implications concerning the nature of the division of domestic work which exists between men and women.

Once one has decided to use the technique of time-budgeting, one still has to decide on the exact design of the project. It is at this stage that analysts must begin to categorize activities and thus define what they understand by the concept of 'work'. Very important in this process of definition is the decision of whether to record only the 'behaviour' of the research subjects or to interrogate them further on the purpose of their activity. The 1974/5 study was completely 'behaviourist' in the above sense. That is, it did not investigate the aim or motive of the activities which the research subjects listed in their diaries. However, as Roy [8] noted, problems arose with this method because the purpose of an activity determines whether it should be placed in the category of professional work, domestic work, leisure or personal care. For example, the action of writing a letter can be part of one's job or of one's domestic duties, for amusement or as part of one's responsiblity in an association. Roy explained that this problem was remedied in the 1985/6 study, the research subjects being required to record the aim of each of their activities so that the analysts could decide whether a certain activity constituted 'work' or 'leisure', for example. Nonetheless, it should be remembered that it remained the responsibility of the analyst, and not the research subject, to decide in the final instance into which category a certain activity should be placed.

Finally, we have to consider the use of the data, once sorted out into the various nomenclatures of activity, to find limited fields of causality between correlating variables. First, it must be noted that the design of the projects limits the scope of subsequent analysis. Taking the differences between the two 'INSEE' time-budget studies once again as an example, the analysts of the 1974/5 study did not have at their disposal information concerning the difference between urban and rural dwellers since the study was only carried out in cities. Furthermore, no direct information on the division and sharing of tasks within households was available because the diary of only one person per household was recorded in 1974/5 whereas in 1985/6, the diaries of couples were collected.

The second difficulty in deducing causal links between variables on the basis of such analyses is that life is not a laboratory. Consequently, one variable cannot be singled out and isolated in order to be tested whilst the others are held constant. This is complicated by the fact that the mass of data collected by a time-budget study can only be analysed piece by piece. Indeed, the analyses concerning domestic work constitute only a part of the overall analysis of the data produced by these national time-budget studies. Thus, within the limits of the data generated, in this case by the 1974/5 time-budget study, we have seen that various analysts have applied the 'demographic' variables of age, gender, number of children and marital status as well as the variable of socio-professional category in order to discover which play the major role in determining both the household division of labour and the amount of domestic work performed by certain categories of people.

However, to decide whether one variable is more important than another on the basis of the figures produced is not a cut and dried process. For example, the analyses of socio-professional categories do show that women from households belonging to the middle classes perform less domestic work than their working class counterparts. However, whether one considers such findings to be 'proof' of the Marxist Feminist and Feminist Marxist proposition that a conflict of interest exists between women from different social classes or whether one prefers to emphasize the still considerable amount of time spent on these activities even by middle class women, (which upholds the Radical Feminist position that there exists solidarity amongst all women) is a matter of choice. Who is to decide whether or not the differences between working and middle class women are significant? How can this be achieved outside the realms of an ideological perspective? The answer is that it cannot. The evidence provided by such statistical analyses cannot settle this dispute as statistical information is open to more than one interpretation.

In conclusion, it must be noted that the choice of design

and the choice of which variables to analyse are influenced by prevailing political and academic preoccupations. It was not until the 'Seventies that time-budget studies were carried out and used to examine the household division of labour. One must assume that this was the result of the theoretical influences coming from the Microeconomists and the political influences exerted by the Feminists. Yannick Lemel (1984) explains that in the 'Seventies, demand became strong for statistical information on household activities. These pressures came, unsurprisingly, from the politicized sphere of feminism and from an academic recognition of the importance of the household in terms of 'enlarged' concepts of consumption; Beckerian notions of the 'productive' household; Marxist Feminist assertions of the 'reproductive' role of domestic labour in capitalism; and Radical Feminist claims that domestic labour is the backbone of an independent mode of production.

However, turning to the 1985/6 time-budget study, Roy [9] explained that the section regarding domestic work was to be employed as part of an attempt to look at the economy in its entirety. She states that it will be used by national accountants for both a macroeconomic evaluation of the non market sphere and for an estimation of the activities of households. Equally, it will be used by 'Publicis' (a market-research company) for a comparison of the image given in advertising of domestic activities and their reality. Furthermore, it will act as the basis for the joint 'INSEE-CNRS' study into domestic production. One can see, therefore, that the demands for information concerning the domestic sphere are no longer coming purely from those interested in matters of female labour, but additionally, from those interested in the more general functioning of the economy and the place of domestic work within that in France. [10]

Thus, the contribution made to the debates on the household division of labour by these time-budget studies is first and foremost to confirm, with the aid of a broad-based statistical study, that domestic work is very important in terms of the time that it consumes, and secondly, to reveal that when domestic work is taken into account, women 'work' longer hours than men. Despite the limitations of these studies in the area of providing causal explanations of the situations which they observe, one cannot deny the usefulness of the descriptive function which they fufil. Indeed, these time-budget studies supply the background to the issue of the household division of labour, whilst the 'qualitative' theorists, which we will now consider, provide the finer detail.

Qualitative analyses of the household division of labour

Presentation of the findings

The studies to be analysed here - those of Michel Glaude & François de Singly (1986), Sabine Chalvon Demersay (1982) and Jacqueline Froger & Jocelyne Peyraut (1982) - are radically different from the time-budget studies. These theorists examine qualitatively the organization of household work. This they achieve principally by interviewing couples, or individuals, on how they organize their domestic work. Such a technique reveals their primary interest in the perceptions of the research subjects in relation to domestic work, as opposed to the behaviour of men and women concerning this area of their lives. I will begin by exploring the work of Chalvon Demersay.

In the context of the Observation du changement social (Observation of social change) project [11], Chalvon Demersay (1982, p. 24) carried out a study intended to identify the 'new model' of marriage and division of domestic labour in eighty households of couples living together (married and unmarried) in the fourteenth arrondissement in Paris. She chose what should be propitious ground for the discovery of such a new model, her research subjects being young, dual earner, professional couples. The task was to find out whether women and men had become interchangeable in their roles as far as employment and domestic labour were concerned.

Chalvon Demersay (1982, p. 25) found that the model of exchange of the husband's salary against the wife's domestic labour no longer existed in her sample. Instead, the partners entered into a very complex system based on reciprocity. This means that they would perform one domestic task in return for another, keeping mental balance sheets of what each had contributed. However, couples testified to the fact that such an arrangement became complicated and unstable. Chalvon Demersay found that many couples gave it up after a time and began to develop either their own specialisms, (these not necessarily being of the traditional mould) or a more strictly defined temporal division of labour.

Nonetheless, Chalvon Demersay notes (1982, p. 31) that despite protestation of good intentions, there still remained a certain inequality in the division of tasks between partners with the men often participating in domestic work without actually taking responsibility for it. More often than not, she found that the domestic work was simply compressed to a minimum with the use of machines;

soliciting outside help; use of restaurants; neglecting repair work; and 'disorder' (but not dirtiness) being accepted as a fact of life. In sum, Chalvon Demersay discovered complex webs of negotiations taking place within the couple which did not always produce completely equitable results.

The second study is that of Froger & Peyraut (1982). They carried out a study on 337 interviewees who were married or living in a couple. They were interested in the correlation between the views expressed by the couples of how domestic work should be organized, how it is organized in their families and their wider opinions and political attitudes. Inductively building up clusters of similar responses, Froger & Peyraut discerned three basic groups of respondents: first, there were those who had interiorized the traditional male/female model: namely, that of the wife unquestioningly taking responsibility for domestic labour whilst her husband assumed the role of breadwinner. More than half the women and only one quarter of the men described their household arrangements in this light. This is a pertinent finding in itself since it reveals that men perceive gender roles to have changed more than do women.

The second group was characterized by a contradiction between the normative views of the couple regarding the division of domestic labour and their actual everyday lives. In practice, there was an adherence to the traditional model outlined above despite a recognition on the part of both partners that this was not 'right' in some way. This often resulted in the husband having guilt feelings about his wife taking responsibility for the domestic work and in consequence, symbolically 'helping out'. As for the wives in this group, they were marked by a consciousness of the injustice to which they were subject. More than half of the men, 40 per cent of the working women and 33 per cent of housewives fell into this category.

In the third group, the couples tended to question the traditional roles, duties and responsibilities of the marriage partners. Moreover, this was reflected in their practices. These couples also registered a high level of indignance at the lack of recognition of the 'invisible work' carried out in the home. Nearly 25 per cent of men, 20 per cent of employed women and only 7 per cent of housewives fell into this category.

The next stage in Froger & Peyraut's analysis was to attempt to link these views regarding the organization of domestic work to the wider world views held by the respondents. Froger & Peyraut explain that the attitudes and the practices linked to the sharing of tasks can be analysed in the light of the 'moral orientations' of the couples concerned. Froger & Peyraut understand these to be attitudes to 'work, to consumption, to leisure time, to social relations and to family models'.

They discovered that the first group of 'traditionalists' tend to see work as a moral obligation. For men, this means professional work and for women, domestic work. Amongst the members of the second group, there is no such commitment to work. Women are not usually happy with their domestic responsibilities and men use the reason (or excuse?) of their careers for not participating more in the home. Unsurprisingly, the third group shows signs of the gamut of 'new' attitudes to work and consumption discussed in Chapter 3, for example, the rejection of work when this is interpreted as narrow careerism, consumption for its own sake and passive, commercial leisure.

Finally, we move on to the work of Glaude & de Singly (1986). They are interested in the power and negotiation involved in domestic organization. First of all, it must be stressed that they are concerned with both the division of decision-making within the couple (for example, where to go on holiday or how to educate children) and the division of concrete tasks. Nonetheless, they (1986, p. 9) stress that 'every activity carries with it a certain degree of decision-making and every decision implies taking on certain responsibilities'. Progressing on the basis of the analogy of the household as small firm, Glaude & de Singly attempt inductively to characterize types of household organization. They (1986, p. 11) explain that by the term 'form of domestic organization' they mean 'the way in which spouses categorize their spatial and symbolic universe into the territory which they share and that which each reserves for him or herself'.

To elicit this information, Glaude & de Singly interviewed a number of women about the domestic organization in their families, distinguishing six areas of decision-making and activity: (i) major decisions; (ii) choice and purchase of major household items; (iii) administration; (iv) supplies; (v) general housework; and (vi) maintenance. Furthermore, they (1986, p. 11) differentiate between those specialisms which give rise to 'the power of organization' and those which bring with them 'the power of execution'. The former relates to decisions concerning the objectives of the couple and the activities which these trigger. Thus, specialization in the areas of 'major decisions' and 'purchasing of major household goods' gives rise to such power. The latter concerns the management of everyday life, resulting from specialization in 'housework', 'maintenance' and 'supplies'.

Nevertheless, the authors argue that all domestic activity gives rise to some sort of power within the couple, even housework, where the decisional factor is more masked. However, this is a far from uncontentious proposition as far as the Feminists are concerned.

Having identified these areas of specialization, Glaude & de Singly continue to determine the degree of specialization of each couple in their sample in each of these areas so defined. Taking an overview, the authors discovered that in more than three out of four households, the wife stated that it was she who was in general charge of washing up and buying children's clothes and who was exclusively responsible for cleaning floors and food preparation. Indeed, the preliminary results of their 1979 research reinforce the conclusions of all the previous studies discussed here: namely, that there is a fairly high degree of specialization in domestic tasks between men and women. However, their novelty is to have found the existence of a basic equality in decision-making between spouses. As a further general conclusion, Glaude & de Singly discovered that the presence of children in a household tended to encourage more specialized and less communitarian models of organization.

On average, then, 'major decisions' (for example, whether or not to buy a flat) were taken in an egalitarian manner as were decisions concering 'purchase of major household items'. However, in all the other areas, the average tendency was towards specialization according to gender. As one could expect, 'supplies' (shopping for day to day items) and 'housework' were the domains of women. Men were found to specialize in one area only - that of 'maintenance'.

However, this was only the average model. Other 'types' of organization emerged from this study which the authors correlated with the socio-professional group of the couples concerned. First, there was the model of the 'Equal Wife' in which, in comparison with the average, women refuse to assume sole repsonsibility for the heaviest housework. This model was found principally amongst teachers and those working in the medical/social professions. Second, there were the models of 'Managing Director Wives' or 'Manager Wives' in which the women took responsibility for major decisions and/or administration respectively in addition to those specialisms found amongst the 'average' women in the sample. These models were found mostly amongst working class families.

Third, Glaude & de Singly found a model of 'Indoor Wives' who were more specialized than average in the practical jobs of supply and housework, but were more or less excluded from decision-making activities. This 'type' is found principally amongst the families of office workers and managers. These are also the socio-professional categories in which one finds the model of 'Petit Patron Wives' in which women take on responsibility for all areas of domestic life including the male specialism, 'maintenance'. Finally, there is the model of the 'Dominated Wife' in which the wife has little or no decision-making role. The only place where she has any authority and specialization is in the kitchen. This form of organization was found in particular in couples in which the cultural and educational balance between the spouses tended to favour the husband.

<u>Relationship to the Microeconomists and Feminists: choices and limitations</u>

The choice common to all three of these studies is methodological in nature. That is, they all follow an inductivist research procedure based on in depth interviews with their research subjects. This method is intended to solicit the research subjects' perceptions of their own lives as much as to learn about the actual behaviour of these persons. In this instance, the aim of these theorists is to discover people's perceptions of the way in which domestic work is shared in their families.

In this section, I will examine the consequences of the inductivist procedure - that is, the choices involved in such studies - in order to discover the relationship of the knowledge produced in this way to the rest of the approaches which arise in the debates on the household division of labour. First, I will examine the choice (made especially by Froger & Peyraut, 1982 and Glaude & de Singly, 1986) to search for variation amongst research subjects and to build up groups of similar respondents inductively as opposed to using preset categories to characterize people's responses, such as class or age. Second, I will consider the implications of using people's perceptions of a situation as opposed to their behaviour as raw data. And third, I will discuss the explanations for the household division of labour which emerge from these inductivist pieces of research.

First, then, Glaude & de Singly (1986) and Froger & Peyraut (1982) look for variation amongst the situations of their research subjects. For example, Glaude & de Singly (1986, p. 9) explain that it is necessary 'to go beyond a unidimensional vision' which places couples along a 'single scale of specialization'. That is to say, they want to show not only that some households are more specialized than others, but also that there exists a qualitative difference in these arrangements which cannot be characterized on the basis of established categories such as social class alone. Indeed, there is a certain refusal on the part of all the 'qualitative' theorists to analyse the research data collected on the basis of preset categories, such as class or age (in contrast to the time-budget studies). Froger & Peyraut inductively create a typology of attitudes to work and household organization. Their research subjects were not segregated according to socio-economic group, for example, prior to the analysis. Furthermore, Glaude & de Singly make no a priori assumptions about the types of organization which exist in various social classes or age groups. Groupings are inductively developed from the data and only subsequently compared with socio-professional group. Their method of analysis does not use 'statistically observable' facts (such as number of children; age; number of household memebers; or socio-economic group) as a foundation for categorization.

Such approaches must be contrasted to those of the committed Feminists who concentrate on the similarity of the situation, either of all women, or of women of specific social classes. One could go so far as to say that the whole structuralist approach rests on finding similarities, not differences between members of preestablished groups. In consequence, the inductivist and qualitative approach of Glaude & de Singly and Froger & Peyraut, by its very nature, belies the 'structuralist' analysis to some extent in that it refuses to analyse the population in terms of classes (gender or capitalist) as a first step even though they may subsequently correlate the groups which have emerged from their findings with such categories.

The second, and perhaps most important point is that Chalvon Demersay, Glaude & de Singly and Froger & Peyraut take the lead in their analyses from the research subjects own perceptions of their personal situation. In contrast to the time-budget studies, these qualitative researchers can differentiate between a husband 'having responsibility for' domestic tasks and merely 'helping out'. Objectively observed, a husband may spend considerable amounts of time at various tasks, but his wife could still perceive herself to be in general charge of them, meaning that the husband retained the right to 'opt out' of his 'duties' at any given moment. Glaude & de Singly (1986), for example, are not interested in the 'objective' behaviour of the couples but the perceptions on the part of wives of the domestic organization of their households. These perceptions, they contend, are more pertinent for the discussion of 'negotiation'. The authors (1986, p. 4) explain that 'the informant that the sociologist uses is an intermediary who is involved in the negotiation of her domestic organization'. Such information is deemed by these theorists to be more important than the neutral description of everyday behaviour provided by time-budgets.

However, this interest in the testimony of the research subjects does not mean that these theorists have no explanatory framework into which they fit their raw data. Thus, even within those approaches which use this descriptive and inductive procedure, there is a notion of causality - or explanation - which gives rise to yet more permutations on ways of explaining the household division of labour. For example, Froger & Peyraut (1982) suggest that the household division of labour which one finds in a couple owes much to the general values and opinions which individuals hold. In other words, they posit the correlation of 'world view' and domestic organization. Indeed, these were the themes discussed in the interviews. Therefore, the agendas even for ethnographic studies such as this are normally set by the theorists and not the research subjects, these agendas being based on the former's explicit or implicit notions of causation.

Glaude & de Singly (1986) develop a complex explanation of the variations in household organization based on the premise that these result from a process of negotiation which takes place between the two marriage partners. In similarity, Chalvon Demersay explains the household division of labour in her sample to be the result of negotiation and of reciprocity. However, Chalvon Demersay does not take her explanation any further whereas Glaude & de Singly attempt to determine the conditions which influence this process of negotiation. According to them, the elaboration of one sort of organization as opposed to another results from: (i) the general culture of the marriage partners (educational level and social position); and (ii) the disparities of cultural and economic wealth between the two partners. They (1986, p. 18) explain that 'domestic power is a commodity appropriated by the spouse who has the most resources'. Women have more chance of appropriating this power if they have a level of education at least comparable to that of their husband or if they have a job or other source of income.

In difference to the Feminists, the analysis of Glaude & de Singly does not take as its point of departure the premise that women are oppressed and exploited. The very notion of 'negotiation' assumes that women have some sort of power to shape the development of their household organization. There is nothing in this analysis to say, for example, that women will always be the losers from this process, nor that to be responsible for domestic work alone constitutes in any way a 'problem' for women. Moreover, the authors do not go into explanations of why women are more likely to be in a relatively weak position in comparison with their husbands as far as education and income are concerned. In fact, one could say that this cut off point which Glaude & de Singly have chosen for themselves is the starting point of the Feminist analysis. In fact, Glaude & de Singly's explanations tend, for the above reasons, towards 'individualism' accepting, as they apparently do, the difference between men and women and refusing to describe society as the outcome of the power relations of class. However, being sociological in focus, Glaude & de Singly's analysis disagrees with the notions that individuals are economic islands operating solely in their own self interest and that the couple is a unit, making rational choices to enhance its economic well-being. This is in contrast to the explanation of the Microeconomists.

In sum, the 'qualititative approaches' do not give unequivocal support to either the Microeconomists or the Feminists. Being ethnographic and humanist in nature, they naturally conflict with the more deterministic and theoretical streak to be found in some, although not all the work of the Feminists. Nonetheless, although Glaude & de Singly in particular lean towards 'individualist' explanations of the household division of labour, they are not of the 'universalist' economistic mould of the Microeconomists.

Conclusions

The results of these 'Empirical Approaches' contribute to the debates on domestic work and the household division of labour in France principally by underlining the fact that domestic work is an important activity in terms of the time which is devoted to it and by providing evidence for the fact that it is indeed women who bear the burden of this type of work. Consequently, these theorists support the assertion that the gender variable is the most important in determining the household division of labour. Finally, they provide more precise details of the exact types of household arrangements which are to be found amongst the French population.

These are very important contributions which have all helped to put domestic work firmly on the academic map in France. However, they have not been able to arbitrate in the theoretical debate between Microeconomists and Feminists (or between various kinds of Feminists). For the most part, this is because the Feminists and Microeconomists already agree that it is women who are principally responsible for domestic work, and that gender is the most significant variable in determining the household division of labour.

Moreover, some of the theorists subsumed under this heading 'contribute' to the debates by adding their own explanations of the household division of labour to those of capitalist or patriarchal functionality and microeconomic rationale. The additional causal factors which they cite include negotiation, reciprocity and the role of ideology/world views. Such factors allow for much more individual diversity than do many of the Feminist analyses, and much more variation of individual reasoning than do the Microeconomists.

Thus, the above analysis yields two general findings: first, that the empirical description provided by these studies cannot help to decide between the competing explanations of the Microeconomists and the Feminists. Since the divisions between these two clusters of theorists are 'politically' motivated in the broadest sense of the term, no amount of empirical work will enable one to decide between them. Second, we can see that despite being firmly grounded in an empirical base, these Empirical theorists cannot avoid making their own assumptions about causality when they attempt to 'explain' reality (as opposed to describe it) which, far from helping one to decide between Feminist and Microeconomist theorists, adds more variations to the reasons why women are responsible for domestic labour.

Notes

1. Yannick Lemel is head of the division 'Populations et Ménages' (Population and household) of the 'INSEE'.
2. This study was carried out by the 'INSEE' within the framework of an international initiative involving ten countries. See, for example, Guilbert, M., Lowit, N., & Creusen, J. (1967).
3. In the case of the 'INSEE' time-budgets - and all the analyses carried out on the basis of these - time spent on 'domestic work' refers to the hours spent in (i) cooking, cleaning, washing, ironing, etc; (ii) childcare and other care for persons; (iii) related travelling time; and (iv) gardening, D.I.Y., car maintenance, sewing, knitting, etc. Thus, 'domestic labour' will

refer to all these activities throughout the discussion of figures produced by these studies. These figures are taken from Grimler, G. & Roy, C. (1987).

4. In reading this seemingly low average for professional work per week, one must remember that this is the average figure for the entire adult population - including students, the unemployed, the retired and part-time workers.
5. Interview conducted in Paris, April 1988.
6. Interview conducted in Paris, April 1987.
7. Comment made at an 'APRE' seminar, reported in Les cahiers de l'APRE, September, 1985, p. 31.
8. Interview conducted in Paris, 1988.
9. In 'Notes for Interviewers', No. 1.
10. The change in emphasis concerning the study of domestic work will be discussed in Chapters 14.
11. This was a 'CNRS' initiative to study issues as they arise in specific locations throughout France. All kinds of informal work were high on the agenda in this project.

7 The Free Market Dualists

Introduction

Having discussed those theorists who concern themselves with the 'domestic' aspect of the informal economy, and in particular its role in the household division of labour, we now move on to examine those theorists who are more interested in the part to be played by the informal economy in the future of work. These theorists are divided into three groups: the Free Market Dualists, the Radicals and the Empirical analysts of this question. This chapter deals with the first of these groups, namely, the Free Market Dualists.

The theorists to be discussed here are Alain Minc (1980, 1982, Nora &, 1980); J. Amado & Christian Stoffaës (1980); Alfred Sauvy (1984); and Lionel Stoléru (1982). They will be christened the 'Free Market Dualist' theorists for the following reasons: 'free market' because they believe in the effiency of the market as the best mechanism for regulating the economy; and 'dualist' because they envisage a society evolving in which two populations exist - one occupied in the formal, the other in the informal labour market. This is their proposal for overcoming the crisis of unemployment without harming the capitalist and productivist structure of the economy.

This discussion will be structured in the following manner. First, I will explore how the Free Market Dualists view the crisis of unemployment which, in their opinion, is impossible to resolve by traditional means. Second, I will analyse the role assigned to informal work activities by the Free Market Dualists in their solutions to this crisis. Third, I will explore the assumptions of causality on which these explanations and solutions are based. And fourth, I will consider the extent to which, in these deliberations, the Free Market Dualists develop a new concept of work.

Presentation of the Free Market Dualist approaches

The nature of the crisis of unemployment

The Free Market Dualists are principally concerned with the problem of mass unemployment. They believe this to be a permanent feature of 'modern' society since, in their view, a return to full employment is not possible, even though it is desirable. However, the Free Market Dualists, realizing that the social dislocation caused by mass unemployment cannot go unchecked, turn to informal work as a solution to this problem. The task of this section is to discuss their reasons for positing that mass unemployment is here to stay and to explore their analyses of how this situation developed.

On the question of the exact nature of the ills besetting the French economy which cause unemployment, there is a difference in emphasis between Sauvy, on the one hand, and Minc, Amado & Stoffaës and Stoléru, on the other. The proposition made by Minc (1980 & 1982), Amado & Stoffaës (1980) and Stoléru (1982) that mass unemployment in France has been caused by rising productivity and low growth is uncontentious. So too is the notion that France, along with other 'mature' industrialized nations, has been the victim of a new world trade balance, characterized by producer countries charging more for raw materials and new manufacturing countries emerging to challenge the market share of the more established ones such as France.

One political option to solve this problem is protectionism, a return to full employment being facilitated by the State planning and protecting the French market. However, since 1983, such an option has been rejected by most politicians and economists in France. Instead, the argument is put forth, from which Minc, Amado & Stoffaës and Stoléru do not dissent, that France must be open and competitive in the world market. However, competitiveness necessitates the further encouragement of increases in productivity.

The rhetoric of most mainstream politicians has been that eventually, such a strategy will lead to a rate of economic growth which is sufficiently rapid to 'soak up' those workers made unemployed through productivity gains. Minc, Amado & Stoffaës and Stoléru all cast doubt on this optimistic outlook. Minc (1980), for example, believes that France will never again enjoy rates of economic growth which would facilitate a significant reduction in unemployment. He (1980, p. 9) explains that 'competitiveness is a necessary but insufficient condition for a real improvement in the employment situation. This is the fundamental premise of the post '73 economy'. The basic assumption is therefore that productivity will continue to outstrip growth in all sectors for the foreseeable future. Minc, back in 1980 (p.4), asserted that growth would need to be around four per cent to stabilize unemployment and between five and six per cent in order to reduce it. Six years later, in 1986, the growth rate was still only two per cent [1] which goes some way to justifying Minc's 1980 predictions. Amado & Stoffaës (1980) add that the development of microelectronics and the computerization of production will permanently reduce the need for manpower. That is, the service sector will not 'soak up' those made unemployed from the manufacturing sector. This is because the service sector too is subject to the same microtechnological revolution as manufacturing industry which reduces the need for service sector employees.

Minc, in his 1982 book, takes these ideas further. He suggests that what France had experienced in the past decade was not just a temporary crisis. Indeed, according to Minc, a process of permanent change had already been set in motion which would lead to what he (1982, p. 231) describes as the 'economy of scarcity'. He asserts that the country will have to adapt to rarity of personal and social income as well as to the rarity of work as we have known it. Continual growth, according to Minc, is a past phenomenon. In sum, on the basis of these predictions for the future of employment, these theorists assert that it is necessary to encourage the growth of the 'informal sector' as a vocational refuge for those marginalized from the formal labour market.

From a slightly different, and definitely more traditionally liberal angle, Sauvy (1984, p. 119-120) lays the blame for mass unemployment at the door of those who instituted the rigidity which plagues the French economy. This rigidity is expressed in the legal controls on employment (that is, redundancy laws, health and safety regulations, minimum wages); in the social security system; and in the general imposition of the State on the lives of individuals which is funded by ever increasing taxation.

However, according to Sauvy, the legislation was not itself the cause of rigidity. In a typically individualist fashion, Sauvy (1984) asserts that the evolution of the market in this direction was the result of a 'general' desire on both sides of industry for stability and security. In the area of work, asserts Sauvy, this means that views on employment become increasingly inflexible. He contends that nowadays, the artisan seeks stability, even if this means that his or her output remains at a lower level than it could have attained if he or she had run a slightly increased risk. Sauvy continues to explain that the employee no longer seeks 'work' as such, but a stable job. Furthermore, the job seeker is encouraged to be choosy by the unemployment benefit system. This search for stability, he continues, is damaging to the economy in that it curtails economic growth and innovation. Sauvy (1984, p. 122) maintains that these attitudes produce a society in which needs go unmet whilst workers claim benefit. His advocacy of informal work, therefore, comes from a belief that it could represent the antedote to this rigid system.

Taking the diagnoses of the 'crisis' of unemployment of Sauvy (1984), Minc (1980 & 1982), Amado & Stoffaës (1980) and Stoléru (1982) together, the reasons why they reject any protectionist programme to reduce unemployment become apparent. None would advocate an even more rigid system of State funded employment creation programmes to cure these economic ills. Trying to roll back the rises in productivity or the internationalization of the economy, or indeed increasing taxation to pay for government schemes, merely reinforces inflexibility. Thus, such ideas are ruled out as solutions to unemployment by the Free Market Dualists.

However, as we have already stated, these theorists do not believe that unemployment can be allowed to continue unchecked. The Free Market Dualists have not been blind to the political and social pressures caused by high, long term unemployment. They stress that the social stability which mass unemployment threatens is a prerequisite for prosperity. Stoléru (1982, p. 200), for example, declares that 'a stable economy cannot be built without a solid social cement'. Equally, in their opinion, the State benefits paid out to the unemployed represented a drain on the competitive sector of industry. They maintain that employment will and should remain the centre of economic activity, but will become a luxury for fewer and fewer people to enjoy. In their search for something to occupy those who will not have the benefit of employment, the Free Market Dualists turn to 'informal' work activities.

The role of the informal economy

The Free Market Dualists, therefore, approach the informal economy from the angle of its usefulness in solving the crisis of unemployment. They contend that the crisis of mass unemployment could be solved by the development of an economic sector based at least in part on informal work activities alongside, and for the benefit of the competitive, hitech sector. Certain informal work activities could form the 'convivial' sector of a 'dual society' (Amado & Stoffaës, 1980), be the basis of the reactivation of 'civil society' within the context of an 'ambivalent society' (Minc, 1982), or constitute part of a newly recognized 'underside of the economy' (Sauvy, 1984). Stoléru (1982) has set out his option of a 'two speed France' in which he divides between the 'the exposed France' and the 'the sheltered France'. The discussion of what the Free Market Dualists mean by these concepts and how they envisage the interaction of the formal and informal sectors of the economy will be presented in this section.

First, I will discuss the nature of the informal sector of the dual economies discussed by these theorists. The type of informal economic activity which interests these theorists includes certain aspects of the 'social economy' (such as the activities of mutual societies and cooperatives), black market work and the activities subsumed under the heading of 'autoproduction'. Taking first the scenario of Amado & Stoffaës (1980, p. 141), they explain that the 'convivial sector' of their 'dual society' would consist of 'organizations isolated from international competition into which new technologies would penetrate more slowly, these being institutions concerned with redistribution'. They (1980, p. 139) explain that there will be an emergence of informal activities which will be 'halfway between the collective and the productive' sectors, including experiments in 'returning to the land and artisanal production'. Although they do not go into detail about how such institutions would be organized, one could assume that they would resemble voluntary organizations and the charitable status of associations.

Second, Minc (1980, p. 13) lists such activities as 'social work, cultural initiatives and community work' as those which could come under the heading of his 'civil society'. It is made clear, however, that people working in such a sector could expect considerably reduced salaries in comparison with those working in the hitech sector. In his 1982 book, Minc (p.233) develops his thinking further, moving away from his former employment-orientated model. He explains that domestic activities, small, directly consumed production, familial self-help, neighbourly service, barter, D.I.Y. and black market work would feature prominently in the activities of 'civil society'. Furthermore, he contends that the 'underground economy' (meaning black market work in this instance) represents a new type of economic reality which is developing alongside more traditional structures for production.

Third, as far as Stoléru (1982) is concerned, although he has an explicit interest in activities of the informal sector as I have defined it, a State subsidized public service sector would also be part of his 'sheltered France'. Stoléru (1982, p. 204) conceptualizes informal activities as being a link between the public and the private sectors, arguing that 'it is time to recognize and to give legitimacy to the third sector, to this informal economy, by making it into one of the links which ties the sheltered France to the exposed France'. He uses the examples of community crèches, black market work, buying products in kit form and voluntary work. He denounces the fact that these are ignored in economic calculations. They are important, in his opinion, because they reduce the income of the State from taxes and they lead to misconceptions about unemployment. He suggests that one should let the informal economy take over services which it is not absolutely necessary for the State to provide.

Turning our attention to Sauvy, he (1984, p. 122) has called black market work the 'essence of liberalism'. Sauvy (1984, p. 274) asserts that black market work, alongside artisanal businesses, constitutes the 'underside of the economy' which is a vital part of the economic scene. Black market work should not, therefore, be criticized for undermining employment and short circuiting the macro-economy of the G.N.P. because it is merely responding, as any other economic activity should do, to 'needs expressed by people'. Black market work, explains Sauvy (1984, p. 274), represents 'the oil in the wheels, the infinite adjustment mechanism' in the economy. Indeed, it is the only mechanism through which one can 'guarantee the utopia of full employment'. In other words, black market work is the elastic in the system which allows a snug fit of supply to demand which is the aim of every economy.

The second question to be asked of the Free Market Dualists is how they expect society to divide itself between the two economic spheres. In accordance with the high priority given to the protection of the 'competitive' sector, Minc (1980), Stoléru (1982) and Amado & Stoffaës (1980) agree that this formal sector would employ those people who were most highly qualified to work in it. Amado & Stoffaës (1980, p. 138) maintain that tomorrow's companies will be obliged to use only highly qualified and specialized human capital and those who are unsuitable 'because of a lack of aptitude or motivation' will be left to one side. Amado & Stoffaës (1980, p. 142) made the highly contentious statement on this matter that the competitive sector would be 'composed of modern men, computer-literate and able to cope with the latest technologies'. The convivial sector, they continue, would be populated 'by less able men' and characterized by lower incomes.

However, the Free Market Dualists would all deny that there would be a hierarchy between the two sectors. 'Equality in difference' is the key to understanding their point of view. For example, Amado & Stoffaës (1980, p. 139) speak of a population divided into two 'sub-groups, complementary but different' constituting a 'voluntarily divided society'. This idea of a voluntary split between the two groups in society is central to the individualist logic of the Free Market Dualists. Minc (1980) and Amado & Stoffaës (1980) assert that the changes they predict will come about because of a fortuitous convergence of economic change (mass unemployment) and a change in attitude towards employment (growing disaffection from employment and consumption for its own sake). Amado & Stoffaës (1980, p. 137) assert that the younger, post war generations are more concerned with free time than with consumption of material goods as certain basic needs are nearing universal saturation. Minc (1980, p. 12) agrees, asserting that unemployment has coincided with 'a growing allergy to traditional employment, above all amongst young people'. Stoléru (1982) is more equivocal on the question of whether two distinct populations would ensue from the developments which he describes or whether individuals would divide their time between the two sectors. He (1982, p. 206) talks about people receiving three kinds of income, an economic income (from formal employment), a social income (from the State) and an individual income (from one's domestic production). He envisages that individuals could choose their own mix between the three according to their tastes and skills.

Sauvy (1984, p. 122), concentrating on black market work, also invokes the liberal logic of individuals making rational choices in accordance with their preferences and capacities. By 'choosing' black market work, he explains, the individual is attempting to escape the prevailing logic of stability in order to satisfy a demand which is not being met by the formal economy. Thereby, he or she creates wealth for him or herself and for the national economy.

One of the methods of encouraging the development of the informal sector would be to change the status of black market work. The question arises for all these theorists of whether (or which kinds of) black market work should be 'whitened', or legalized, and to what extent. For Sauvy (1984), promoting the role of black market work does not mean 'whitening' it completely as this would entail a frontal assault on the social security system. Instead, Sauvy (1984, p. 143) suggests that the State should lessen or abolish V.A.T. and social security contributions pertaining to work carried out in servicing or household repairs by individuals. This move would be accompanied by a squeeze on unemployment benefits. Correspondingly, the unemployed should be allowed to undertake household repair and servicing work for money without loss of benefits. Such a measure would encourage 'legal' small businesses whilst maintaining the supremacy of the large company. The black economy could nurture would-be entrepreneurs.

Stoléru (1982) was a leading light in the campaign against black market work in the late 'Seventies. [2] However, this was in the context of wanting to reform the law concerning black market work. He (1982, p. 205) suggests that one should legalize certain types of black market work, meaning that 'certain simple and fair conditions should be laid down which would permit someone to unblock his neighbour's washbasin legally'. He argues that this would be a source of economic activity and jobs. Minc (1982, p. 182) agrees with these propositions, saying that 'it is necessary ... to call on the State to whiten black market work and to accept the underground economy and no longer to use it as a shameful and inadmissible way of coping with the recession'.

In conclusion, then, the Free Market Dualists argue that the informal sector could be a help, as opposed to a hindrance or threat, to the competitive sector. Its development is intended to satisfy social and political demands for work and income without interfering with economic growth. This, as I will discuss later, is in stark contrast to the plans for informal work activities advocated by the Radical theorists and is a product of the Free Market Dualists' acceptance of the logic of the free market, capitalist economy. Minc (1980, p. 3) argues that the activities of 'civil society' should be encouraged 'as long as they do not cast a shadow over the competitiveness of those economic sectors which are engaged in international competition'. Moreover, Amado & Stoffaës (1980) assert that the high performance sector, due to its rigidity and fragility, would have to be embedded in a large, 'traditional' sector which would generate 'employment' even if this were badly paid.

As I will discuss in the following section, these attitudes towards the market, industry and the informal sector are all closely linked to the choices made by the theorists concerning explanation of the crises and the ideology on which their scenarios for the future are based.

Evaluating the Free Market Dualist approaches

The responsibility of this section is to map out the ways in which the Free Market Dualist analysis is both 'individualist' and 'universalist' in nature. First, these theorists are 'universalist' in their approach because they fit the informal economy into an all embracing conception both of the crises besetting the French economy and society and of the solution to these crises. Second, both their definition of the crisis of unemployment and their choice of scenario for the future of work reflect their 'individualist' leanings in theoretical and ideological terms. In both cases, this 'individualism' is primarily expressed as an acceptance of the fundaments of capitalism and of the free market. Indeed, the essential difference between them and the Radical theorists (to be discussed in the next chapter) is the extent to which they accept the present socio-economic and political order.

This is apparent in the definition which the Free Market Dualists offer of the crisis in which the French economy finds itself. First and foremost, although they predict the relative failure of French industry in the international market (that is, failure to prevent mass unemployment), they do not put into question the efficiency (or morality) of the existing system of world production and distribution. In other words, neither the need to persist in the struggle for economic growth, nor the central question of the high priority placed on economic goals in society is critically examined.

Furthermore, technological progress and the rises in productivity which it engenders whipped along by international competition cannot and must not be challenged, according to these theorists. Conversely, and as we shall see in the next Chapter, the need to put this system into question is what characterizes the analyses of the Radicals. Indeed, for the Free Market Dualists, the informal economy is one side of what Godard (1985, p. 327) has termed the 'dualism of the last resort', a means of alleviating the economic crisis 'without having any impact on the logic of the organization of, or the value placed on the competitive and high technology economic sectors which are subject to international competition'.

A further aspect of the 'individualism' of the Free Market Dualists in this case is the question of people's lack of initiative and the petrifying role of the State in this process. Sauvy, in particular, argues that it is the constraints placed on the market by the State which are causing recession. Indeed, Sauvy advocates black market work as a solution to these problems for the very reason that it is not subject to the constraints imposed by labour legislation and taxation. This means that black market workers can operate in a fashion which approximates to the liberal theory of economic exchange much more closely than does regular employment.

Thus, the role accorded to the informal economy by the Free Market Dualists in their solution to economic crisis is a product of their faith in the market and the mechanisms of capitalism. Minc (1980, p. 14) maintains that what is required to solve the crisis is 'flexibility, mobility and decentralization'. The Free Market Dualists posit that the main obstacle to this is the State and its labour and social security legislation. Thus, the 'informal economy' is perceived by the protagonists of this perspective to be more anti-State than anti-market since it is the State which blocks more diversified and dualist work patterns. Amado & Stoffaës (1980, p. 143) go so far as to say that frequently, 'social legislation backfires against those which it was meant to protect. In many cases, it bears a large proportion of the responsibility for unemployment'.

Thus, the scenario of the Free Market Dualists is one in which the market is given more prominence, not less. Indeed, they have this in common with the Microeconomists. For example, Minc (1982, p. 180) asserts that all activities rely on the market law of exchange and that 'the market is the natural state of society. Everything which seeks to constrain it excessively, or even to abolish it, causes it to reappear on the peripheries'. Nonetheless, this 'new liberalism' in France is one which concludes from experience that the market, left to itself, will go off the rails, especially in creating unacceptable poverty and concentration of firms. Thus, these Free Market Dualist theorists reach the consensus position that the State must exist, but be circumscribed to specific areas and wherever possible, problems should be solved within the bounds of market mechanisms. Such a view encourages the examination of 'informal' solutions rather than reliance on the panacea of 'more State intervention' to solve problems.

The final expression of the individualist view of society

espoused by the Free Market Dualists is the way in which they envisage the population dividing itself between between the 'formal' and 'informal' sectors of the economy. Amado & Stoffaës are the most extreme in this case. They assume first, that some people are more capable than others of working in the hitech sector and second, that a natural selection process will take place which will sort people out into two distinct populations of workers who will devote themselves wholeheartedly to one sector or the other.

Stoléru and Minc are more flexible and more ambivalent as to whether or not two 'nations' will rise from the ashes of the economic crisis. Indeed, they leave open the possibility that individuals will want, and be able to divide their time between the formal and informal spheres. However, if division there will be, they believe that it will come about amicably because of the fragmentation of values in French society over the last two decades. Minc (1982, p. 152) explains that 'sociological analysis has been able to show that consensus in France means agreeing that nobody agrees. This tolerance for the right to be different is the key to the policies that must be followed'. Thus, people could devote themselves entirely to one sector or the other, or choose a mix between the two. Stoléru (1982, p.192) wants to encourage part time work, parental leave and the like, whereas Amado & Stoffaes (1980, p. 138) seem to suggest that those involved in the productive sector will have to be totally committed to it if France is to compete successfully in the world market.

The Free Market Dualists assume that a change in attitudes has come about which means that many people will want to work exclusively in the convivial sector - in large enough quantities to avoid social conflict. The individual is therefore assumed to be making voluntary, rational choices according to personal preference and abilities. Minc's (1982, p 169) hope is that at the time when supply of jobs is becoming ever more restricted, demand will modify also because of the post '68 shift in social values.

The insistence of these theorists that this division will come about amicably according to personal preferences and capacities is further evidence that they believe in an 'exchange' model of society in which concepts such as 'disadvantage' and 'oppression' do not feature. Indeed, their uncritical approach to the free market assumes that rational beings are exercizing their freedom of choice according to their personal capacities. Competition, international and personal, is the most efficient way of producing wealth, which must remain, therefore, the primary goal of work. This attitude to 'actually existing' capitalism explains the Free Market Dualists' attitude to the role and purpose of informal work activities and, indeed, their concept of work. This question will be explored in the following section.

A new concept of work?

In contrast to those theorists interested in the 'household division of labour', the Free Market Dualists are not proposing a conceptual change to extend the meaning of 'work' in theoretical analyses and quantifications. They are proposing a new, practical organization of work in society which will make more use, (and acknowledge certain aspects) of the informal sector. However, the question must be posed here of whether these theorists undermine the centrality of the concept which equates 'work' solely with 'employment'. The answer to this question is linked to whether they consider informal work to be playing a 'compensatory' or 'challenging' role in society.

What do theorists such as Minc want to provide in the informal sector if it is not purposeful activity for the unemployed? Without wishing to deny that these theorists are proposing that a new generation has emerged with new needs to be derived from work other than an income, it must be remembered that their prime aim is to protect the competitive sector of the economy. Thus, they wish to unburden this sector from the taxes levied by the State and used to pay unemployment benefits. They do not wish the State to redistribute income, so the only means left to avoid social conflict provoked by the poverty resulting from unemployment is to provide the population with work of some sort, informal or not.

It is true that these theorists wish to change social attitudes to unemployment and encourage the unemployed to become active in the convivial sector. However, it is hard to see this as innovatory in terms of how society perceives work in general when such convivial activities are reserved for the marginalized in society. If the core of competitive industries remains protected, it will mean that the 'second' sector will always be second best.

As we have discovered, the primary concern of these theorists is 'unemployment' and the possible social unrest that it could cause. They wish to use the informal economy to stabilize the system whose cornerstone is employment. Thus, the main obstacle to the development of a new concept of work arising from the analyses of these theorists in any form is their insistence on protecting the 'core' economic sector: that is, the private, competitive hitech core in which the primary aim of work is the creation of profit and the dominant relationship within which work is carried out is employment. This is the consequence of their uncritical acceptance of the efficiency and rationality of the free market. If the competitive sector is to remain so protected and of such high status, then it is hard to imagine that it will not cast a shadow over the 'marginalized' informal sector. The Free Market Dualists do not want to use the hitech sector so much to free people's time for more creative activity as to protect it by couching it in an informal base.

Indeed, it is not so much the concept of work, but of unemployment that Minc and Amado & Stoffaës in particular wish to transform. It should be remembered that the State, in its stipulation that whilst claiming benefit one must be 'seeking work' and doing very little else, reinforces the massive cleavage which exists between work/employment, on the one hand, and unemployment/idleness on the other. Minc (1980, p. 14), in particular, believes that the relevant legislation must be changed in order to create more opportunities for the unemployed to augment their income through their own initiative.

Further evidence, however, of the way in which the Free Market Dualists cling to employment is their particular interest in that form of informal work which most closely resembles not only employment, but also the small business, free exchanging model of the economy: namely, black market work. Minc (1980, p. 13) for example, calls for 'the creation of new structures in which a new type of <u>employment</u> could find expression'. The black market system mixes aspirations for more liberty at work with an appetite for material gain. Although Minc (1980 & 1982) and Stoléru (1982) do consider what we have termed 'autoproduction', Amado & Stoffaes do not. Indeed, all of these theorists are primarily interested in those activities which most nearly approximate 'employment' as it exists at present. This is a manifestation of the Free Market Dualists' overall acceptance of the 'formal' economic sphere and all that goes with it.

Sauvy (1984) goes so far as to say that the aim of work is nothing more or less than the creation of concrete, material wealth. He (1984, p. 277) comments that 'employment, or more precisely, work, is, in the economy, the enemy, or at least the passive as opposed to the active which is the creation of wealth'. 'Work' is a disutility to be minimized in relation to the utility derived from it. Sauvy (1984, p. 278) continues that the aims of 'familial, tribal, capitalist and socialist economies' are the same: 'to satisy the needs of people. Work is not an aim in itself: it must respond to need'. Although Sauvy is more extreme - or explicit - in these views than some of the other Free Market Dualists, his essential argument is an important one to contrast with the propositions of the Radical theorists. The Radical theorists call for participation in informal activity for all citizens, not only because of its economic aspect of creating material wealth but because it is a means of compensating the alienation common to much of the 'work' carried out within the context of employment.

Therefore, in conclusion, one can say that the Free Market Dualists, despite advocating the development of the informal sector, do little to undermine practically - and thus conceptually - the centrality of employment in economic and political life. Informal work, they hope, will buoy up a flagging economic system, despite, one might add, having a strong enough logic of its own to compensate the shortfalls of this system.

Conclusions

Thus, the Free Market Dualists are concerned about the destabilizing effects of unemployment and advocate informal work as a refuge for the marginalized in society - although some recognize that eventually, more general change may come about on the basis of this. The free market productivist system, therefore, is not put into question. In fact, the aim of the Free Market Dualists is to enhance its performance. Thus, employment remains at the core of the organization of work which they envisage. This is not so for the Radical theorists for whom employment, far from being a sacred cow, is a primary target for their criticisms.

What is significant is that the Free Market Dualist theorists imply that this change will come about spontaneously. That is, that the unemployed will find it relatively easy to pour their energies into the informal economy and derive some sort of income or satisfaction of need from it. It is this assumption which will be put to the test by the Empirical researchers.

Notes

1. Source: OECD, 'Economic Outlook', December 1986.
2. For a detailed discussion of this campaign and previous government policy, see Klatzmann, 1979 and 1982.

8 The Radicals

Introduction

In common with the Free Market Dualists, the Radical theorists are interested in the informal economy primarily in terms of the role that it could play in the future development of work. Thus, their approach is 'universalist' in the sense that their study of the informal economy is embedded in a broader canvas of social analysis, critique and prediction. However, the appraisal of the present day problems of 'work' made by the Radicals are very different from those of the Free Market Dualists, relying as they do on the key concepts of oppression, exploitation and alienation to describe society. One can group under the heading 'Radicals' the following theorists: Brice Lalonde & Dominique Simmonet (1978); Phillippe Lebreton (1978); The 'EPPEM' collective (1977) [1]; André Gorz (1982 a & b, 1985 & 1986); the ADRET collective (1977); Ingmar Granstedt (1980); Guy Aznar (1978, 1981 & 1987); Yona Friedman (1978 & 1982); Jacques Delors (1979) (& Gaudin, 1979) (& Foucauld, 1980) (and the 'Echanges et Projets' group, 1980); Guy Roustang (1982 & 1987); Ignacy Sachs (1980 & 1983); and Pierre Rosanvallon (1980), along with a marginal group of more 'descriptive' analysts: Jocelyne Gaudin (& Greffe, 1980) (& Schiray, 1984); Michel Schiray (& Vinaver, 1980); and Xavier Greffe (1981).

The discussion of this group of theorists will be structured similarly to that of the Free Market Dualist cluster. First, I will explore the way in which the Radical theorists perceive the nature of the present day problems of 'work'. Second, I will analyse the role which the Radicals assign to the informal economy in solving these problems. Third, I will explore the assumptions of causality on which these explanations and solutions are based. And fourth, I will consider the extent to which, in these deliberations, the Radical theorists develop a new concept of work.

Presentation of the Radical approaches

The nature of the problems of work

The Radical theorists discuss the problems of 'work' in terms of a number of more general social and economic crises. They are all agreed at a basic level of analysis on the nature of these crises. Thus, in a first section, I will address these common diagnoses of the social and economic disorders which affect the organization of work. Some theorists do not go beyond this level of analysis of the crises. However, other theorists enter into a causal explanation of why these crises have come about. They explain them in terms of 'capitalism' or of 'technology', or refer to them as symptoms of the 'ecological' crisis and of Humankind's distorted relationship to Nature. Thus, in a further three sections, I will discuss, in detail how various sub-groups of theorists proceed with their analyses.

The description of the crises which is accepted by all the Radical theorists rests on three principal assertions. First, the Radical theorists maintain that most people are unsatisfied with their employment. This is for two related reasons: first, because employment is often stultifying and alienating and second, because full time employment does not allow people the freedom to compensate for this lack of satisfaction outside working hours. Both these problems flow from the Radical theorists' second observation that society, in pursuing economic growth for its own sake rather than as a means to an end, has lost its way. Third, and finally, the Radical theorists are all agreed that the crisis of unemployment puts into question our current organization of work.

First, then, according to the Radical theorists, the world of employment in itself does not provide opportunities for personal growth for the majority of the population. What makes matters even worse is that this organization of work over structures people's time. It does not leave them enough space free of the obligations of their employment to compensate for the deficiencies of their jobs outside working hours. Aznar (1981, p. 39) assesses this situation in the following manner: he asserts that 'any society which proposes that its citizens spend the whole of their time, energy and empathy engaged in an activity which cannot, by its very nature, soak up this energy, is fundamentally perverse'. Moreover, Aznar [2] explained that the genesis of his own interest in matters relating to the organization of work sprang from his realization that many people were suffering a general malaise concerning their way of life. He declared that in his work as a marekt research consultant, he saw people who were 'suffering distress in relation to their lives' and who, responding to the question 'what would you ideally like to do' did not answer by saying that they did not want to work, but rather that they wanted a 'different kind of work'.

Likewise, Delors and his 'Echanges et Projets' group (1980) expound the idea that people want freedom from time-discipline. These theorists (1980, p. 70) use economic reasoning to explain this trend. They argue that products are offered on the market which require much time for consumption, such as those services related to culture, sports, and leisure. In order for these sectors to grow and be successful, their products must be offered to a broad base of consumers. Thus, workers demand, and are given, more free time in order to consume these services. In being granted this time, they experience freedom from time discipline. Delors & 'Echanges et Projets' (1980, p. 71) continue

> Knowing that one can take on other kinds of roles influences one's way of approaching one's professional role, and also leads inevitably to the reduction in the importance of employment in comparison with other activities; to the questioning of the primacy accorded to work time;and to the creation of a demand for more 'free' time.

Second, and in addition to the arguments that employment is often stifling and that it occupies too major a part of people's lives, there is the criticism of present day social and economic organization that economic growth is no longer viewed as a means to an end, but has become an end in itself. In consequence, argue the Radical theorists, an individual's work, as embodied in employment, no longer responds to the needs of the consumer of the goods and services which he or she creates, but to the needs of production itself. Radical theorists break with accepted wisdom in that they do not consider these two 'needs' to be mutually compatible. Friedmann (1982, p. 89), for example, defines a concept of 'socially useful work' which is work that is indispensable 'for a society in a state of emergency' [3]. She estimates that only thirty-five to forty per cent of the economically active population [4] are engaged in such production. The rest are obliged to produce essentially 'unnecessary' goods in order to earn the income necessary to personal survival. Gorz (1985, p. 58) is in agreement with this observation, suggesting that 'for a section of the population, only the production of inessentials allows them access to necessities'. Gorz, along with the rest of the Radical theorists, is of the opinion that no one should have to work at such 'production' to earn the money necessary for survival.

The third common aspect of the Radical theorists' analysis is to link these cultural dissatisfactions to the most socially pressing of the post '73 economic problems: namely, the unemployment crisis. However, in contrast to the Free Market Dualists, the Radical theorists assert that unemployment represents an opportunity for much needed change, even though this opportunity seems to be cloaked in disaster. For example, Aznar [5] suggested that it is a good thing that full time employment for all is now a thing of the past. Sachs (1980) suggests that the current economic crisis has put into question the more or less tacit assumption made by nearly all previous economic schools of thought that it was enough to manipulate the macropolitics of economic growth in order to facilitate the microdevelopment of the economic, social and cultural spheres of life. He (1980, p. 50) declares that

> Today, because of the economic crisis, we are beginning to realize just how much it has cost us to have turned economic growth into an end in itself and to have gambled above all on its never ending continuation, whereas growth constitutes a necessary, but by no means sufficient condition for development.

Thus, the crisis of unemployment puts into question first and foremost the justification of subjugating all social goals to the economic aim of continued growth.

However, although these basic points are agreed upon by all the Radical theorists, divergences loom as some of them attempt to define the 'cause' of these problems. Why did 'economic growth' become such an all powerful rationale? What function does time-discipline fulfil? These questions, and others like them, divide various sub-groups of Radical theorists from one another. First and foremost, there is a sub-group of theorists - notably Roustang, Sachs, Friedman and Aznar - who stop at this juncture. For them, the problems outlined above are part of a certain logic, a certain rationale. For example, Aznar [6] was adamant that the problems of work should not be reduced to a simple question of capitalism: 'it goes beyond the question of who owns the factories. We must forget capital!', he declared. Sachs (1980, p. 59) adopts a similar approach, regarding the problem not as one of 'the means of production', but one of 'malconsumption'. In other words, his explanation is quite simply that some people over consume and some under consume. Roustang (1987, p. 14) believes that due to technological progress and the relative saturation of consumer durables, it will be more and more difficult to reduce unemployment significantly. Given this state of affairs, it is best to use the opportunity so presented to change the way we work in a positive manner.

Others, however, choose to delve further to expose the roots of these problems, citing 'technology', 'capitalism' or 'Humankind's relationship to Nature' as explanatory factors. The first option adopted is to examine in more detail the role of industrial technology in creating these problems. This is the choice of Granstedt. Talking of the crisis of unemployment, he (1980, p. 9) explains that it is 'due to the radical imbalance in our means of production' and that 'the tools spawned by the industrial revolution lead to world economic instability'. He maintains that the problem of employment is one of a rigid and complicated system of world wide interdependence which does not provide individuals with the possibility of freedom of action.

Granstedt accepts that other factors - such as inherited culture or the distribution of power - have their part to play in these crises. Nevertheless, he (1980, p. 17-18) maintains that 'of the three, today it is the structure of our tools' which is predominant. In other words, even if these 'tools' evolved in conjunction with capitalism, we now have to deal essentially with a crisis of the 'means' of production as opposed to the 'mode' of production. Despite this focus on 'technology', it is clear that Granstedt's position derives from the 'New Left' changes described in Chapter 3 which proposed that it was not enough to transfer the management of the infrastructure of capitalism to the 'socialist' state because this industrial infrastructure itself is a source of alienation and oppression.

The second option open to Radical theorists who want to unearth the cause of the problems of time-discipline, productivism and unemployment is to look towards the role played by capitalism. Notably, this option is taken up by Delors, Gorz and the ADRET collective. Delors, for example, concentrates on the topic of time-discipline. He (& 'Echanges et Projets', 1980, p. 67) alleges that the whole history of industrialism has been characterized by the struggle of workers to control their work time in the face of employers who have continually attempted to make sure that their employees reserve all their energies for their job.

The need to consume commodities is strongly linked to this time-discipline because prolonged working hours in themselves ensure that people do not have the opportunity to 'opt out' of the cycle of work, production and consumption to satify their needs in an autonomous manner. Thus, as Gorz (1982a, p. 82) explains, 'only with capitalism does work, or the heteronomous exchange of exchange values, become a full time activity and the self supply of goods and services become a marginal or subordinate activity'. If people did have the time to produce goods and services for themselves (thereby short circuiting the capitalist market), this would lead to a loss of profit and affect capital accumulation.

On the question of people's dissatisfaction with their jobs, Gorz (1982a, p. 2) asserts that the worker is alienated from his or her product because the primary objective of production under capitalism is to create exchange values as opposed to use values. The employee produces goods not to use or enjoy him or herself but to be sold by his or her capitalist employer. The employee is compensated for the labour which he or she exerts by a wage. In sum, workers sell their labour power, and not the fruits of it. This estrangement of workers from the products which they create results in the alienation of workers from their activity. Indeed, the ever greater value placed on commodities leads to a corresponding devaluation of the human world and of people's creative capacities. As a consequence of selling their labour power (as opposed to its product), individuals become unhappy in their work as they are restrained from developing their mental and physical capacities or feeling any bond with the product of their labour. It is in this way that the capitalist system is at the root of these feelings of alienation.

Nonetheless, Gorz (1982a, p. 100) and the ADRET collective (1977, p. 108) do not lose sight of the fact that scale and remoteness are at the heart of alienation in employment. However, they perceive these as flowing from the capitalist rationale of 'accumulation'. The centrality of the pursuit of economic growth and the concentration of the various aspects of life into ever larger and more remotely controlled units - especially employment - is explained by these theorists with reference to capitalism.

And what of the crisis of unemployment? Gorz (1985, p. 9-10), for example, explains the crisis of unemployment in Marxist terminology. He maintains that sooner or later, profit had to begin to fall. The more that one deploys capital to produce a certain volume of commodities, the more the profit that is extracted from those commodities diminishes in relation to the mass of capital used. The mass of capital cannot grow to infinity. If profits begin to fall, crisis sets in: machinery cannot be renewed; the production of machinery decreases; a reduction in production ensues. In Marxist terms, this is a case of over accumulation. That is, the amount of capital deployed for production becomes so great that capital cannot reproduce itself at a normal rhythm. The value of capital falls, and with the closure of factories, can eventually be destroyed.

Gorz (1985, p. vii) believes that society is approaching a crossroads brought about by technological developments (these being the major contributing factor to unemployment) which are leading capitalism into crisis. He calls the technology of the industrial revolution a 'one-way street'. It dictated the way that work had to be organized. Conversely, the microtechnologies, he argues, 'herald the abolition of work' as they provide a 'crossroads' which gives society the opportunity to turn off its capitalist path. Gorz (1985, p. vii) explains that

> [Ricardo and Marx] predicted ... a social order where the efficacy of technology would abolish work, the logic of capital and commodity relations to reveal disposable time as the measure of true wealth: the micro-electronic revolution is pulling us in that direction.

Nevertheless, Gorz does not think that this will inevitably happen: the terms on which this technology is introduced must be socialist terms. There is nothing to say that the microtechnologies cannot, and are not being pressed into the service of capitalism.

The ADRET collective (1977), however, does not agree that these possibilities have only just presented themselves. On the contrary, technological advances could always have been channelled towards freeing people from 'necessary' productive activity instead of always being attuned to the demands of industrial growth. Productivity gains could always have been, at least partially, expressed in a reduction in working hours. In using these gains purely to raise production, notes the ADRET collective (1977, p. 102)

> a choice of civilization was made: namely, to use the possibilities opened up by the prodigious development of technology over the last one hundred years, not to reduce working time, but to increase production. ... This was the choice of a productivist and consumerist society.

Third, and lastly, certain other Radical theorists explain that the problems laid out at the beginning of this section can be traced back to Humankind's relationship to Nature and the ecological crisis which this has engendered. This is the view of Lalonde & Simmonet (1978), Lebreton (1978) and the 'EPPEM' collective (1977). The dissatisfaction manifested by people with their employment is not explained by the 'ecologists' as the consequence of the 'capitalist' organization of work. Instead, these theorists highlight the problem of the concentration of work into larger and larger scale units. Indeed, in their opinion, it is the scale of institutions alone which renders work alienating. The target of their criticism is bureaucracy and technocracy in themselves and not just as manifestations of capitalism. Thus, society is bedevilled by its ossified, over complex organization which ignores the lessons offered by the planetary ecosystem. These show that it is diversity and flexibility which ensure stability. Accordingly, this sub-group of Radical theorists argues that the way of working embodied in employment contradicts these 'natural' principles.

Moreover, the 'ecologists' argue that to have more, society is willing to work more. This creates the conditions which result in consumption becoming the aim of existence. Lalonde & Simmonet (1978, p. 128) conclude that work is 'the drug which we consume the most willingly', the new opium of the people, perhaps. In true ecologist terminology, Lalonde & Simmonet (1978, p. 134) describe this whole cycle as a waste of human energy. It is a waste because this energy, used for the production of unnecessary goods and services in stifling and alienating conditions, could and should be put to the development of human autonomy in all aspects of life.

As for the question of the crisis of unemployment, Lalonde & Simmonet (1978) understand this to be a manifestation of a wider 'ecological' crisis, the heart of which is lack of harmony with nature on which human society is, indeed, dependent. Lalonde & Simmonet (1978, p. 61) explain that human economy at present does not work with Nature; it attempts to replace it. Growth in human productivity is accompanied by a decline in the productivity of the natural world, setting in motion a cancelling out process which most people refuse to take into consideration.

Moreover, for Lebreton (1978, p. 148-9), (who expresses the general line of thought of these 'ecologists') the impending crises are part of Nature's contingency plans to establish equilibrium in the face of Humankind's parasitic plunderings. He argues that with the use of 'tools' and 'money', an artificial process was set in motion for which 'Nature had not prepared the necessary regulatory mechanisms'. However, Lebreton is of the opinion that in the long term, the impetus of material constraints will oblige people to reset their objectives, including those concerning work.

In sum, all the Radical theorists are convinced that society must, or will change dramatically since it is, in this latter quarter of the twentieth century, at a particularly vital stage in its development. The developments in question include changes in social attitudes, especially to work; the unemployment crisis; the new technologies; environmental destruction and the inevitable crisis of capitalism. Whereas the Free Market Dualists turn to the informal economy as a means to solve the unemployment crisis without unduly affecting the core capitalist and productivist sector, the Radical theorists - whilst considering a return to full employment to be on the whole impossible - also see such a reinstatement of the status quo to be undesirable. However, just as different causal factors are emphasised by different Radical theorists in explaining the genesis of these crises, so too is there variation concerning the future scenarios for society suggested by these theorists and thus, concerning the role that they attribute to informal work in the future of the economy. It is the role of the informal economy in these scenarios that I will now explore.

<u>The role of the informal economy</u>

The role assigned to the informal economy in solving these crises by the various Radical theorists is dependent upon their respective choices of future scenario. The kind of informal activities in which these theorists are interested; the relationship which these activities are said to have to the State and to the formal labour market; and the precise difficulties which such activities are meant to overcome are all choices which can be traced back to this scenario.

The Radical theorists are not only, or indeed necessarily concerned with informal work activities as they exist today, but in the possible emergence or reinforcement of a category of work which one could call 'autonomous' in the future. Reminding ourselves of the definition of this category of activity, 'autonomous' work does not refer to a tangible, empirically observable category of activity. Instead, the notion is linked to utopian visions of what work could be in the future. Thus, autonomous work is a conceptual, as opposed to a concrete phenomenon. It suggests that a type of work should come about in the future over which the producer will have a large degree of control and in which creativity and conviviality will be the driving forces. In sum, 'autonomous' work is creative, controllable and socially useful. It has a purpose for the person performing it other than the earning of a wage.

On the whole, the most 'reformist' of the Radical theorists have a vision of 'autonomous' work which merges with forms of informal activity which exist at present, as well as with the activities of such organizations as cooperatives, associations and the like. The most 'radical' of the Radical theorists do not explicitly refer to types of informal work which exist today since this does not fit their aim of calling for a complete redrawing of the boundaries which divide various categories of activities from one another.

Godard (1985, p. 327) has dubbed the type of scenario envisaged by the majority of Radical theorists as the 'dualism of the socialistic alternative', meaning a dualism which attempts to find new forms of autonomy and sociability in the allocation of work between an informal and a formal sector. What unites all the Radical theorists is their wish to put an end to, or at least considerably reduce the domination of 'heteronomous' work over our lives and to introduce more autonomous work into them. Heteronomous work is understood as that over which individuals have little or no control.

There are three separate (but connected) future scenarios for work envisaged by the Radical theorists. First, there is the 'socialist' scenario in which the State would take control of heteronomous production and designate the boundaries between the autonomous and heteronomous spheres of life. Second, there is a scenario which rests on the more libertarian and ecologist ideal of changes in work patterns coming about through piecemeal initiatives. Accordingly, the autonomous sphere would develop as a result of civil society nibbling away at the domains of the formal market and the State. The third scenario is based on a more pragmatic, social democratic solution to the crises. Such a solution would produce a mixed economy in which the needs of industry would be balanced with people's need for autonomy and creativity. I will begin the discussion with an examination of the first of these.

Autonomous work in the socialist scenario. Broadly speaking, in this section I will be discussing the work of Gorz (1982a & 1985) and the ADRET collective (1977) and, to a lesser extent, that of Granstedt (1980). On the whole, these theorists want to bring about an 'autogestionnaire' society in which the informal economy would play a major part. What renders this in particular a 'socialist' scenario is the fact that these theorists believe that the State would retain an important role in organizing the essential (heteronomous) work on which society as a whole relies for the production of its staple goods.

Gorz (1985, p. 56), for example, calls for a new balance between three types of work: heteronomous work; small scale cooperative and communal free entreprise; and autonomous, household based activity. ADRET (1977, p. 114) creates similar categories, distinguishing between 'liberated work' and 'constrained work', the criteria for the difference between them being the presence or absence of creativity; the identity of the beneficiairies of the goods or services produced; the scale of operation; and whether what is produced is intended for exchange or use. Granstedt (1980, p. 15) differentiates between the 'integrated productive system' and the 'autonomous productive system', the former being based on what amounts to industrial technology, and the latter on a smaller scale sets of 'tools' which the individual can oversee and control.

As an example of the kind of scenario envisaged by these theorists, one can examine the propositions of the ADRET collective (1977). The ADRET collective (1977, p. 145) suggests a pattern for the organization of work in which each person would perform an average of two hours a day of 'constrained work' (which could be translated into so many days a week, months a year, and so on, according to individual tastes and circumstances). In conjunction with such an organization of work, there would be an absolute ceiling placed on the amount of goods and services produced in this manner. This would be possible without a drastic reduction in living standards both by manufacturing more durable products as well as by distributing wealth more fairly which would alleviate poverty without incurring the need for growth in the economy.

Granstedt (1980, p. 17-20) argues that a reorientation of technology is the solution. He asserts that the 'integrated productive system' and the 'autonomous productive system' are essentially two different kinds of tools: the first needs large scale organized action for it to function whilst the second can function on an individual or autonomous basis. Granstedt argues that the balance between these two types of tools should be redressed. He insists that scientific progress can be applied to the development of both types of technology. Furthermore, the two types of technology are complementary in the sense that they can and do exist side by side, but they are rivals in the sense that the relative importance of each can fluctuate. The problem today is that the 'integrated system' has become too dominant. In Granstedt's scenario, the 'integrated tools' would be used only for the production of socially necessary goods within a zero growth economy. The 'autonomous system' would be the domain of any supplementary production of goods and services desired by individuals or small communities.

As underlined in the introduction to this section, Gorz, the ADRET collective and Granstedt contend (along with most Radical theorists) that, although it can be reduced, 'heteronomous' production cannot be eradicated completely if Western society is not to slip back into the 'realm of necessity', characteristic of preindustrial times. Gorz (1985, p. 56) declares that 'subsistence production, even when autonomous, belongs to the sphere of necessity' whereas 'real autonomy is the space to do what is not absolutely necessary, or the space to do nothing, to dream'. Only 'heteronomous' work, using the newest technologies, can provide this space in which people can realize their creative capacities. The ADRET collective (1977, p. 10) agrees that poverty, or the everyday fight for survival, cannot be liberatory because when people are engaged in such a struggle, they do not have the opportunity to enjoy diversified and creative activity. It is the mass production of staple goods which can provide this opportunity, although this does not have to be performed according to a capitalist logic. 'Heteronomous' work, suggests Gorz (1985, p. 56), is not to be equated solely with capitalist wage labour which results in the production of marketable commodities. The notion of 'heteronomous' activity simply refers to work which is out of the control of the individual. As such, there is no reason why such an organization of labour could not be pressed into the service of producing socially necessary use values.

Such a new organization of work, argue these three theorists, cannot develop without change in the way in which society and the economy is organized. It cannot come about within a productivist/growth economy fuelled by the capitalist profit motive. Thus, the role of the market economy is in some doubt in this scenario, being replaced for the most part by the State which, it is argued, would organize 'heteronomous' work. Furthermore, explains Gorz (1982a, p. 105), it would be the State which would provide a basic income for citizens as well as the collective tools with which they could perform autonomous work. He continues to explain that just as there needs to be a dualism of autonomous and heteronomous work, life and human relationships must be similarly divided into a heteronomous and autonomous sphere. Gorz refutes the possibility of the complete self-management of society. He rejects it as a myth because a community without some objectified rules is open to domination by a powerful leader or sub-group. Gorz (1982a, p. 112) observes that

> The objectification of a set of obligations external to each individual, yet common to them all, is the only means of protecting the members of the community from the personal power of a leader. The existence of a State, separate from civil society ... is thus the essential prerequisite to the autonomy of civil society.

Gorz (1985) admits that these are major revisions of the self-management principle, but stresses the need for practicality. He (1985, p. 76) maintains that 'the aims of self-management are aspirations, not a global, coherent and operational concept of the nature and functioning of society'. Gorz makes the assumption that it is objectively impossible to live harmoniously without rules because social groupings are too vast and too complex to be overseen by the individual. Granstedt (1980, p. 21) also argues that if the two modes of production (autonomous and heteronomous) are to survive side by side, the State must organize the boundaries and arbitrate between them. Indeed, it is the role accorded to the State by these theorists which makes theirs an essentially 'socialist' scenario.

Gorz (1982a & 1985) takes his ideas further down the 'socialist' road, detailing the steps which could bring his particular scenario about. Following in a specifically Marxist tradition, Gorz asserts that the crisis of unemployment has encouraged the development of a new class of individuals who will take the place of the traditional standard bearers of revolution - the industrial proletariat. According to Gorz, it is no longer the industrial proletariat, but this 'new' class which has the most 'objective' interest in social and economic revolution because it is they who are most deprived by the present economic system and particularly, by its organization of work. This new historical subject is the 'non-class' of post industrial proletarians.

Gorz (1982a, p. 68) explains that 'this non-class encompasses all those who have been expelled from production by the abolition of work, or those whose capacities are underemployed as a result of the industrialization of intellectual work'. More precisely, these people have no job security or class identity; they work casually and part time and are generally over qualified for the work which they perform. Consequently, they experience work as a blank interval to be endured in order to earn their living. Gorz (1982a, p. 6) posits that this 'new historical subject' has emerged because of the loss of ability to identify with one's work. The fact that work has become a nondescript task without personal involvement and which is interchangeable with any other has led to the disappearance of any sense of belonging to a class (hence the expression 'non-class'). Consequently, the objective for the workers of this class becomes a matter of how to free themselves from their work (which contrasts with the aims of the industrial proletariat whose objective it has been to enhance the quality and status of their work). Thus, Gorz singles out this 'non-class' because it is they who experience employment, when they have it, not as an activity which gives them working class identity, but as alienation pure and simple.

Gorz posits that 'work' has lost its meaning because we are 'producing in order to work' rather than 'working in order to produce' which is the natural order of things. This inversion is experienced most profoundly by the non-class of post-industrial proletarians. They perceive themselves as external to the production of society and see no point in taking over its machine-like structure. What matters to them is the appropriation of autonomy outside the realms of employment which would allow self-development. Therefore, argues Gorz, it is this 'non-class' who have the most to gain from the development of 'autonomous' activities'. He (1982a, p. 74) explains that

> The logic of capital has brought us to the threshold of liberation. But it can only be crossed at the price of a radical break in which productivism is replaced by a different rationality. This rupture can only come from individuals themselves ... Only the non-class of non-producers is capable of such an act. For it alone embodies what lies beyond productivism: the rejection of the accumulation ethic and the dissolution of all classes.

Granstedt, like Gorz, looks to the unemployed for the lead in bringing about a new organization of work even though he does not build a complete theory around this idea. He (1980, p. 232) explains that 'permantently high unemployment represents the first chance to escape from the industrial impass'. It is this assumption that the unemployed and marginalized will have a large part to play in the evolution of a new organization of work which is put under the microscope of the Empirical Approaches, as we will see in the following chapter.

Autonomous work, ecological principles and the libertarian ideal. This group of theorists - Lalonde & Simmonet (1978), Lebreton (1978) and the 'EPPEM' collective (1977) - advocate the encouragement of 'autonomous' work not only as a means of improving people's quality of life, but because such diversified and decentralized activity is much more in harmony with the ecological principles by which they set so much store. These are dispersion, diffusion, diversity and dilution which they contrast to the principles of concentration and simplification which dominate France's present day industrial economy. Thus, they posit that growing autonomy on the part of individuals to work according to their own needs and desires (instead of according to those of industry), will result in a more diversified society and economy which will be more 'ecologically' viable. 'Autogestion', therefore, is essential to environmental protection as it would allow society to become less concentrated and less ossified, more diverse and flexible and as such, in keeping with and more responsive to the needs of the planetary ecosystem. For these theorists, therefore, encouraging autonomous work is necessary to avoid environmental disaster as well as to provide a more fulfilling life for individuals. However, there is no contradiction in satifying the needs of the planet and those of Humankind in the eyes of these theorists because they believe that Humankind could live better if it lived more in accordance with the principles of Nature.

So, in this scenario, what form would this autonomous activity take? And how would it be related to other forms of activity? Lalonde & Simmonet (1978, p. 128) differentiate between 'l'activité franche' (free activity) which is done for oneself, for pleasure or out of necessity and 'le travail aliéné' (alienated work) in which the product, organization and distribution of work is out of the control of the individual. They (1978, p. 134) lay down plans for a society which balances a sector of mass production (which, as we have seen in the 'socialist' scenario, would produce socially necessary goods) with a multiplicity of autonomous activities. Furthermore, they stress the need both for decentralization as well as for participation of citizens in managing their own lives, work and society. This would entail all citizens partaking not just in menial jobs, but also in professions which are now closed and specialized.

But, who will balance the spheres of 'alienated work' and 'free activity' in this 'ecologist' scenario'? The State? Lalonde & Simmonet (1978) do not put so much faith in the State as do Gorz, the ADRET collective and Granstedt. They agree that certain activities must be carried out at the regional or national level, but they believe that the era of the Nation-State is being revolutionized in that the various agents of civil society will continuously chip away at the edifice of the State. Lalonde & Simmonet (1978, p. 171) believe that there will be a continual battle between 'a central, State run sphere and the plethora of local, community or private autonomous activities'. They believe the mission of ecologists to be to organize 'this duel in such a way as to favour all the Davids over Goliath'. Thus, the State, and other centralized institutional bodies, will continue to exist, but the duty of civil society will be continual vigilance since the good will and self-restraint of these can at no stage be trusted.

Lebreton (1978) resolves the problem of managing (and restricting) a centralized sphere which produces enough basic commodities to safeguard material living standards in that he is not so convinced of the need to keep these living standards at present levels. Concomitantly, he does not place so much importance on the retention of the heteronomous sphere of production as Lalonde & Simmonet (1978) and the advocates of the socialist scenario. In other words, Lebreton favours a greater withdrawal from socially organized production and a higher degree of material austerity than do the other Radical theorists discussed this far. Thus, his proposal is not for a 'dualistic scenario' of the type preferred by the majority of the Radical theorists. Rather, he envisages a more universally 'self-sufficient' and deinustrialized solution to the energy and unemployment crises.

In sum, it must be stressed that when the ADRET collective (1977), Gorz (1982a & 1985), Granstedt (1980), Lalonde & Simmonet (1978), Lebreton (1978) and the 'EPPEM' collective (1977), speak of autonomous work, this is a conceptualization of a type of work which has a specific relationship to its opposite, 'heteronomous' work, in a future scenario. It has very little to do with how they perceive the relationship which exists at present between current forms of informal economic activity (namely, black market work, domestic work and voluntary work) and the formal market system. Nevertheless, some interpret certain aspects of present day informal economic activity to be localized rebellions against the alienating system of employment. Bosquet [7] (1980, p. 40), for example, suggests that an individual who chooses artisanal black market work is rebelling against the strict time-discipline of capitalism. He suggests that black market work is considered dangerous by employers' associations because it threatens to liberate the worker to exchange his or her labour without the intermediary of the employer.

Equally, participation in domestic activities is seen as compensation for the alienating effects of the employment sphere. Lalonde & Simmonet (1978, p. 37) suggest that such activities as 'D.I.Y., gardening, artisanal production and assembling products from kits' have become fashionable and are enjoying a new lease of life just when 'it seemed that they were going to be forgotten in the euphoria of waste'. Furthermore, Lalonde & Simmonet (1978, p. 129) deem the products of such activities to be infinitely more 'useful' than those of many formal employment activities: they assert that 'looking after children and preparing food', for example, are tasks which are 'fundamental' to survival.

Gorz (1982a, p. 80) suggests that the growth in domestic activities represents 'a sphere of autonomy' which has been 'wrested from a world governed by the principles of productivity, agression, competition and hierarchical discipline'. Familial activities have the advantage of being ends in themselves. Gorz disagrees with the notion that the rise in the number of people participating in production within the home denotes an 'individualization' of society, claiming instead that it is representative of a 'cultural mutation announcing the transition to post industrial society'.

However, Lalonde & Simmonet are not blinded with enthusiasm for the development of domestic production within the current social and economic structure. They (1978, p. 131) assert that 'not only have autonomous activities been mutilated and imprisoned in the confined space of the urban appartment', but also those which have survived have been 'contaminated and colonized by the commodities and the ideologies of alienated work'. No activity, so the argument goes, can remain totally immune from the prevailing capitalist or industrialist system.

Thus, a certain ambiguity reigns on the matter of evaluating the role played by present day informal economic activities for these two sub-groups of Radical theorists. The third sub-group of Radicals is more directly interested in the various forms of informal work which exist at present. However, as we will see, they too have doubts about the role - potential or actual - which these activities can play in tranforming the ways in which we 'work'.

Coexistence with capitalism: the informal economy and the social democratic scenario. The theorists to be discussed under this heading put forth a scenario in which work in the public (State), private (market) and civil (autonomous) spheres coexist and in which there is a more flexible organization of work time. Delors (1979) (& Gaudin, 1979) (& Foucauld, 1980) (& Echanges & Projets, 1980), Aznar (1978 & 1981), Sachs (1980 & 1983), Rosanvallon (1980) Roustang (1982 & 1987), Schiray & Vinaver (1980), Gaudin (& Greffe, 1980) (& Schiray, 1984), and Greffe (1981) all call for a new balance between employment, on the one hand, and more autonomous activities, on the other. However, in comparison with the theorists whom we have discussed in the previous two sections, they do not believe that such a scenario necessitates either a drastic reduction of the capitalist market sphere or 'zero' economic growth.

Thus, we are dealing here with the moderate wing of the Radical group, this being the reason why I have labelled its future scenario 'social democratic'. This position has developed in the post '79 recessionary period. Its theorists are interested not so much in a new form of work which we might label 'autonomous', but rather in the way in which informal activities as they exist at present can be developed alongside employment. These, they hope, will be an innovative antedote to the recession and the problem of mass unemployment. Indeed, the idea is to create employment in a liberatory way which encourages flexibility and creativity. Schiray & Vinaver (1980, p. 66), for example, advocate that informal activities be taken into account in the planning of the economy. Planning, they argue, should aim to maximize individuals' opportunities to choose the way in which they wish to satisy their needs rather than to favour exclusively the growth of market goods and services.

Thus, these theorists maintain that the three spheres of the State, private enterprise and autonomous, informal, or non profit making activity can live harmoniously together. Delors, for example, (1979, p. 147-8) explains that being a socialist, he believes that one should 'act empirically'. If that means recognizing that the State has a role to play, and the market sector too, then so be it. Roustang (1987, p. 12) goes so far as to suggest that any policy to encourage informal work should seek to avoid harming the entrepreneurial vitality of private companies. Likewise, Aznar [8] contends that the productivity of capitalism, which creates wealth, and the redistributory role of the State constitute the essential backdrop to the liberty of the individual to produce autonomously. In addition, Sachs (1980, p. 59) advocates the encouragement of 'ways of life which integrate into activities of market production and consumption those which take place outside the market sphere'. Similarly, Rosanvallon (1980, p. 24) calls for a 'pluralist scenario' which mixes a cocktail of these three spheres. However, he emphasizes that if people eventually do enjoy the freedom to choose between market, State and informal means of meeting their needs, change in the way in which the State and market mechanisms operate will inevitably ensue.

However, although there is a recognition amongst these theorists that the market will continue to function, Sachs (1983, p. 60), for example, believes that the structures of consumption, production and employment would have to be redefined simultaneously with a definition of the aims of growth. That is, although these theorists do not, on the whole, advocate 'zero growth', they realize that their scenarios entail a new balance between economic and social goals. Roustang (1987, p. 91), for example, asserts that 'what is essential is to think afresh about the interaction of the economic with the non economic sphere'.

Of what, then, would the 'third', 'autonomous' or 'informal' sector be composed, according to these theorists? Delors (1979, p. 151) explains that the 'third' sector would consist of the production of goods and services in conditions close to those of artisanal or cooperative production. These new production units would be small, decentralized and created by individuals or small groups who wanted to experiment with new forms of work to satisfy economic and social needs.

According to Aznar (1978, p. 69), this autonomous sector of activity must provide the opportunity to partake in 'le travail impliqué' (personally involving work) which is work with which the individual can identify and which allows him or her to invest part of him or herself in the product of his or her labour. When people have time free of their employment, contends Aznar, they want to engage in an activity in which it is possible to 'invest part of themselves'.

It should be noted, nonetheless, that these theorists are not necessarily as commited to the 'informal sphere' as those who advocate the 'socialist' and 'ecologist' scenarios. For example, Roustang (1987, p. 100) contends that 'there is no reason to favour either market production or informal production'. He asserts that one should maintain a neutral position in order to find the right balance between all forms of activity according to circumstance. This opinion is indicative of the position taken by the majority who advocate this 'social democratic' scenario:

namely, that it must be individuals who choose whether or not to specialize in market production or autonomous production, or to find their own personal balance between the two spheres. In order for people to have the opportunity to do this, a new organization of time must be brought about based primarily on the possibility of work sharing, part time work, flexible retirement ages and time made available for education throughout one's working life.

Similarly, Delors argues that the self-management of society must be based on the self-regulation of time. That is, everyone must have the right, in the first instance, to choose their own work time. Delors & Foucauld (1980, p. xiii) contend that such a revolution in the organization of time would permit 'a successful formula for the sharing out of employment'. In agreement with these propositions is Aznar (1981, p. 55) who advocates a society in which couples, for example, could pool their incomes from two part time jobs; education and employment or retirement and employment could be alternated; or a second activity could be brought into play such as self-provisioning, black market work, or the establishment of 'microcompanies'.

Indeed, it is part time work and work sharing which will solve the problem of unemployment, according to these theorists. Roustang (1982, p. 230) asserts that unemployment could be reduced effectively by the sharing of employment and the development of activities outside work. Furthermore, Rosanvallon (1980) declared that mass unemployment had not caused social dislocation because of the existence of the informal economy. He asserted that the unemployed were already making use of opportunities offered by the black labour market and by domestic production to save themselves from penury. Indeed, it was these assertions which generated widespread interest in his work on this subject in France, putting his proposals for a 'pluralist society' rather in the shade.

However, despite advocating this scenario, some theorists have their doubts that the capitalist market system would accept such competition from the autonomous, informal sphere. This 'autonomous' production would necessarily substitute the need for a proportion of the present consumption of commodities produced in the market sphere. For example, Gaudin & Greffe (1980, p. 99) argue that capitalism would tolerate such autonomous production only if it were to remain marginal since 'the logic of capital accumulation is incompatible with that of work sharing and the informal economy'. Greffe [9] expressed doubt that the non official economies, as they exist at present, are sufficiently independent from the formal market and State sphere to fulfil anything but a colonized role.

The next chapter discusses the 'Empirical Approaches' to the role that the informal economy could play in the future of work. One of the principal aims of these discussions will be to examine whether or not empirical research has provided any evidence with which to evaluate the likelihood of these various scenarios coming to fruition. However, in order for such an evaluation to be possible, we must be clear about the assumptions on which all these scenarios are based.

First and foremost, all the Radical theorists credit the informal sector with a degree of strength and independence vis à vis the formal State and market economies. According to those of an 'ecologist' or 'socialist' persuasion, it is the cycle of 'employment - wage - consumption' which precludes most self-provisioning. Indeed, if people produce goods and services autonomously for themselves and for others in their families or their communities, this cycle is disrupted. The conclusion drawn from this observation is that autonomous production undermines and ultimately challenges the capitalist/industrialist system. To a lesser extent, the 'social democrats' of this Radical group, despite believing that the opportunities for autonomous work can be increased without totally reversing either the productivist or capitalist logic of the economy, concede that the realization of their scenarios would entail certain changes of emphasis in the goals of production. Some even conclude that in the final analysis, capitalism could not tolerate the existence of an 'autonomous' rival. For all the Radical theorists, therefore, the informal sector is distinctly different from the formal economic sectors and can provide, on the one hand, wealth and on the other hand, creative and satisfying activity for individuals where the formal economy fails.

Second, moreover, all the Radical theorists posit that the unemployed will be amongst the first to take up opportunities to work informally. Nonetheless, most of these theorists stress the necessity for institutional and practical changes to be brought about to allow those marginalized from formal production to work 'autonomously' or informally. Although all the Radical theorists, albeit to different degrees, believe that informal activities as they are performed today can provide a basis for more autonomous working patterns, this does not mean that they believe that as of now, people in general, and the unemployed in particular, have the choice of working informally. Thus, Empirical research showing the lack of opportunity to work informally, especially amongst the unemployed, would not nullify the possibility of the Radical scenarios being realized.

Therefore, in comparing these scenarios with the findings of the Empirical researchers, we must remember that the Radical theorists do specify certain measures which would have to be implemented in order for their scenarios to come into being. The ADRET collective (1977, p. 146), for example, points out that at the moment, if people want to produce certain goods and services autonomously, they have to buy the raw materials and more importantly, the tools necessary for that production individually. The expense which this incurs, and the infrequency with which the tools in particular would be likely to be used, renders informal production impracticable for those with fewest financial means. Thus, the ADRET collective maintains that the necessary tools for informal production would have to be made available by the State, or bought on a communal basis, perhaps with the State encouraging this through special credit schemes. Without such a policy being applied, the theorists warn, freedom from employment (in the form of joblessness) would mean sad idleness because at present, only employment provides access to the tools of production. Likewise, Schiray & Vinaver (1980, p. 70) explain that in order to widen access to informal production, one would have to take into account such factors as 'access to physical resources, space, buildings, production facilities, the availability of finance and also time and information'.

More importantly, many of the theorists take up the question of the system of remuneration (distribution of the fruits of heteronomous work) which their scenarios raise. If people were to work a two hour day, for example, in the framework of a highly productive economy, the system of remuneration could no longer be based on the principle of the exchange of labour time for income. Gorz suggests that life and citizens would have to be paid instead of workers and work so that everyone could reap the benefits of the automated production process. Enough heteronomous work would be performed by the members of society to cover everyone's basic needs and income would be received by each individual to satisfy those same needs. Gorz (1986, p. 61) maintains that

> a social income should be the counterpart of social productivity and not a welfare benefit. ... It is a question of guaranteeing an income which will not go down with the decrease in the amount of time worked. It is not work itself from which income should be independent, but from the amount of time which it socially necessary to devote to work.

Aznar (1987, p. 8), too, proposes a system of 'three incomes', these being 'the work wage', 'the second pay cheque' (composed of a 'social income' and an 'automation income') and the products of autonomous working.

Third, the Radical scenario hinges on the assumption that people will warm to non material values, such as creativity, 'whole person' relationships and autonomous conditions of working, in decentralized communities and that they will want, or be able to separate the improvement of their quality of life from that of their quantity of possessions. The corollary of this is the assumption that deep down, people are ready to reject consumerist values. This is an example of the 'faith' in Human nature held by these theorists - that is, the faith that the majority of people hold the same views as they do. It is also an expression of the faith which they put in the informal economy to provide these satisfactions. Empirical research will be able to reveal whether people who engage in informal work do so for such reasons as the need to be creative and, indeed, whether these people actually experience informal work in this positive manner.

Finally, it is one thing to say that people want autonomy, and that one way to provide this is through informal work, but it is quite another thing to say that existing informal activities can solve the problems of the market economy, especially in the field of unemployment. Greffe[10] maintains that although unemployment will not be solved by the informal economy, it is true that 'people are demanding more autonomy' and that these demands could be satisfied in the informal sector. Thus, in examining the findings of the 'Empirical Approaches', it will be necessary to differentiate between evidence which throws light on whether or not the informal sector can compensate for joblessness and that which reveals the extent to which informal work provides opportunities for autonomy.

In conclusion, the scenario which the Radical theorists favour could be entitled a 'Janus' scenario since it draws inspiration from past modes of production and applies them to the future. Indeed, the concept of dualism is fundamental to the Radical scenarios for the future of work. The backwards looking dimension is that which searches for a return to autonomy and the directness of producing personal use values. This is an echo from the nineteenth century anarchist tradition which itself harked back to precapitalist agricultural and craft communities where harmony and cooperation and the intrinsic values of creative and useful labour supposedly reigned. Nonetheless, the forwards looking dimension is the Radical theorists' insistence on preserving heteronomous work since this is a means of creating relatively painlessly the material affluence characteristic of the capitalist stage of development. The aim of this scenario, therefore, is to have the best of both worlds: creativity and community coupled with freedom from scarcity.

At the level of choice of scenario and the role of the informal economy in that scenario, there is agreement that a new balance between formal employment and other kinds of useful activity should be struck. However, there is a basic difference over whether or not such a change would entail the end of 'market' production (or to what extent this should be protected) and whether or not economic growth is a necessary or desirable phenomenon. Furthermore, the reasons for the ecologists' preference for autonomous activities are not the same in all respects as those of the socialists. More sceptical still of the ability of informal work to live up to any of these expectations are Gaudin, Schiray, Vinaver and Greffe.

Evaluating the Radical approaches

These Radical theorists have in common the implicit or explicit critique of the 'structure' of society. It is this which informs their choices of explanation, scenario and evaluation of the role of the informal economy. Nonetheless, structuralism means different things to different theorists. First, there is a difference between those Radical theorists who are firmly 'structuralist' in their analyses and others whose analyses and scenarios tend towards those of the Free Market Dualists. Second, amongst the most strongly structuralist theorists, there is disagreement concerning the exact nature of the structure which shapes society. This is either 'capitalism' (in which case it is the owners of the means of production who constitute the most important determining variable in social and economic structure), or 'industrialism' (in which case it is the means of production themselves which constitute the determining social and economic force).

First to be discussed are those theorists whose analyses tend to bridge the gap between the notions of the most extreme Radicals and those of the Free Market Dualists. These theorists are Delors, Aznar, Sachs, Rosanvallon, Roustang, Gaudin, Greffe, Schiray and Vinaver. It is not so much their choice of explanation of the crises which divides these theorists from Gorz, the ADRET collective, Granstedt, Lebreton, Lalonde & Simmonet and the 'EPPEM' collective as the role which they accord to the capitalist market in their favoured scenario. These theorists think it possible to reform capitalism through the introduction of a more flexible time cadre and new opportunities for creative activity. Nonetheless, to believe that informal work could exist cheek by jowl with capitalist market production implies a certain favourable evaluation of the capitalist system: namely, that if capitalism can be reformed and the consumerist and time-disciplined aspects of this system altered, then capitalism and the play of the free market cannot be the root cause of all the ills in society. Thus, there is an implicit agreement between these theorists, on the one hand, and Free Market Dualist theorists, on the other, that the market is a natural structure that must be retained. However, in the opinion of even these Radical theorists, people should be encouraged to work informally as an exercise in the fulfilment of certain positive goals - not just as a relatively cheap and expedient way of keeping the unemployed off the streets.

The remainder of the theorists (that is, Gorz, the ADRET collective, Lebreton, Granstedt, Lalonde & Simmonet and the 'EPPEM' collective) do not share this view of the market and the prevailing structure of society. Rather, they are of the opinion that the crises are 'systemic', that is, insurmountable without some degree of fundamental change of the capitalist/industrialist system. For example, the ADRET collective (1977, p. 175) observes, that 'the absurdities and the injustices' of society 'are not the result of mistakes, but are necessary to the survival of the system'. Thus, they conclude that autonomous work cannot survive in such surroundings.

However, the description of this offending system is a cause of disagreement amongst these theorists. The divisions between them are very similar in nature to those to be found amongst Feminist theorists. That is to say, we are dealing in both these instances with challenges to the centrality of the concept of capitalism from 'post '68' ideological positions. In the case of the Feminists, of course, the competing structure is that of patriarchy. In the case of the Radicals, it is the relationship between the economic system of capitalism and the broader systems of 'industrialism' and 'productivism' which is at issue. The choice between 'capitalism' and 'industrialism' is related to the way in which the various Radical theorists define the relations of oppression which exist in society. They emphasize either the oppression of class by class; Nature by Huamnkind; or Humankind by a technico-cultural system.

I will first consider those theorists who characterize the

structure of society in terms of Humankind's relationship with Nature and criticize the 'industrial' and 'productivist', (as opposed to the 'capitalist') system. They are Lebreton, Lalonde & Simmonet and the 'EPPEM' collective, this being the group of theorists whom I have already dubbed the 'ecologist' wing of the Radical group. In their opinion, humanity, as a homogenous unit, exploits Nature. Although they accept that this unit is internally divided - by class, race and gender - this does not alter the fact that people, taken as a group, exploit the natural world. Indeed, Lalonde & Simmonet (1978, p. 61) criticize many social scientists for only studying intra-human conflicts, ignoring the conflict in which Humans have entered with their environment.

Given this analysis, it follows that these theorists describe 'capitalism' as the most rational and efficient form of domination and exploitation of Nature and natural resources. For Lebreton (1978, p. 275), being perhaps one of the most radical 'ecologists', capitalism is just one manifestation of the 'socio-energetic' system which is industrial society, characterized by 'giganticism, complexity and speed'. That is, society is governed by a logic which is more all embracing than the profit and capital accumulation motives: this logic is productivism, which simply means the ethic of creating as much as one can, as fast as one can. Thus, the way to remedy the crises, of which dissatisfaction with employment and unemployment are a part, according to these theorists, is for Humankind to realize that it belongs to, and is not master of Nature.

For these theorists, capitalism is a sub-set of productivism since a system can be productivist without being based on private profit. Equally, capitalism is a sub-set of industrialism, the latter being a manifestation of a scientist, positivist paradigm where rationality and effiency rule, but not necessarily private profit. Influenced by technological determinism, productivism is seen in terms of the unacceptably large scale of machinery and institutions. The definitions of the crises which these theorists make, therefore, stem from their assertion that 'productivist' society has attempted to supplant Nature instead of working with it. As the authors of 'EPPEM' (1977, p. 14) explain, 'the technical and social choices which are being taken contradict the principles of physical and human ecology'. In sum, these theorists posit that 'society' is dependent upon the maintenance of the natural environment, but argue that Humankind refuses to accept this.

Lalonde & Simmonet (1978) and Lebreton (1978) suggest that the characteristics which set humans apart from the rest of the living world is their consciousness, their ability to act by using language, tools and society and later, an efficient mode of exchange, namely, money. These used in a controlled fashion could enhance the human experience. However, by an unspecified mechanism, but definitely against our conscious will, these tools have turned against us. Lebreton (1978, p. 31) asserts that

> not only does human machinery transform the environment, but by a dialectical process, the transformed environment acts on the actor. ... Thus, just when we think that we have perfectly mastered our creation, like the sorcerers' apprentice, we find ourselves becoming more and more constrained by it to the point where we ask ourselves who is the master and who the slave?

Thus, since we derive no long lasting benefit from our attempts to subjugate Nature, according to these theorists, we must realize that we are part, and not master of Nature and that as such, we must live in Harmony with it since human society is a sub-set of the ecosystem.

For those of a more Marxist persuasion (namely, Gorz and the 'ADRET' collective) the challenges to their analyses arising from these 'ecologist' theorists have not gone unheeded. In fact, it was the realization that it is necessary to change the technology and productivist logic of industrial society and not just the ownership of its means of production in order to bring about a truly 'socialist' society which prompted 'socialists' to consider the question of autonomous work.

However, these theorists consider the concepts of capitalism and productivism to be interchangeable. According to their analyses, profit remains the driving force of productivism and consequently, productivism has not got a logic or rationale independent from that of capitalism. Gorz (1985) explains this position, saying that each company attempts to make its machinery profitable as quickly as possible in order to be in a position to install more and better machinery, ('better' meaning that fewer workers are required to attain the same volume of production). Thus, in advanced capitalism, increasingly refined and expensive machinery produces more goods with fewer workers. Total labour costs reduce whilst the burden of capital increases (that is, the level of profit necessary to make existing machinery pay for itself). In Marxist terminology, this means that the organic composition of capital increases - that is, more capital is used for the same amount of production. Consequently, profits and production have to keep rising in order to repay loans and to renew machinery.

Indeed, it is capitalist competition which fuels the fires of the expansion of industry. Thus, it is the need to make profit which leads to the continual striving for economic growth.

Therefore, although the ADRET collective and Gorz are concerned about environmental crisis and the productivist society, in their opinion these are products of the capitalist system and the accumulation of surplus value (and not vice versa). This is the point of interpretation which separates them from Lebreton, Lalonde & Simmonet and the 'EPPEM' collective.

Finally, the notion of 'industrialism', in particular, raises the question of the role played by the 'means' of production, in other words, the nature of the technology itself, in shaping society. Granstedt (1980) is the Radical theorist who leans most heavily towards technological determinism in his analyses. However, the role of the 'technological' structure of industrialism as a determinant (as opposed to the class structure of capitalism) comes into play in the work of the ADRET collective and Gorz as well as in that of the 'ecologists' since they all stress that no profound change in society can take place without the dominance of large scale industrial complexes being challenged.

In fact, for all the Radical theorists, industrialism is more than a technical system and capitalism more than a question of ownership. They are involved in a symbiotic relationship. It is people who choose the technology to be used; however, once this technology is in place, it in turn shapes the structure of society. The argument goes that the 'choice' of direction of technical progress is made from a limited range of alternatives which is dependent on the extent of our knowledge and manipulative capacities. Once established, this technology becomes part of the infrastructure of society, playing an important and influential role in the shaping of social and economic patterns.

The theorists who have their roots in the Marxist tradition tend towards citing the bourgeoisie as the modellers of our technological system. Thus, they broaden out the notion of 'capitalism' so that it engulfs industrialism. Industrial technology is shaped by, and benefits the dominant, property owning class above all. Within such a logic, industrialism, as a technical system, is an integral part of capitalism, the profit motive still reigning supreme. Thus, as Gorz (1985, p. 2) argues,

> To talk of an industrialist civilisation is not to ignore

or deny its essentially capitalist character. The fact that industrialism is common to both capitalism and socialism emphasises the importance and implications of this notion.

Leaving aside the differences amongst the Radical theorists in order to concentrate on their similarities, the essential factor which separates the Radical theorists as a group from the Free Market Dualist theorists concerns the way in which the two sides define the 'crises' which French society faces and which, in particular, affect the future of work. For the Free Market Dualists, the crisis is one of mass unemployment: in their opinion, if unemployment had not risen to such heights, there would have been no crisis or need for change. This does not concur with the propositions of the Radical theorists. To differing degrees, the Radical theorists posit that even without the occurence of the crisis of mass unemployment, there would still have been a need to transform work patterns. In their view, high unemployment only constitutes a spur to long needed action. Indeed, some see unemployment as a golden opportunity for progress rather than a crisis in itself.

In sum, amongst the Radical theorists, a certain optimism reigns which is founded on the notion that the problems of the social structure can be transcended. As a consequence of the structuralist analytical framework which informs their studies, the Radical theorists believe that the ills of modern society can be remedied. To posit that a societal 'structure' exists which influences behaviour infers that society is a historical phenomenon, liable to change and development, as opposed to a static entity which is directly, or indirectly the product of human nature. This belief is reflected in their scenario for the future which suggests that given suitable conditions, humans could live more harmoniously with each other and with Nature.

A new concept of work?

Just as with the Free Market Dualists, but in contrast to the Microeconomists and Feminists, the Radical theorists do not propose a conceptual change to the meaning of 'work'. Instead, they propose a whole new organization of 'work' in society which would make use of certain aspects of the informal sector. However, the Radicals' analyses have conceptual spin-offs in that their proposals contradict some of the traditional assumptions concerning the characteristics which render an activity 'work'.

The first assumption which they question is that any activity which produces wealth, or 'value', is useful, and therefore, constitutes 'work'. The Radical theorists undermine this assumption in two ways: first, by suggesting that much activity which is performed outside the realms of employment is useful and therefore 'work', and second, by maintaining that not all economic production (work) is useful in the sense that it contributes to well-being, even if it creates monetary wealth. For example, some Radical theorists assert that much activity carried out under the social relations of employment is not productive because it is ecologically counter-productive. That is, it is activity which destroys the natural world which is the ultimate provider of all riches. These theorists advocate that work be redefined on the basis of a distinction between those activities which increase well-being and those which detract from it. Such a distinction completely cuts across the traditional differences between work and leisure.

Second, underlying the analyses of the Radical theorists is the notion that 'work' should be an act of creation, an activity which brings its own rewards and fulfilment. For the Radicals, such a notion appears to have been lost in a society in which 'work' equals selling one's time for a wage and in which employment has become an activity for deferred gratification, separated in space and time from the rest of life. In fact, the whole notion of 'work', in that instance, conjures up the image of an activity which is constrained, an effort, and which, in the last resort, one would prefer not to do.

The very aim of the Radical scenarios is to bring back a creative element to work. Thus, for these theorists, 'work' should not be characterized as an activity which one would prefer not to have to do. They criticize the 'deferred gratification' principle of 'working' solely that one may possess or consume. Moreover, they interpret disaffection from work as disaffection from the brutalizing and redundant nature of modern day employment which has neither intellectual control nor emotional proximity. The other side of the coin of brutalizing labour - namely, commodified leisure and compensatory consumption - are no answers, they assert: creativity and participation must be brought back into all aspects of society.

In their analyses, the Radical theorists undermine the consumerist ethic which conceives of consumption of market commodities as reward for the constraints and effort of employment. In the contemporary work ethic, work, far from yielding its benefits in Heaven (as is the notion inherent in the Protestant work ethic), tantalizingly spreads them out before our eyes in this world. 'Work', in this instance, is the cost of consumption, hence the neoclassical economic concept of work as a cost incurred in pursuit of utility. It is therefore to be minimized wherever possible, implying, when taken to its logical conclusion, that 'having' (consumption), is to be prized over and above 'doing' (production/work).

The Radical theorists, on the whole, posit that satisfaction should be rediscovered in the act of creating. In fact, they reach backwards towards the medieval ethic of craftsmanship and creativity. One could say that the scenarios of the Radical theorists are far from Hedonistic since they advocate a strong work ethic, even if this is not the Protestant work ethic of unrelenting toil as penance for past or original sins. It is an ethic of creativity based on the notion that all people have a natural tendency to create which is at present stifled.

Indeed, the Radical scenarios spring from a positive faith in Man's destiny as a creator and from the notion that 'industrialism', despite 'creating' products on a scale hitherto unknown, constrains our creative capacities as individuals. Lalonde & Simmonet (1978), for example, fuse the concepts of pleasure and necessity together in their 'activité franche' whereas traditionally, necessity has been perceived to be the preserve of production and employment whereas pleasure is confined to leisure and consumption. This is quintessential of the Radicals' affirmation that work should be organized in such a way as to provide 'pleasure in production'.

Aznar (1978, p. 61), accepting the difficulty in using the category of activity 'work' to express and conceptualize such innovative ideas, proffers a new way of dividing between types of activity which completely cuts across our notions of 'work' and 'leisure'. He proposes, on the one hand, the notion of 'le travail impliqué' which is activity in the end project of which one can invest part of oneself and from which one gains fulfilment. On the other hand, he develops (1981, p. 69) the notion of 'l'entravail' which is everything that is done out of necessity and has no personal meaning for the individual carrying it out.

Nonetheless, there is the possibility that the positive value accredited to 'creativity' could represent a conflict of interest for those Radical theorists of an 'ecologist' persuasion. Although Lalonde & Simmonet (1978, p. 36) assert that 'the desire to be autonomous combines with a taste for Nature and with a willingness to reconcile oneself with its materials, its animals, its rhythms and its mechanisms', one could still ask whether autonomous work is essentially good for Humankind and for Nature? Is it not the case, according to ecologists, that human creative urges have led to the environmental dangers inherent in industrialism?

Lalonde & Simmonet (1978) explain the domination of Nature as a perversion of the positive urge to create and act upon the world. This suggestion leaves open the possibility of positive change. Lebreton is less equivocal in his vision of 'work'. His is a vision which is not so concerned with 'personal fulfilment' as with the return to the question of 'ends'. In his opinion, by subordinating the means to these ends with our ingenuity, an equilibrium could be found which would allow a lasting cohabitation between humans and the biosphere. This he calls 'ecogestion' (ecomanagement). For him, when hard decisions have to be made, the natural constraints imposed by the ecosystem will have to be our first consideration and not the fulfilment of the human need to act upon the world.

In conclusion, we can see that in their advocacy of an organization of work which makes use of the informal sector, these theorists attack the concept that work can be defined solely as that activity which contributes to the G.N.P., and, furthermore, that work is a functional activity for deferred gratification. In consequence, their aim is not to advocate the inclusion of informal economic activity in the G.N.P. as proof of its economic importance, but to question the importance placed on the notion of G.N.P. and the implications that accompany this judgement.

Conclusions

In sum, the Radical theorists criticize the alienating aspects of employment, time-discipline and the high priority placed on economic growth. Some theorists - Aznar, Sachs, Roustang, Schiray, Greffe, Vinaver and Gaudin - take these problems as given. Granstedt lays them at the door of technology. Delors, Gorz and the ADRET collective cite capitalism as the culprit whilst Lebreton, Lalonde & Simmonet and the 'EPPEM' collective blame Humankind's relationship with nature. Unemployment is seen by all more as an ideal opportunity for change rather than as a problem. This is their principal difference from the Free Market Dualists.

As far as choice of scenario and the role of 'autonomous' work is concerned, we have witnessed the emergence of an old division between a social democratic and socialist scenario. However, in this instance, these are both imbued with an 'autogestionnaire' spirit. Moreover, they are both challenged by an ecologist, libertarian scenario. In these scenarios, all give a place to 'autonomous' work, the questions being: first, should it coexist with the market or only with the State?; and second, should informal work respond first and foremost to human need, or should it be moulded in order to correspond more to the needs of the environment? However, a shadow also hangs over all these scenarios, namely, the power of the informal sphere to play any of these roles.

The explanation and definitions of the structure of society proposed by these theorists challenge the centrality of Marxist concepts of capitalism and the power of the ownership of the means of production to determine the nature of society. These are part of the ideological and political shifts outlined in Chapter 3, namely, those of the political ecology movement and the New Left in which industrialism and its underlying logic, productivism, are criticized.

Furthermore, this wholesale questioning of the industrial organization of society by these theorists radically influences how they define 'work'. The main notions which they question are that work is an unpleasant activity performed for deferred gratification and that its aim is the augmenting of the G.N.P.. They stress the need to fulfil people's desire to be creative and perform useful activities. However, the connotations which go with the word 'work' itself have led one theorist, at least, to develop a new vocabulary for distinguishing between different types of activity.

The Radical scenarios are thus predicated first, on people wanting more creative activity and second, for some theorists, the unemployed being the vanguard of change. Indeed, they share these propositions with the Free Market Dualists. Moreover, it is these propositions, in particular which are scrutinized by the Empirical theorists, the discussion of which will form the basis of the following chapter.

Notes

1. A collective book was written by a group of French ecologists. It was entitled 'Les Ecologistes Présentés par Eux-Mêmes'. Thus, the shorthand to describe them will be the 'EPPEM' collective. The theorists are: B. Charbonneau; F. Chanial; M. Chanial; J.P. Dupuy; S. Fernex; M. Gerber; G. Klein; E. Kressmann; B. Lalonde; R. de Miller; L. Samuel; D. Steinbach; P. Tourbe; & A. Waechter.

2. Interview conducted in Paris in April 1988. Aznar runs a market research business in which he interviews many people about their opinions and attitudes.
3. That is, production of food, some energy, some clothing, repair, transport, education and health
4. That is, all those who are employed, self-employed or registered unemployed (seeking work).
5. Interview conducted in Paris, 1987.
6. Interview conducted in Paris, 1988.
7. Gorz's journalistic alias.
8. Interview conducted in Paris, 1988.
9. Interview conducted in Paris, April 1987.
10. Interview conducted in Paris, April 1987.

9 Empirical studies of the informal economy and the future of work

Introduction

Both the Radicals and the Free Market Dualists work within a 'universalist' methodological framework, concerning themselves with the role to be played by the informal economy in the general social and economic changes which they predict and advocate. In contrast, the theorists to be discussed in this Chapter adopt an empirical methodological approach. Indeed, it is their aim to observe the characteristics of the informal economy and informal workers as they exist in various circumscribed situations in the present day.

Many of these Empirical analyses of the informal economy have been influenced by the theoretical debates instigated by the Radicals and the Free Market Dualists in the early 'Eighties. The theorists of both these clusters, as we have seen, were optimistic vis à vis the potential for developing and extending the scope of informal work activities. On the one hand, the Free Market Dualists believed that the informal economy could remove the unemployed from the dole queues and from the streets without placing an onerous financial burden on the State. On the other hand, some Radicals interpreted the apparent growth of various forms of informal economic activity as a seed of discontent with consumer society and the stultifying nature of many formal, paid jobs. The Empirical theorists (to differing extents and in various ways) put these assumptions to the test of empirical investigation.

Given that a variety of questions is addressed by these Empirical theorists, I have sub-divided them, for the purposes of this discussion, according to the principal issue which they investigate. From this process, four groups of theorists emerge. First, there is a group of theorists who study the relationship between the unemployed and the informal economy, examining the extent to which the unemployed compensate for their loss of income with black market or domestic activity. Both the Radicals and Free Market Dualists base their predictions for the future of work on the hypothesis that the unemployed will save themselves from penury and develop new 'autonomous' lifestyles through the medium of informal work. The findings of these Empirical studies will reveal whether or not such propositions are justified.

Second, there are several theorists who have studied the informal economy as it is manifested in small communities. The reasoning behind this choice of subject is that small communities - in this case, a steel-making village in Lorraine, a commuter village near Lille and a new town in the Paris region - are propitious places for the informal economy to thrive. With this in mind, these researchers seek evidence for the growth (or survival) of informal production in such settings. Once again, it will be interesting to compare the findings of this research with the predictions and prescriptions made by the Radicals and Free Market Dualists.

Third, there are various quantitative and qualitative studies of black market work to be taken into account. This group of theorists addresses such issues as whether the value of the 'underground economy' is growing and what the motives of those who undertake black market work are. The findings of the studies which concern themselves with the motivation of black market workers will be particularly useful to compare with the assertions made by the Radical theorists that by choosing to work independently in the black market, workers are rebuking the capitalist system of employment.

Finally, I will consider the work of theorists who have calculated, in macroeconomic terms, the contribution of domestic work to the national economy and the degree to which production has been transferred from the market to the non market sector, or vice versa. The analyses of this group of researchers rely on the idea that wealth and well-being are not created by formal production alone. It will be seen that the results of these analyses are relevant both to the hypotheses of the Feminists as well as to those of the Free Market Dualists and the Radicals.

The procedure for analysis in each section will be, in the first instance, to sketch out the major findings of the various research projects. Thereafter, I will proceed to a discussion of the choices involved in the design of these projects. I will conclude with a discussion of what limitations these choices place on the significance of these findings when comparing them with the work of the Free Market Dualists and Radicals. I will begin with the question of the 'unemployed and the informal economy'.

The unemployed and the informal economy

Presentation of the findings

The studies to be discussed here are those undertaken by Rashid Foudi, François Stankiewicz & Nicolas Vaneecloo (1982) and Marie-Annicke Barthe (1985 a & b). A small contribution to our understadning of the informal economy is also made by Fournier, Glaude & Reynaud (1984) in their study of the budgets of unemployed working class families. [1] Both major studies look for evidence to support the proposition that the unemployed are engaging in more black market and domestic work than those in employment. They both work on the basic hypothesis that unemployment is a permissive condition for the development of informal work as it provides the disposable time and the financial motivation for such activity to take place.

The aim of both of these studies is to explore the strategies for 'getting by' employed by the household when one or more of its members becomes unemployed. Foudi, Stankiewicz & Vaneecloo (1982, p. 20) interviewed ninety-four men between the ages of twenty-five and fifty who had all been registered at the 'ANPE' for more than three months. They came from the area around Lille, a region of high unemployment. Barthe (1985b, p. 19) interviewed eighty-one men and women aged under fifty-five living in the working class estates of the Parisian suburb of Orly-Choisy. This area is described by Barthe (1985b, p. 19) as a modern day 'pocket' of poverty. Thus, both of these are not only samples of the unemployed, but of the urban unemployed, the significance of which will become clear after the discussion in the following section of the incidence of informal work in small communities.

Barthe (1985b, p. 23) and Foudi, Stankiewicz & Vaneecloo

(1982, p. 23-30) discuss the alternative sources of income available to the domestic unit. [2] They include the income derived from black market work as well as the savings on expenditure gained by producing goods and services by domestic work. In the case of black market work, Foudi, Stankiewicz & Vaneecloo (1982, p. 49) discovered that nearly half of the sample (that is, forty out of ninety-four interviewees) attested to having carried out black market work whilst being unemployed. Barthe (1985a, p. 45) found that forty per cent of her sample had done so. However, Foudi, Stankiewicz & Vaneecloo (1982, p. 48) stress the fact that only fifteen respondents derived either 'essential' income (essential being defined as at least fifty per cent of the 'SMIC' ['salaire minimum interprofessionnelle de croissance', or minimum wage]) or 'significant' income (more than twenty-five per cent of the 'SMIC') from black market work. Thus, hardly any of Foudi, Stankiewicz & Vaneecloo's sample could support themselves on the revenue derived from black market work alone.

Furthermore, it was found by both studies that black market work is not a viable option for all the urban unemployed regardless of their skills and experience. Foudi, Stankiewicz & Vaneecloo (1982, p. 50-53) discovered that the previous work experience of the individual is the most important determinant in whether or not he or she has the opportunity to take up black market work during unemployment. Both skills and know-how as well as a nexus of social contacts with potential employers is required: in other words, one must have a skill to offer and be able to find demand for that skill. Foudi, Stankiewicz & Vaneecloo explain, however, that unemployment limits access to such necessary social networks, and prevents people from creating them.

Likewise, both studies found that the longer one is unemployed, the more one loses the social network which allows one to perform black market work. Foudi, Stankiewicz & Vaneecloo (1982, p. 50) found that in twelve cases, people undertook less black market work after they were made unemployed than when they were in employment because they no longer had the tools of their trade at their disposal from work; because the risk of losing their unemployment benefit was too great; and finally, because they came up against a lack of demand. An important reason for lack of demand, suggests Barthe (1985a, p. 46), is that if a particular locality has been hard hit by unemployment, no one has the money to employ black market workers. Barthe is therefore well justified in concluding that in the black labour market, the same inequalities of access exist as in the regular labour market. In sum, those living in unemployment black spots, with fewest qualifications, can prosper neither in the formal, nor indeed in the informal sector.

In the case of domestic production, no significant increase of level of activity was found amongst the unemployed either. Foudi, Stankiewicz & Vaneecloo (1982, p. 57-60) discovered that twenty-one of their respondents had suspended all refurbishment of their house or flat owing to lack of funds. In only four cases did such activity increase. The results produced by Fournier et al (1984, p. 47) support this finding. They explain that the unemployed spent only half the amount of money on major D.I.Y. tasks in comparison with the amount spent by the employed working class. The same pattern was detected for car maintenance.

Neither Foudi, Stankiewicz & Vaneecloo nor Barthe discovered any increased rate of participation in activities such as knitting and sewing, gardening, making preserves or keeping livestock after unemployment. The reasons given by the respondents for this 'lack' [3] of domestic production are similar in nature to those encountered in black market work. First, Barthe (1985b, p. 31) found that particularly in the case of activities such as sewing and knitting, many of her sample lacked the necessary skills to undertake such production. They had never learnt them.

The second reason relates to the need for a certain infrastructure to perform certain kinds of domestic production. Take the example of gardening. As far as gardening is concerned, the unemployed working class is less likely to have a garden than their employed counterparts. If one does not possess a garden, then unemployed or not, one cannot grow one's own vegetables. Fournier et al (1984, p. 47) discovered that only thirty-one per cent of unemployed working class families had kitchen gardens, in contrast to forty-three per cent of the employed working class. However, Foudi, Stankiewicz & Vaneecloo (1982, p. 59) and Barthe (1985b, p. 31) found that self-provisioning increased by only seven per cent after unemployment even amongst those households which did possess a garden.

Thus, from these findings, it appears that the urban unemployed are not massively involved in either domestic or black market work. Although the permissive conditions of time and motivation exist amongst unemployed people, lack of skills, tools, raw materials and social networks all contribute to the impossibility for many of the unemployed to 'help themselves' in this way. In fact, Foudi, Stankiewicz & Vaneecloo (1982, p. 78-81) found that what was more important to the unemployed than 'l'autoproduction' and black market work were the loans and gifts which they received from other family members - indeed, an informal network of redistribution of income rather than informal production was revealed.

In the following section, I will discuss the limitations of the work of Barthe and Foudi, Stankiewicz & Vaneecloo inherent in the choice of method and design of their projects. Subsequently, I will assess how this affects the extent to which we can use their findings to evaluate the validity of the propositions of the Radical and Free Market Dualist theorists.

Relationship to the Free Market Dualists and Radicals: choices and limitations

The work of Foudi, Stankiewicz & Vaneecloo and Barthe falls under the category 'Empirical Approaches' because both studies wish to observe the experiences of the unemployed in the informal economy in the field. Neither attempts to fit its observations into a universal theory or critique of society, or a plan for the future of work. However, that is not to say that in designing their projects, these theorists have not had to make choices which limit the scope of their findings. The nature of these limitations will determine the extent to which they can be used to evaluate the propositions of the Free Market Dualist and Radical theorists. Indeed, it was the environment created by the theoretical propositions of the Free Market Dualists and Radicals, coupled with press and government assertions that the unemployed were engaging in undeclared work whilst claiming benefit in the late 'Seventies and early 'Eighties, which prompted Foudi, Stankiewicz & Vaneecloo and Barthe to choose to observe this particular phenomenon. In fact, these theorists are testing the hypothesis that the unemployed compensate for their lack of income with informal work.

It is clear that these two studies provide no evidence to lend support to the proposition that the unemployed are ardent informal workers. As Stankiewicz [4] explained, in the early 'Eighties, there was an idea that black market work was easy and that anyone could do it. He argued that one of the interesting aspects of his own study was to show that there are, in fact, many obstacles to engaging in such activity.

Although the samples used by Foudi, Stankiewicz & Vaneecloo and Barthe were relatively small, and thus, provide no 'proof', statistically speaking, of the trends which they describe, their findings are highly significant because they throw doubt on the hypothesis - which was very strong in the late 'Seventies and early 'Eighties - that the free time and financial need experienced by the unemployed are the only necessary conditions for informal work to take place. The propositions for the future of work of the Free Market Dualists rely heavily on the assumption that the unemployed will find it easy to generate income through informal sources. However, in view of the findings of Foudi, Stankiewicz & Vaneecloo and Barthe that the most marginalized from the formal labour market are those least likely to be able to convert to some kind of informal activity, this seems rather unlikely.

Equally, these findings throw doubt upon some of the Radicals' hypotheses. For example, how will Gorz's 'non-class of post-industrial proletarians', (constituted partially from the unemployed) develop the class consciousness which will enable them to become the new engineers of social revolution, if, as these Empirical studies show, the social networks necessary for the development of class consciousness are broken down by unemployment? More generally, there is a tendency amongst Radical theorists to suggest that 'informal labour markets' are more open to all citizens than their formal counterparts. However, Foudi, Stankiewicz & Vaneecloo and Barthe detect the same inequalities of access depending on skill, education, social networks and economic environment pervading the domestic and black market sectors as one might find on the formal labour market. Indeed, these doubts stopped many of the Free Market Dualists and Radicals in their theoretical tracks, resulting in a decline in the number of publications of these persuasions appearing from the mid 'Eighties onwards in France.

Nonetheless, before hastening to conclude that these two Empirical studies are the objective measuring sticks with which to beat the hypotheses of the Radicals and Free Market Dualists, it must be remembered that the studies of Foudi, Stankiewicz & Vaneecloo and Barthe carry with them their own assumptions and limitations which reduce their power to undermine the propositions of the Free Market Dualists and Radicals. The principal choice made by Foudi, Stankiewicz & Vaneecloo and Barthe - a consequence of their training as economists - is to emphasise the financial strategies of the unemployed for 'getting by'. Therefore, the two studies treat informal work purely as a form of financial compensation for income lost through unemployment. Many Radical theorists, however, conclude that it is not only the unemployed who would benefit from increased opportunities to work 'autonomously', but also people who find themselves in stultifying, repetitive jobs. Such an assertion stems from the Radicals' belief that work must fulfil needs which are not ultimately pecuniary - notably, needs for creativity and meaning in life. Furthermore, the findings of Foudi, Stankiewicz & Vaneecloo and Barthe do not preclude the possibility of the State providing the urban unemployed with the infrastructure - for example, allotments or community workshops - to enable them to 'help themselves'. In fact, these findings underline the need for policy changes if either the Free Market Dualist or Radical scenario is ever to be realized.

Finally, both Foudi, Stankiewicz & Vaneecloo and Barthe agree [5] that there could exist more propitious environments for informal work to take place than urban working class settlements, and more ardent informal workers than the registered unemployed. Whether this is true or not will be put to the test in the following sections.

The informal economy and small communities

Presentation of the findings

The studies to be discussed here are those of Claire Legrain (1982), Didier Cornuel & Bruno Duriez (1985) and Sophie Tievant (1982). [6] Their analyses concern the network of exchange of informally produced goods and services - and their size and importance in qualitative terms - in various 'small', or non urban communities. These are first, a steel village in the region of Lorraine; second, a commuter village near Lille; and third, a new town in the Paris region respectively. I will start by presenting the findings of Legrain (1982).

Legrain (1982) made a study of the village of Grand Failly situated in Lorraine, a region in which agriculture and the steel industry combine. Indeed, many villagers from Grand Failly work in the steel industry. At the time of Legrain's study, the local steel works had imposed a twenty-five per cent reduction in hours and wages on its workers. Thus, the most interesting of her descriptions for the purposes of this book concerns the way in which villagers employed in the steel industry compensated for this loss of income by working 'informally'.

Legrain was 'revisiting' Grand Failly more than a decade after an extensive study concerning the degree to which remote rural villages had been affected by modernization in France was carried out there by Lemarche, Rogers & Karnoouh (1970). One could have expected Legrain to discover a decline in the amount of informal activity taking place in this village in comparison with that which was recorded in

1970. However, she (1982, p. 186) claims to have found the informal side of village life to be alive and well. Legrain notes that to compensate for their loss of income, the steel workers of Grand Failly increased their domestic production, even selling some of the surplus to their fellow villagers. Furthermore, they filled their spare time by working on the black labour market, especially on farms.

Moreover, amongst the population of the village at large, Legrain discovered that wood burning stoves were gaining in popularity as energy prices rose and that much of the refurbishment of housing that was taking place was being carried out informally. As Legrain (1982, p. 186) points out, 'the informal economy represented a means of improving the standard of living of the villagers and of staying in the village'. In partial explanation of this level of informal activity, Legrain (1982) insists that there was a very strong work ethic prevailing in the village which praised doing something for oneself over and above consumption. Indeed, participation in the informal economy was an integral part of participation in the social network of the village.

The social importance of participation in a network of informal production and exchange is revealed also by Cornuel & Duriez's (1985) analysis of the informal economy in a commuter village in the area around Lille. Indeed, they discovered that social and economic considerations go hand in hand in maintaining informal production and exchange in the village. First, Cornuel and Duriez insist that economic motivations have a large part to play in people's choice of taking part in informal exchanges. In the case of black market work, they assert that the economic benefits from the point of view of the worker include the lack of deductions to pay and work regulations to consider; and from the point of view of the consumer, they suggest that the quality of the service received on the black market is often higher than one could expect to obtain for the same money on the formal market.

However, agreeing with Barthe (1985) and Foudi, Stankiewicz & Vaneecloo (1982) that for informal exchanges to take place, a cohesive social network is necessary, Cornuel & Duriez (1985, p. 173) discovered that getting things done or generating income on the informal market has its cost in the time that it takes to maintain these social networks. Indeed, Cornuel & Duriez found that the newcomers to the community (these being fairly numerous given that they were studying a commuter village) had been obliged to devote much time to the task of integrating themselves into local exchange networks.

Cornuel & Duriez not only discovered that informal exchanges of labour need a nexus of social relationships in order to exist; they ascertained that, in turn, informal exchanges reinforced the closeness of the relationship between villagers and represented a means of drawing in the newcomers in order to maintain village solidarity. Cornuel & Duriez [7] asserted that

> the very existence of informal activities is founded on a network of relationships and the very existence of this network can become in itself the aim of the informal activities. That is to say, they are not purely economic exchanges. Rather, they serve to maintain and preserve the relationships between the members of a community.

For Cornuel & Duriez, therefore, the informal exchange of goods and services in the village is not so much an alternative means of wealth creation, but of social solidarity. Whether the social network exists for the benefit of informal exchange or vice versa is not in question. Working on this basis, Cornuel & Duriez (1985, p. 187) assert that the village is the ideal location for informal work to take place because it has a set of social relations distinct, but not independent from or in direct conflict with the 'capitalist relations of production and political relationships organized within the apparatus of the State'. The authors claim that at the level of the nation as a whole, the specialization of social networks according to economic, political and other functions leaves the State with the main responsibility for ensuring the cohesion of the national community. If informal exchanges are similarly inscribed in the logic of social cohesion, then their main competitor must be the State. Hence, they conclude that the informal sector is more anti-State than anti-economic.

In the third study, Tievant (1982, p. 61) investigates the non market exchanges which take place in a new town in the Paris region - Saint-Cévry. According to Tievant, a new town is a place where the social relations existing between the inhabitants have a chance to develop in an innovative way because they have to be constructed anew. In fact, Tievant discovered that some of the inhabitants of Saint-Cévry had moved there in order to do just that. Tievant (1982, p. 63) employed the very qualitative method of 'networking' to accumulate her sample of around thirty interviewees. This is a method which initially selects one person on which to base the sample and traces his or her social contacts in order to build up a picture of the interactions which exist in a certain community. In so doing, Tievant wanted to find out first, what goods and services were circulating between domestic groups in the town; second, which domestic groups were involved in these exchanges; and third, how and why such exchange was taking place.

On the question of the types of goods and services circulating between households, Tievant discovered the following categories: those based on the use of collective equipment; specialized services needing specific skills; services based on the transmission of technical or artistic skills; and the production of goods. Thus, echoing Foudi, Stankiewicz & Vaneecloo and Barthe, Tievant (1982, p. 118) explains that informal exchanges develop on the basis of a network of social contacts, skill, time, and access to necessary equipment.

On the matter of who was taking part in such exchanges, Tievant (1982, p. 67-68) detected two types of inhabitants in the town: first, there were the pioneers and militants who had moved there to create a new life. They were young, middle class and very active in associations. Second, there were those who had ended up in the town by accident and who had only very limited relationships with their new neighbours. Thus, once again, the inequality of access to informal market networks is emphasized by the results of this study.

Finally, as regards the reasons why people take part in such exchange, Tievant (1982, p. 99) maintains that they are not purely economic, saying that it was not 'in economic rationality that one could find the justification for the exchanges practised at Saint-Cevry'. She continues that 'if this circulation of goods and services does not respond to an economic necessity', then it must have an 'essentially symbolic function'. Tievant maintains that informal exchange of goods and services has as much, if not more to do with maintaining a sense of community and social solidarity than with economic rationality.

Thus, we can see from these three studies that social networks are very important for the performing of informal work. This coincides with the assertions of Foudi, Stankiewicz & Vaneecloo and Barthe. These theorists were, however, struck by the lack of such networks in the urban communities of their studies. In contrast, in the communities studied here, it seems that these social networks have held on more tenaciously, whilst in Tievant's new town, such networks have been consciously recreated by groups of committed individuals.

Relationship to the Free Market Dualists and Radicals: choices and limitations

The studies of Legrain, Cornuel & Duriez and Tievant fall under the category of 'Empirical Approaches' because they are all qualitative (or, ethnographic) studies which observe the everyday practices of specific groups of people. This does not mean, however, that they are devoid of any explanatory framework within which to analyse informal activity. For example, Tievant employs as an explanatory framework the concept of reciprocity.[8] She asserts that the difference between market and non market exchange can be explained as the difference between formalized and less formalized reciprocity. That is, formal exchange - being that which is considered to be 'economic' - relies on a system whereby one receives a set return for one's work, calculated in monetary values. At the other extreme of non market exchange, there is a more general, uncalculated balance sheet of recompense in kind for work performed.

Thus, just as Foudi, Stankiewicz & Vanecloo and Barthe, as economists, employed an 'economic' framework of interpretation (expressed by their interest in informal work as a means of compensating for lost income) these theorists, being sociologists and anthropologists for the most part, explore the question of informal work in terms of its place in the 'social fabric' of the community. Indeed, it is from this primary interest that their focus on small communities (as opposed to the unemployed) springs.

Given their sociological and anthropological bent and their interest in the social cohesion of communities, one is led to ask oneself why these theorists chose to employ the notions of 'the informal economy' and 'the informal exchange of goods and services' as opposed to that of 'sociability' to describe their object of study. The answer is that in the early 'Eighties, the 'informal economy' was a fashionable idea in France, and one which figured highly on the agenda of the Observation du Changement Social project of which all these studies are a part.[9] Indeed, the genesis of the field of inquiry of the informal economy has been the renaming of various phenomena which were once classified as 'social' with 'economic' concepts and titles.

As regards what these studies tell us about the informal economy in terms of the future of work, the first point to note is that they support the findings of Foudi, Stankiewicz & Vaneecloo and Barthe in that they reveal that various conditions need to be fufilled in order for people to undertake informal work and participate in informal exchanges. The fact that these conditions are met for some people, but not for others, means that inequality of access to the informal, as well as to the formal economic sector exists.

This is illustrated by the differences between the experiences of the unemployed of Orly-Choisy (Barthe, 1985) and Lille (Foudi, Stankiewicz & Vaneecloo, 1982), on the one hand, and those of the steel workers of Grand Failly (Legrain, 1982) who were working short time, on the other. First, the workers of Grand Failly were in receipt of a reasonable - albeit reduced - income with which to purchase the materials and tools which are vital to domestic production and to one's ability to work on the black market. In contrast, the urban unemployed of Paris and Lille had no such 'capital' to invest in informal production. Second, an informal social network existed in the village of Grand Failly into which the steel workers could integrate themselves in times of hardship. This social network, in conjunction with the survival of an agricultural sector alongside the steel industry, provided the demand for black market work in the village. No such economic and social safety net existed for the urban unemployed of Lille and Orly-Choisy. Additionally, living in a rural setting as opposed to an urban one, the steel workers of Grand Failly possessed the infrastructure, - for example, kitchen gardens - which is necessary for domestic production to take place. Moreoever, the inhabitants of Grand Failly seemed to retain more of the necessary traditional skills required for such production.

Likewise, the inequalities of exchange in the informal sphere come to the fore in Tievant's study. She notes that some parts of the population of the new town of Saint-Cévry were excluded from the circuits of the 'the parallel economy'. These were notably those who were older, not from 'professional' backgrounds and who did not share the particular political profile of the most active members of the informal networks.

Thus, the conclusions that we must draw both from the studies of the relationship of the unemployed to the informal economy and from the studies of informal work as it is carried out in small communities are that many of the requirements of the formal labour market are demanded of workers in the informal sphere. This means that this informal sphere cannot provide a haven for those excluded from employment. Such a conclusion casts doubt on the Free Market Dualist proposition that the unemployed will all be able to help themselves through informal production. For the Radicals, this means that much planning and conscious change would have to come about for their various scenarios to be realized.

Although these findings must be rather disappointing reading for the Radical theorists, it should not be forgotten that they contain at least a slight glimmer of hope for them. That is, these studies have revealed that people will put a great deal of effort into maintaining small scale networks of sociability and reciprocity, and that informal production and exchange play a part in maintaining these, all of which gives credence to the Radical notion that people need to belong to communities of human proportions, and to feel some kind of personal implication in the work which they perform.

Quantitative and qualitative approaches to black market work

Black market work is the category of informal work which has excited the most controversy in France. Although the question has been raised periodically throughout this century, it was as the recession began to bite hard in 1979/1980 that the latest wave of protest reached its peak. As the recession hit, politicians, the press and in particular, employers' associations in the building industry began to cast around for likely scapegoats for their problems: one such scapegoat was black market workers. Black market work was condemned for being a drain on the economy, its critics maintaining that if one takes into account the existence of black market work, then unemployment and inflation are overestimated, growth underestimated, and at the extreme, economic stagnation is but a statistical illusion. A major campaign against black market work was launched in 1979, interestingly enough by the man who three years later was advocating certain aspects of black market work to be encouraged: namely, Lionel Stoléru. He explained (1979, p. 39) that the main objective of his campaign was to reply to the worries of artisanal businessmen who were facing unfair competition from their black market rivals.

The assumption underlying all these assertions is that black market work has undergone a massive expansion since the onset of the recession. Thus, it was on the basis of this assumption, and in the hostile atmosphere which surrounded black market work, as well as in the context of the more positive propositions of the Free Market Dualists and the Radicals, that certain quantitative as well as qualitative studies of black market work were carried out in the 'Seventies and 'Eighties.

Quantitative approaches

Presentation of the findings. A series of articles and government and employers' association reports on black market work were published in the 'Seventies and early 'Eighties in France [10] which bandied around many figures calculating the amount of black market work taking place. For the most part, these were derivations from several foreign macroeconomic attempts to put a figure on the size of the 'underground economy'. [11] These macroeconomic evaluations employ 'indirect' methods to calculate the dimensions of this economy. That is, they arrive at a potential figure representing the size of the 'black economy' by analysing discrepancies in the recorded economic facts which they have to hand. [12] The first quantitative approach is the monetary approach of Gutmann (1977). This calculation assumes that black market transactions take place in cash money as opposed to bank money (cheques, transfers and the like). Furthermore, it supposes that declared economic activity takes place in stable proportions between cash and bank money. Thus, to calculate the magnitude of the black economy, the evolution of the relationship between the mass of bank notes in circulation and the mass of bank deposits is examined.

It is obvious, however, that this method of calculation is ruled by the idea that the black economy is growing. It supposes that one can pinpoint a past period in which black market work did not exist from which one can deduce the 'stable proportions' between bank and cash money transactions characteristic of an economy comprised only of declared activity. Thus, a calculation such as Gutmann's can only show whether the black economy has grown (or declined). It cannot provide us with information about the absolute size of this economy, or the range and scope of its activities.

The second approach is the fiscal approach. This uses figures of proven tax fraud to estimate the volume of transactions on which the interested parties do not pay tax. Third, and finally, there is the national accounts approach. This method of calculation, on the one hand, totals up incomes, and on the other, production output. Any discrepancy between these can be taken as the undeclared income earned from working on declared production (that is, the black market work carried out within registered businesses). This method cannot, therefore, detect the 'private' black market work which takes place between individuals; that is, the undeclared income from undetectable production. The results produced by these methods paint a picture of an 'underground economy' which ranges in size from ten per cent to around thirty-one per cent of G.N.P. of the industrialized countries, including France.[13]

Relationship to the Free Market Dualists and Radicals: choices and limitations. The quantitative macroeconomic approach, taken as a whole, has a number of shortcomings. First, it faces the practical difficulty of discovering the amount of work which, by its very nature, is hidden from official statistics. Greffe (1981, p. 103), for example, notes that 'one can easily imagine the difficulty involved in grasping the reality of an activity of which one of the principal motivations is precisely to evade the official observation and registration machinery'. This means that there is much room for manoeuvre (or, one could suggest, guesswork) on the part of those performing such calculations. Moroever, the discrepancies which exist in the figures produced by such studies mean that politicians and other interested parties have a range of statistics from which to choose to support their particular argument. Indeed, this confusion has helped to stir up some of the periodic hysteria concerning black market work.

Second, this agregate, macroeconomic approach to measuring black market work has no regard for differentiating between legal, but undeclared work and criminal activity, nor between types of black economic activity. This results, as Laë (1987, p. 19) points out, in undeclared painting and decorating and poker playing being put in the same category. However, this is not a problem for those who carry out such studies because they have no concern for the details and specific characteristics of black market work. Their only interest is to produce an agregate figure to show that the 'black economy' represents an important source of competition for the formal economy.

Thus, such measurements reveal very little about the characteristics of black market work, such as what forms it takes and why people engage in it at all. It is the assertion of the inadequacy of these purely statistical approaches which prompted Jean-François Laë (1987) and Lebars, Camus, Cosset & Nottola (1980) to carry out their qualitative analyses of the subject. It is to the work of these theorists that I now turn.

Qualitative studies

Presentation of the findings. Two studies are of interest in this section: they are those carried out by Lebars, Camus,

Cosset & Nottola (1980) and by Jean-François Laë (1987). They both attempt to dig beneath the surface of economic reasoning to explain why individuals are motivated to perform black market work.

Lebars et al (1980) carried out an analysis of the socio-economic causes of the development of black market work in the building trade.[14] They (1980, p. 30) interviewed black market workers (working for individuals, not registered firms) and their employers in the trades of plumbing, electrics, carpentry and painting and decorating. The interviewees were mainly young men aged between twenty-three and forty-three of which the majority had had a professional training. [15] Lebars et al (1980, p. 63) discovered that amongst those black market workers interviewed, eighty per cent were motivated by financial factors. Of the sample, twenty per cent desperately needed the income derived from black market work whilst sixty per cent explained that it provided them with non essential income only. The three most important economic reasons for undertaking black market work given by the respondents were first, that they wanted extra income on top of their wages; second, that the burden of tax and social security was too high for them to set up in regular business; and third, that it was impossible for them to find legal employment. Only a very small number expressed dissatisfaction with their regular work (when they had any), this perhaps being explained by their level of professional qualification and skill.

The social factors influencing the interviewees' decisions were found to be of secondary importance in the majority of cases. The principal 'social' reasons for undertaking black market work were the following: independence; pride in completing a whole job as opposed to merely executing parcellized tasks; equality with the employer when he or she is a private individual; and lastly, the possibility of planning one's own work time. Thus, although these 'social factors' were not of primary importance, they imply that such work provides additional creative and social outlets to regular employment.

Laë (1987, p. 8) worked with a very small group of thirty-one black market workers who had all been engaged in black market work for over two years. Like Tievant, Laë employed a system of networking and following up informal contacts in order to gather his sample. Using detailed interviews with these people about their background, professional experience and work practices and patterns, Laë (1987, p. 30-34) aimed to build up a profile of their lives and reasons for working on the black market.

Four 'profiles' of types of black market workers emerged

from this sample. He labels them in the following way: first, 'les salariés' (the employed); second, 'les artisans' (artisans); third, 'les petits noirs' (small time black market workers); and fourth, 'les all blacks' (full time black market workers).

First 'les salariés' are those who accumulate black market work on top of their regular employment. Laë notes that their situations are very difficult to reduce to a common denominator. However, he maintains that on average, the members of this group derive twenty-seven per cent of their total income from black market work, or 23,000 Francs per person per year in 1985. Second, 'les artisans' are mainly young people working alone, or in pairs, occasionally employing a third person, it being impossible for them to sustain their business on declared work alone. Many of them turned to black market work when they were on the point of falling drastically into debt. Black market work represents twnety-eight per cent of their yearly income, or 20,400 Francs in 1985. Third, 'les petits noirs' have had employment of a precarious nature and limited duration in the past, but not in the year of study, 1985. Their sole source of income is black work and they live, for the most part, on a very tight budget, approximately 20,000 to 40,000 Francs per year in 1985. Fourth, 'les all-blacks' are people who deal solely in black market work, but in difference to the 'petits noirs', they make a more reasonable living from it, around 67,000 Francs per year in 1985. However, this sort of turnover is not enough for them to set up in business on a regular basis.

Laë (1987, p. 46-52) is interested in the combination of the social and economic reasons why these various categories of people decide to enter the field of black market work. He suggests first, that for the 'petits noirs' and the 'all-blacks', black market work is a means of economic survival. It is their sole source of income. Second, the prospect of gaining a practical apprenticeship is high on the list of the priorities of the 'petits noirs' and the 'all-blacks', and it is also a major factor in the reasoning of the 'salariés'. Third, for 'les artisans', turning to the black market was their only way of avoiding bankruptcy. Fourth, Laë discovered the less than noble reason voiced by all his respondents that they entered into black market work in order to undercut the competition and 'steal' clients; and fifth, for all but the 'artisans', of course, black market work was perceived by the interviewees as a means by which to establish a regular business.

However 'financial' all these reasons appear, Laë (1987, p. 68) asserts that although money is important, 'it is not the absolute determining factor' in the decisions of his research participants to undertake black market work. Social reasons have their part to play also. Thus, black market work, according to Laë, is not the simple product of insufficient resources, lack of employment or the limits of the market economy. Social factors intervene in these economic choices, such as one's honour, self-image at work and wish to avoid routine. The economy - formal or informal - he continues, rests on the fear of boredom, the desire to be independent and the pleasure of negotiating and trading. These social factors lie at the heart of the individual's desire to work. For those reasons, Laë explains that the majority of black market workers should be understood not in their marginalized relationship to formal employment but in their relationship to regular self-emloyed artisans. This is not surprising since three of the four main clusters of black market workers which emerge from his study are characterized not so much by their inability to find paid employment, but by their inability to establish or sustain a regular business.

<u>Relationship to the Free Market Dualists and Radicals: choices and limitations.</u> The studies of Lebars, Camus, Cosset & Nottola (1980) and Laë (1987) fall under the category of 'Empirical Approaches' because, once again, these theorists have gone into the field to observe the phenomenon of black market work. This they chose to do because, despite there having been much discussion of the subject during the late 'Seventies and 'Eighties, very little was actually known about the characteristics of black market workers. In fact, Lebars et al and Laë set out explicitly to test the assumptions, first, that it is the unemployed who engage in black market work, and second, that it is the mounting burden of taxation alone which has encouraged the rise of black market work, if indeed a rise there has been. These assumptions, they believed, were based on ignorance of how and why black market work is actually carried out. Lebars et al (1980, p. 1) explain that

> the study originated from the realization that the statements coming from certain professional circles, and to a lesser extent, from the administration, according to which black market work is uniquely a negative and socially condemnable practice, did not in any way explain why this type of activity exists and why it appears to have been developing in recent years.

Laë (1987, p. 168) adds that one cannot capture the reality of black market work merely by examining economic trends concerning incomes, exchange of goods and expenditure. There are personal motivations and lifestyles to be taken into account as well.

Comparing the findings of these theorists with those of Foudi, Stankiewicz & Vaneecloo, Barthe, Cornuel & Duriez, Legrain and Tievant, we see that they lend further support to the assertion that people require certain skills in order to enter into informal production. Indeed, Lebars et al and Laë both stress that black market workers are skilled and highly employable, often combining black market activity with a regular job or business interest. In sum, they underline the fact that black market work is not an easy alternative to employment. In his analyses of the professional backgrounds of his thirty-one interviewees, Laë (1987) found that due to their knowledge and experience, they were some of the best placed people to gain employment. He (1987, p. 164) notes that

> it is not the retrenchment of the labour market which prevents [black market workers from getting a job], it is not the slow-down in certain industrial sectors which pushes them into black market work, their professional know-how and their social dexterity make them extremely employable.

What, then, do these findings mean for the propositions of the Free Market Dualists and the Radicals? As far as the Free Market Dualists are concerned, the observations, notably made by Laë, that the lifestyle of the black market worker relates more to that of the 'artisan' than to that of the unemployed casts further doubt upon the ability of the black market sector to cater for the needs of the unemployed. However, the very fact that Laë does find some people who 'choose' this marginal existence, and can survive on it, may be taken by the Free Market Dualists and, especially Sauvy (1984), as evidence that informal work does, in fact, take some of the pressure from the social security system and reflect the need of people to take risks and to be independent from the State - in a word, entrepreneurial.

As regards the Radicals, it is the motivations of the black market workers discovered by these studies which are of interest. Some Radical theorists - especially Gorz - have asserted that individuals turn to black market work as a reaction against capitalism. It is true to say that the social factors listed as motivations by Lebars et al seem to tally with this notion. For example, some of their interviewees commented that they enjoyed black market work because they were able to see the job right through to the end (as opposed to working on parcellized tasks). Nonetheless, the results of this study did not completely reinforce the validity of the notions of the Radicals. It must be remembered that only very few of the research subjects expressed discontent with their regular employment, and that the social factors cited as motivations by black market workers were secondary to the economic ones in eighty per cent of cases.

Furthermore, Laë (1987, p. 166) found evidence amongst 'full time' black market workers that they chose their particular lifestyle because they wanted more freedom than the employment available to them could offer. Such a finding can be used to support either the Radical or Free Market Dualist view of society since both these clusters of theorists criticize the system of stable and inflexible employment, but for different reasons. On the one hand, the Radicals, for example Gorz, assert that 'employment' (and the constraints on the freedom of the worker which it entails) is a problem because it is the means by which capital exploits and controls labour through time-discipline and de-skilling. On the other hand, the Free Market Dualists, and especially Sauvy, criticize rigid systems of stable employment because they stifle entreprise on both sides of the industrial divide. Thus, for Gorz, if an individual chooses the 'freedom' of black market work, this constitutes a reaction against the 'capitalist system' which alienates him or her from his or her work. For Sauvy, however, such a choice is a sign that certain individuals want to strike out on their own, free of the chains on their enterprise with which the State has shackled them.

These contradictory interpretations of Laë's observation stem from the contradictory views of capitalism which these two sets of theorists hold. On the one hand, in the 'negative' view of Gorz, capitalism needs docile employees in order to survive. Thus, any assertion of independence on the part of workers is a threat to the stability of capitalism. On the other hand, according to the 'positive' assessment of Sauvy, capitalism needs a population with initiative in order to thrive. Thus, such 'enterprising' behaviour is interpreted as a justification of the free market system. Therefore, it is clear that empirical observation and recording of the motivations of workers is open to a range of interpretations.

In sum, whilst the Free Market Dualists and Radicals talk of black market work in terms of the role that it can play in future social and economic change, these Empirical studies stress the 'normality' of black market work. That is, neither of these studies provide evidence to suggest that the number of black market workers is growing, or that their motives for engaging in black market work relate directly to unemployment and the recession. Moreover, they suggest that black market workers are often frustrated artisans and small business persons, not potential social revolutionaries, although, as we have seen, this is a question which is open to interpretation. Indeed, one could posit that there has always been a minority of people who choose to work in this fashion alongside the formal structures of employment.

The contribution of domestic work to the national economy

Presentation of the findings

The contribution made by this group of researchers - Pierre Kendé (1975 & 1978); Ann Chadeau & Annie Fouquet (1981); Ann Chadeau & Caroline Roy (1985); and Daniel Stoclet (1983) - is to have calculated in monetary terms the contribution of domestic work to the national economy and to have examined the shifting balance between market and non market production. In so doing, they span the preoccupations not only of the Radicals and Free Market Dualists, but also the Feminists, and to a lesser extent, the Microeconomists. First and foremost, this is because the notion that there is a domestic - or more generally, non monetary - input into the creation of wealth and well-being is an assertion which all theorists who study the informal economy would endorse.

All of these theorists employ macroeconomic methods to evaluate the extent of domestic production. First, Kendé (1975 & 1978) and Chadeau & Fouquet (1981) evaluate the amount of domestic work which is carried out in France by according a price to the value of the time which is devoted to the domestic production process. On the one hand, Kendé calculates the contribution made by domestic production to the standard of living of individual families whilst on the other, Chadeau & Fouquet estimate the value of such production in terms comparable with the G.N.P.. Second, Chadeau & Roy (1985) measure domestic production in terms of the value of its output of goods and services. Their interest is the shifting balance between market and domestic production. This is also the primary interest of Stoclet (1983) who uses time-budget and other economic indicators in his attempts to assess the nature of the transfer of production from the market to the non market sector, and vice versa. I will begin, however, with a discussion of the work of Pierre Kendé.

The traditional method applied to evaluate standards of living and levels of consumption of households was to measure their expenditure on market goods and services. However, such a method did not take into account what households produce for themselves. It is this omission which Kendé attempted to rectify. Studying sixty households composed of couples with two to four school age children in the Paris region, Kendé calculates the number and value of the goods and services produced within the household for its own consumption. This, in conjunction with 'regular' consumption, constitutes the 'consommation réelle' (real level of consumption) of households. He (1975, p. 8) defines 'la consommation réelle' as the 'sum of socially valued resources that a consumption unit uses during a determined period'.

Kendé calculates the value of domestic work on the basis of how much the producers of comparable goods and services are paid on the labour market, evaluating the cost of different domestic tasks one by one. Kendé (1978, p. 238-9) gave each activity a separate tarif (valid in Paris for 1974), ranging from forty-five Francs an hour for the work of a painter to three Francs an hour for that of a childminder, the most common tarif being ten0 Francs an hour for a housekeeper. Kendé found that, on average, the total domestic work of a household in which the wife stayed at home was worth 26,830 Francs per household per year. In households where the wife was employed, domestic work was worth on average 24,200 Francs per household per year. Such amounts are at least equivalent to what one could have earned on the formal labour market at the time, and as such, considerable.

From such findings, Kendé (1978, p. 243) concludes that 'domestic production, far from attenuating differences in incomes, tends rather to accentuate them'. That is, he found that self-provisioning in goods and services within the household did not reduce the differences in standards of living between the poorest and wealthiest families (in terms of household income), but mirrored them. For example, the difference in the incomes of dual, as opposed to single income families of similar socio-professional categories could not be overcome by the extra domestic production which a housewife could achieve in comparison with her employed counterpart.

Second is the analysis of Ann Chadeau & Annie Fouquet (1981). Chadeau & Fouquet are not interested in the contribution made by domestic production to the standards of living of particular households. Rather, their interest is in the overall contribution made by domestic work to the economy in terms of the G.N.P. In their attempt to estimate the monetary value of domestic work in France for 1975, Chadeau & Fouquet (1981, p. 36-41) tested three methods of calculation. Two of these methods rely on the principle of the 'manque à dépenser' (lack of necessity to spend). That is, they measure what the household would have to pay for certain goods and services if it did not produce them itself. The third method rests on the principle of the 'manque à gagner' (the opportunity cost model) based on the same premises as those employed by the Microeconomists)(see Chapter 4). In other words, it calculates what those individuals performing domestic work could earn on the market in the time that they devote to their domestic duties.

The first of the two methods which apply the 'manque à dépenser' principle assesses how much it would cost to employ what amounts to one domestic servant to carry out all the domestic tasks that household members usually perform themselves: this is termed the 'global method'. The second method evaluates how much each task would cost to be carried out by individual specialists: this is labelled the 'product by product' method (this latter being the same as that employed by Kendé).

Applying the 'global' method, Chadeau & Fouquet value domestic work at 640 billion Francs, or fifty per cent of G. D.P for France for 1975. [16] In the second 'product by product' method, there is a complication: the market price of substitutes for domestically produced goods and services covers not only the price of labour, but raw materials, V.A.T., depreciation of capital, overheads and the like. Thus, one has to evaluate not the price of the goods and services produced themselves but the wage rates paid to the 'specialists' who produce each of them. For example, Chadeau & Fouquet used the hourly wage rate of a mechanic for time spent on car repairs carried out at home and that of a childminder for childcare. According to this method, domestic work was worth 826 billion Francs, or sixty-five per cent of G.D.P. in 1975 in France.

The final method - that of 'opportunity cost' - is calculated on the basis of the amount per hour an individual may have earned on the market had she or he devoted the time spent on domestic labour to paid work instead. The value of an hour of the individual's time is assessed according to his or her qualifications, work experience, training and so on. This method produces the figure for the value of domestic work of 634 billion Francs for 1975, or fifty per cent of G.D.P.. Thus, it tallies with the result arrived at by the 'global' method. The principal conclusion to be drawn from these studies is that the 'value' of domestic work is, according to all these methods, highly significant.

Ann Chadeau [17] explained that after her attempt (with Annie Fouquet) to measure the value of domestic work through the medium of time, she realized that such a method only measured input of effort. It could not take into account the productivity of that time and thus revealed very little about the value of the goods and services actually produced. Thus, with Caroline Roy, she proceeded to outline a method for measuring the output of domestic production by estimating the value added to the raw materials purchased on the market by domestic work. The third study which I will examine in this section constitutes their first steps towards this goal.

Chadeau & Roy (1985, p. 1) assert that by using monetary in conjunction with non monetary indicators - National accounts data combined with the results of Household Surveys - modes of production and trends of domestic output can be traced. Their method involves categorizing final consumption commodities according to the role which they play in the production process which takes place in the household. Chadeau & Roy's (1985, p. 8) categories are the following: first, there are substitute products. These are market products which substitute the need for similar domestic production. Second, we have complementary products which cannot be produced by households themselves but are used in domestic production. Finally, there are pure final consumption products which can be neither produced by households, nor serve in any further productive process before being consumed.

By studying the trends of consumption of each of these types of products in conjunction with time-budget data, Chadeau & Roy attempt to identify whether (and which sorts of) domestic production is increasing or declining. For example, an increase in the consumption of a substitute product would indicate a decrease in household production whilst increased purchase of complementary products would be a sign that household production is on the rise. The results of a pilot survey reveal that there has been, in the past fifteen years, a rise in preference for packaged foodstuffs (substitute products) and a rise in household production of laundry services (indicated by a rise in complementary products such as washing machines). This, then, is a method highly suited to discussions of 'market - non market' transfers, this being the preoccupation of Stoclet, whose work I will discuss next.

The fourth analysis to be presented here is that of Daniel Stoclet (1983). Stoclet, in similarity to Chadeau & Roy, studies indicators which are liable to reveal which functions are being transferred to, and those which are being transferred away from the non market sector. Although he refers to the time-budget studies carried out by INSEE and a time-budget carried out by the CESP (Centre d'Etudes des Supports de Publicité) in 1979, he bases many of his arguments on statistics concerning the consumption of certain goods and services necessary to, or substitutes for domestic labour. These categories of indicators are directly related to those used by Chadeau & Roy: namely, the consumption of the raw materials necessary for domestic production; the comparative consumption of items which require no further work before they can be consumed and those which require some input from domestic labour; the consumption of the 'tools' of domestic production; and finally, the evolution of the consumption of services capable of substituting domestically produced services.

In examining these indicators, Stoclet (1983, p. 121) emphasizes the fact that the trends concerning market - non market transfers are gender specific. Stoclet posits that in their everyday housework tasks, women have resorted increasingly to the market, whereas men have increased their domestic activities, such as gardening, D.I.Y. and car maintenance. Stoclet explains this situation by the fact that women's time is becoming increasingly constrained by employment, whereas for men, employment is taking up less and less of their time (see Chapter 3).

However, in the case of those women who remain housewives, Stoclet notes that the decrease in the domestic labour burden in terms of the time [18] which is absolutely necessary for the care of the family means that they have more time to devote to 'leisure' activities. These 'leisure' activities, however, are often related to domestic activities. He (1983, p. 131) maintains that 'economically inactive women also have recourse increasingly to the market and thereby gain time for leisure, cultural activities, cooking, or needlework which then take on a new meaning as a hobby'. In other words, housewives, freed from the necessity to produce certain goods and services at home, have chosen to return to certain traditional activities, such as breadmaking or needlework. Consequently, these activities have taken on the character of leisure pursuits as opposed to domestic labour. He finds evidence for the rise in this 'leisure' production in statistics concerning, for example, the rate of consumption of machines such as yoghurt and spaghetti makers which has risen in the past few years. In sum, Stoclet argues that for the most part, any detectable increase in self-provisioning is attributable to increased leisure time and increased wealth, a point which is very important when assessing the work of the Free Market Dualist and Radical theorists.

Relationship to the Free Market Dualists and Radicals: choices and limitations

These four studies fall under the category of the 'Empirical Approaches' because their analyses are based primarily on measurement, either of domestic production in absolute terms, or in terms of the balance between domestic and market production. However, what these theorists choose to measure, and the method of measurement which they adopt, are not value free decisions. Indeed, certain influences are at work which affect these choices. It is these influences which will be discussed first of all. Furthermore, the choices of what to measure and how to measure it put limitations on the degree to which such results can be used to evaluate the validity of other theories. A discussion of these limitations will constitute the second part of this section.

The influences which have aroused interest in measuring non market, domestic production in macroeconomic terms relate to dissatisfaction with traditional economic models - notably, those associated with the G.N.P. First, in the early 'Seventies, criticisms emerged concerning the ability of such models to evalute 'real' standards of living and well-being in France. Kendé's (1975) work was, in fact, part a CNRS project launched in 1973 which aimed to develop models for evaluating well-being which relied less on measurements of material consumption than had previous models.

Second, there was impatience on the part of feminists that macroeconomic assessments of economic activity ignored the contribution to society that women make through their domestic work. Indeed, it was the feminist movement which demanded that the contribution of women's domestic work be recognized in macroeconomic terms. Chadeau & Fouquet in particular contextualize their work in this way. They (1981, p. 34) explain that 'faced with the upsurge of feminist ideas in the 'Seventies, extremely varied currents of public opinion converged on the necessity to recognize domestic labour as a real form of work which was both useful and productive'.

For example, Michel (1978, p. 12) called for the introduction of a new statistical index (originally created by J. Sabran) - the 'P.F.B.', 'produit familial brut' (Gross Familial Product) - into the national accounts. She asserted that if such a statistic were presented to the public, the assumption that standards of living are merely the results of market production and consumption would be challenged. Michel explained that such a challenge was necessary in order to make women's contribution to well-being in society visible.

Third, one cannot discount the influence exercised over Chadeau & Roy and Stoclet by the propositions made by the Free Market Dualists and the Radicals that a major shift from market to non market production was occuring as a way of compensating for falling standards of living provoked by the recession. Consequently, the methods employed by Chadeau & Roy and Stoclet are designed to allow the investigation of trends in the balance between the market and the non market sectors.

Having established the factors which aroused interest amongst these economists in the monetary evaluation of domestic production, it is now necessary to examine the problems which arise when one attempts this calculation and the limitations which such problems place on the pertinence of these results. The first difficulty encountered by these theorists is their definition of 'work'. All the theorists considered here have to overcome the hurdle of deciding which activities constitute 'domestic work' as opposed to 'leisure' in order to be able to estimate the value of this work. All opt for a roughly similar definition. This stipulates, first, that to be deemed 'domestic work', an activity must have a viable market substitute (in any case, if an activity did not have such an equivalent, measurement in monetary terms would be impossible). Second, and most importantly, this definition states that an activity constitutes domestic production/work only when the service or product to which it gives rise could be produced to the same effect by someone from outside the household who could expect financial compensation for his or her effort.

Whilst realizing that these theorists have had to develop a working definition which allows them to carry out their evaluations, the limitations of such a definition should not be overlooked. First and foremost it must be noted that only the person involved is able to decide whether or not he or she derives pleasure from the performance a certain activity, and thus, whether or not it would be possible for another person to perform that activity to the same end. It is not a decision that a researcher can make by observing behaviour alone. Take the example of gardening. There is no doubt that both the 'service' of gardening - employing a gardener - and the tangible products of gardening - fruit, vegetables and flowers - are readily available on the market. In other words, from an objective standpoint, gardening has a market substitute. However, are these products really substitutes to the person who gains pleasure from the act of participating in this activity? This pleasure cannot be purchased on the market, but does this render the act of 'gardening' in this instance ineligible to be included in the concept of work and thus in the measurement of 'productive' activity?

In fact, Stoclet touches on this point in saying that domestic work is 'work' for women because it constitutes their duty whilst for men certain domestic activities have taken on the character of leisure because they are a matter of choice, carried out, for the most part, because of the feeling of satisfaction which their achievement brings. Stoclet (1983, p. 128) explains that

> For women, the time taken up by domestic work reduces dramatically when they are employed whereas for men, the reduction of work time brings with it an increase in leisure time which they can devote to D.I.Y.; thus, we could say that domestic life is women's work and men's leisure.

It seems, therefore, that many, particularly non routine domestic activities, do indeed constitute leisure pursuits for many of the people who undertake them, although this does not undermine their usefulness or detract from the fact that they contribute to standards of living. The ambiguity of status of these activities does not, however, lend itself to a definition which can be easily employed by these particular theorists. They have had to simplify their definition of work in order to make it operational. Indeed, this is an example of how in order to squeeze domestic work into units of measurement appropriate to activities performed under the social and economic relations of employment, these theorists have had to ignore some of its subtleties.

A further set of problems occurs when the theorists attempt to match domestic services to their market counterparts. That is, the choice of which wage rates to apply to domestic production is far from being a straightforward and neutral question. The major problem which arises in all of the methods of calculation based on input of time is that such calculations reflect the lowly status both of women on the labour market and of their routine domestic work in society at large. This is the result of using equivalent values borrowed from the formal labour market to assess the 'worth' of domestic work, and especially the routine cooking, cleaning and childcare which falls mainly on women. In fact, such calculations express the prejudices against women's domestic labour which have led to its exclusion from macroeconomic models in the first place.

Taking the case of the 'global method' of Chadeau & Fouquet, this measures the value of domestic labour on the basis of the wages paid to a domestic helper. However, the low wage rates common in the profession of 'domestic helper' mirror the low social value accorded to unpaid routine domestic work. Moreover, this 'profession' is overwhelmingly female, its low wage rates predicated upon the low value of women in the labour market. Chadeau & Fouquet note that this method underestimates the value of many of the more specialized domestic tasks, for example, house and car maintenance and administrative activities. This is unsurprising considering that these activities have their market substitutes in male dominated sectors of the labour market.

With this point in mind, one can explain why the 'product by product' method (the same method as that used by Kendé) sets a value for domestic labour which is higher than that set by the other two. By using specialist wage rates, and rates current in traditionally male spheres of employment, one can raise the overall value of domestic labour. What emerges, therefore, is the divergent social and economic standing of different individuals and different professions. This is explicit in the 'opportunity cost' approach. According to this analysis, the time spent on domestic labour by men and highly qualified and/or employed women is worth more than that of unqualified housewives. This is despite the fact that housewives have 'specialized' in domestic work. Thus, it is not so much the value of domestic labour as that of domestic labourers which is being calculated.

The most stark example of the problems with these evaluations of domestic labour is that in 1975 in France, in terms of hours, domestic labour outstripped professional work by approximately twelve per cent, but in monetary terms, it was only worth between fifty and sixty-five per cent of G.D.P.. It seems, therefore, that evaluating domestic labour with the tools of, and in comparison with the formal labour market, can only reproduce the hierarchy between domestic labour and employment activities and serve to reflect the lowly status of domestic labour and those normally responsible for it - namely, women.

The limitations of the approaches described above do not, however, reduce their most important impact which is symbolic. For example, taking into account the statements made by Chadeau & Fouquet (1981, p. 42) that calculations such as theirs must remain in the realm of 'the fictional economy', one could wonder whether Chadeau & Fouquet's analysis was intended to be scientifically accurate or to reflect reality. It seems more likely that it was an academic exercise intended for political effect. In an interview with the Marxist Feminist review Des Femmes en Mouvement, Chadeau (1981, p. 25) explains that 'the fact of having given a monetary value to these hours of work, even if none of the methods are satisfactory, is still important: a thousand billion francs is enough to make an impact which could change reality'. Therefore, the accuracy of the figures in terms of their relationship to a certain reality was not of paramount importance - so long as they were high enough for people to sit up and take notice, which, if the press coverage of the publication of the report is anything to go by, they certainly did. Chadeau [19] herself explained that putting a value on domestic work was important because 'it shows in Francs - and the public takes notice of monetary values - the importance of this work which was effectively hidden'.

The final point to discuss is whether or not those who speak of market - non market transfers offer any evidence to support either the Free Market Dualist or Radical propositions concerning the growth of the informal economy. The answer to that question is negative. There is no evidence to suggest that there has been a concerted shift towards informal production in the market - non market sector balance, with transfers in both directions having been pinpointed by these theorists. Moreover, the message which comes from the other Empirical researchers is reinforced: namely, that the non market sector cannot compensate for the deficiencies of the market sphere because it is in no way an independent entity. The factor which emerges most starkly from these studies is that the informal sector is dependent on the formal sector for its raw materials.

Indeed, for Stoclet (1983, p. 143), the fact that people are doing more things for themselves in the home is in keeping with the general trend of rising living standards based on the market economy. The whole hypothesis that increased domestic production is compensating in some way for a lack of financial resources supposes that in an earlier period, households were employing people to perform the tasks - such as painting and decorating - that they now perform for themselves. The hypothesis which Stoclet puts forward, in contrast, suggests that the jobs that are now being carried out by households themselves were left undone in the past because of lack of finance. The increase in money spent on D.I.Y. materials, for example, is therefore an expression of people's rising expectations vis a vis the surroundings in which they live, not their inability to pay for professional services. It is the extra income which people receive which allows them to buy the tools and materials which they require to improve their homes. D.I.Y. is therefore the product of growing resources in time and money. Once again, informal production does not appear to be the saviour of the most marginalized from society. Indeed, self-provisioning appears to be part of the sphere of non necessity.

In sum, therefore, these studies all use the symbolic power of monetary values to reinforce the importance of non market (domestic) production and thus women's contribution to society. However, in so doing, they reinforce the idea found amongst the Feminists and Microeconomists that informal activity is central and essential to the economic structure as it stands today and is not independent from it.

Conclusions

The Empirical Approaches listed here have made several important contributions to the debates on the role of the informal economy in the future of work. The studies concerning the informal economy and the unemployed, the informal economy and small communities and the practices of black market workers have all concluded that time and financial need are not sufficient conditions to allow people to engage in informal production of the domestic or black market kind. They have all shown that tools, materials and a certain infrastructure (all of which require money to be spent on them) are necessary, not to mention appropriate skills, in order for informal production to take place. Moreover, they have shown that if one is to take part in informal exchanges, one needs to be part of a social network since it is this network which provides 'customers' or 'trading partners'. Consequently, these studies, taken as a whole, have shown that the same inequalities in all the areas listed above can and do exist in the informal sector, just as they exist in the formal labour market.

Furthermore, the studies of black market workers in particular have shown that the motivations of people who engage in informal production are 'normal' in the sense of not necessarily running against the grain of capitalist society. For example, they have shown that people engage in black market work for monetary reward, for the sense of being productive and even entrepreneurial, and in the case of the village communities, because to do so constitutes an integral part of village life.

In sum, these Empirical analyses suggest that the gulf between the formal and informal sector is not as great as some of the Radical and Free Market Dualist theorists apparently assume. Indeed, the final group of theorists discussed in this Chapter explicitly work on the basis of this assertion, calculating the great contribution that informal work makes to the 'economy' as it exists today. Moreover, the work on market - non market transfers carried out by Stoclet and Chadeau & Roy underlines the points made above that there is nothing innovatory about the coexistence of the informal and formal sectors, or that from time to time, in the wake of changing circumstances, various activities will move from one sphere to the other.

This series of results concerning the close relationship between formal and informal production has undermined, to some extent, the optimism concerning the future of informal work which the Radicals, and to a lesser extent, the Free Market Dualists, appear to hold. Thus, these findings, suggesting as they do that the informal economy cannot be an economic and social panacea for the problems concerning work which France and other Western industrialized countries have been facing for the past fifteen years, have contributed to a reduction in interest in the subject on the part of Radical and Free Market Dualist theorists from the mid Eighties onwards, a point which will be discussed further in in Chapter 12. The studies do not contradict the notion that it might be a good thing, from many points of view, to encourage the development of more autonomous forms of work. However, they reinforce and underline the need for planned change to make this happen since their results suggest that the prerequisites for informal production to take place are too numerous for this to come about spontaneously.

Notes

1. Source of information: Budgets de Familles, 1979, INSEE.
2. They are: the declared activity of the household members; the income derived from black market work; the goods and services produced by domestic activities; the use of savings and loans; help from institutions, neighbours or friends; or crime.
3. That is, 'lack' in comparison with what one might have expected.

4. Interview conducted in Lille, April 1988.
5. Interview conducted in Lille, April 1988 (Foudi & Stankiewicz) and interview conducted in Paris, April 1987 (Barthe).
6. All of whom have produced their analyses within the context of the O.C.S. - Observation du changement social - project. See '9' below.
7. Interview conducted in Lille, April 1988
8. As developed by the anthropologists of primitive society Sahlins (1976) and Mauss (1973).
9. Many of the studies here are part of a major CNRS project carried out in the early 'Eighties called the Observation du changement social which had quite an interest in the informal economy. Stankiewicz (interview, 1988) explains that the heart of this project was to observe social change in a localized fashion. The idea came from certain sociologists who wanted to counter-balance the preference for general analyses of social change which existed in French social science until that time. Duriez (interview, 1988) said that this project represented a change in the 'problematique' in France towards studying local situations instead of the universal social evolutions.
10. The campaign against black market work is well covered by Klatzmann (1979). Some of the reports on black market work include: Soupa (1971); Metton (1979); Delorozoy (1980); Bouniol (1980); Chambre de commerce et de l'industrie (1980); Tanzi (1982); and the Conseil économique et social (1983).
11. See Chapter 1 for an explanation of the difference between 'black market work' and the 'underground economy'.
12. See Heerjte and Barthelemy (1984) for a detailed discussion of their methods.
13. See Chapter 2 for a full breakdown of the figures relating to the underground economy produced by these studies.
14. Lebars et al (1980, 1) define black market work as 'an activity accomplished outside the institutional framework, infringing work regualtions and escaping, by its clandestine nature, the paying of associated social and fiscal obligations'.
15. 'CAP' (Certificat d'aptitude professionnelle) (certificate of professional aptitude): fifty per cent; 'BT' (Brevet technique) (technical diploma): ten per cent; 'BTS' (Brevet technique supérieur) (advanced technical diploma): ten per cent; none: thirty per cent.

16. This figure does not take into account the effect of tax and social security contributions which would be deducted from the wages of the individuals carrying out this work if it were, in fact, paid.
17. Interview conducted in Paris, April 1988.
18. By a comparison of INSEE 1966 and 1974/5 and CESP 1979 time-budget studies.
19. Interview conducted in Paris, April 1988.

PART 3
LESSONS TO BE LEARNT FROM THE FRENCH DEBATES

10 What do we 'know' about the informal economy in France?

Introduction

The hypothesis which informs this analysis of the contibutions made to the informal economy debates by French theorists posits that all understanding and interpretation passes through a screen or filter of values, ideological and political affiliations and theoretical convictions. Hence, there is no one objective standpoint from which analysis of the informal economy can be undertaken. It is essential to recognize this if one is to assess in as unbiased a way as possible the lessons which can be learnt about the informal economy from the contributions of French theorists.

That said, there are certain 'facts' concerning the informal economy which have an empirical or statistical grounding and which are not disputed from any quarter. Equally, there are certain evaluations of the informal economy over which a general consensus of interpretation reigns. These points of consensus, or peaceful coexistence of views relating to different aspects of the informal economy could be said to constitute what we 'know' about the subject. For all that, there are other issues regarding various aspects of informal economic activity which provoke heated debate amongst theorists. This Chapter will, therefore, on the one hand, outline what 'knowledge' of the informal economy has been produced by French theorists, and on the other hand, clarify the nature of the ideological choices which provoke irresolvable conflicts between them.

This discussion will be structured in the following manner. First, I will outline the areas of consensus regarding the informal economy which exist between the theorists. Thereafter, I will investigate the three broad areas in which divergence and conflict arises. Thus, second, I will explore conflicts arising out of the choices of explanation made by the theorists. Third, I will examine those stemming from their choice of method. And finally, I will pursue the question of the different ways in which the theorists explain the role - potential or actual - fulfilled in society and in the economy by the various types of informal economic activity.

Points of consensus: what do we 'know' about the informal economy?

There is one point on which all the French theorists who study the informal economy are agreed: namely, that wealth and well-being are not produced by activity in the formal sector of the economy alone, but require other inputs - namely, from the domestic, voluntary and black market sectors. However, whether this means that informal economic activities should be encouraged and developed or reduced in importance is another, more contentious issue which will be discussed a little later.

Taking first those theorists who are primarily interested in the household division of labour, there is a broad consensus that domestic work is a very important activity in terms of the time devoted to it. This simple observation informs the theoretical models of the Feminists and Microeconomists, and is borne out by the statistical and ethnographic results of the Empirical studies. Moreover, they all acknowledge that the responsibility for domestic labour falls squarely on the shoulders of women. Accordingly, it is agreed that the most significant variable in determining responsibility for domestic work is the gender variable, being more important than those of age and class. [1] Furthermore, there is agreement that women cannot earn as much on the formal labour market as men. This is a factor which plays a decisive role in women taking on the domestic responsibilities of the household or family unit. Indeed, these findings from France correspond very closely to the general consensus in the English language literature (see Williams, 1988). Consequently, until such time as either socio-economic or politico-ideological factors emerge to disturb this consensus, we could say that these statements constitute 'knowledge' in this subject area. However, if one attempts to explain the relationship of women vis à vis domestic work set out above, the differences between the Microeconomists and Feminists and between them and the Empiricists begin to emerge.

As far as the theorists whose main interest is the role of the informal economy in the future of work are concerned, the Free Market Dualists and Radicals agree, on the whole, that unemployment is a major problem; that France will never return to a state of 'full' employment as this was understood in the 'Sixties; and that the informal economy could play a part in the solution to this problem. However, above and beyond these bare bones of analysis, divergence occurs between these theorists. The main contentious issue between the Free Market Dualists and the Radicals concerns the question of whether the crisis of unemployment is a disaster pure and simple or an opportunity cloaked in disaster, as will be discussed in more depth later.

In sum, it must be said that the points of consensus amongst French theorists concerning the informal economy are rather limited. The reasons for this will be become apparent in the following discussions.

Conflicts concerning explanation

As we have seen in our discussions, the debates concerning the informal economy in France revolve around two separate, but related questions - that of the household division of labour and that of the role of the informal economy in the future of work. In exploring the conflicts concerning the explanation of why informal economic activity is structured as it is, we will therefore first compare the Microeconomists with the Feminists, and then the Free Market Dualists with the Radicals. Having discovered the major issues which divide them, we will move on to examine the extent to which the individualist orientation of the Microeconomists and Free Market Dualists unites them in spite of their differing preoccupations. Likewise, we will subsequently look at the relationship between the structuralist analyses of the Radicals and the Feminists.

Taking first the disagreements between the Microeconomists and the Feminists concerning why it is women who carry the burden of domestic labour, the question which divides them is that of whether or not women have any choice in marrying, having children and assuming domestic responsibilities. Whereas the Microeconomists assert that whatever the constraints which come to bear on them, women always have a choice in these matters, the Feminists cannot accept this simplistic adherence to an absolute definition of 'choice'. For them, the 'constraints' on women are such that the very concept of 'choice' becomes meaningless. The sanctions awaiting most women who refuse the socially accepted path of marriage and children are too great.

This question of degree of choice enjoyed by women cannot be separated from the theorists' evaluation of women's present day situation in France. Divergence of opinion occurs between those who find this situation tolerable, on the one hand, and those who find this state of affairs intolerable and insist on the need for change, on the other. Indeed, the less tolerable a theorist perceives the inequalities and injustices in society to be, the less likely he or she is to accept that this situation can be the product of individuals' choices. To perceive society as the outcome of the sum of individuals' choices implies that if inequality and exploitation exist, this is ultimately the product of human nature and not the perversion of it by a social 'structure'.

Not striving to decide which of these two approaches (Microeconomist or Feminist) is most 'truthful' or most 'appropriate' offers one the opportunity to examine more closely the ideological and political motivations which underlie each position. Thus, it is possible to reveal that the discord between the Microeconomist and Feminist theorists concerning the degree of choice exercised by women results from their respective 'individualist' or 'structualist' orientations, as well as from their gender politics. Consequently, the conclusion that we must draw is that the argument over the existence or absence of 'choice' in women's lives can only become a stale one in academic terms. That is not to say that either side should refrain from trying to win over as large a following as possible to its views. However, it should be remembered that one is dealing with a matter of moral and political conviction, and not one which can be resolved by further theorizing and empirical research as we will discuss in a little more detail later.

Second, then, we move onto the disagreements and conflicts which persist between the Free Market Dualists and the Radicals in France. These arise primarily from two conflicting evaluations of the capitalist/industrialist system and the sacrosanctity of economic growth and international competition. These differing evaluations are reflected in differences of opinion concerning unemployment. Whereas the Free Market Dualists are of the opinion that unemployment is the only crisis, the Radicals argue that it is but one manifestation of other, more deep rooted crises, such as those of environmental destruction and alienation from industrial society.

As a consequence of these conflicting assessments of present day society, the scenarios proposed by the Free Market Dualists, on the one hand, and the Radicals on the other, also vary. That of the Free Market Dualists is designed to safeguard the capitalist system; enhance economic growth; and secure France's place in the world market. Overall, the aim of the Radicals is to change this system drastically even though there are subtle differences between them concerning the degree and type of change demanded.

It is important to note that in their explanations, one cannot differentiate between the Radicals and the Free Market Dualists on the basis of a traditional Left-Right split. The difference between 'Left' and 'Right' can, in traditional terms, be summed up as the difference between collectivism and free entreprise, state regulation and the market. However, as we have seen, both the Radicals, on the Left, and the Free Market Dualists, on the Right, denounce State domination of the lives of individuals. Indeed, what the Free Market Dualists and the Radicals have in common is a suspicion of the State - although, naturally for different reasons. Purely by concentrating on the informal economy as a solution to the problems of work, both the Free Market Dualists and Radicals are suggesting that a certain degree of disengagement on the part of the State is desirable.

Having examined both the Microeconomists and Feminists, and the Free Market Dualists and Radicals, we can see that the conflicts between the individualist and structuralist camps are manifested in similar, if not identical ways between both sets of theorists. These are disagreements first, over the degree of choice exercised by individuals in deciding whether or not to devote themselves to certain kinds of activity; second, over the extent to which individuals can be described as different but complementary, or divided by various forms of structurally-determined inequality (this inequality being the result of oppression); and third, over the degree of acceptance or rejection of the present organization of the economy and society.

First, then, as far as the measure of choice enjoyed by individuals in their lives is concerned, the 'individualists' (the Microeconomists and the Free Market Dualists) argue that society is composed of free and legally equal individuals exchanging goods and services on the market. For that reason, they consider everyone to be in a position to choose, within certain constraints, what they want to do in life. Microeconomists argue that women 'choose' to devote themselves to domestic work. Family models and the division of labour between spouses are products of individuals acting 'rationally' (that is, in accordance with their own interests, given the options open to them). For example, women may assume the role of housewife motivated by the desire for children within the constraints of their potential salary weighed up against the cost of childcare.

The Free Market Dualists argue that the 'dual society' will evolve without social tension because some individuals will freely choose the quieter life of working informally, accepting the disadvantage of a lower 'material' standard of living in preference to earning higher salaries in the rat race of employment in the hitech competitive sector. In the opinion of both the Microeconomists and the Free Market Dualists, even if some people are more successful than others, this is ultimately a product of the choices that they have made in the light of the constraints which have come to bear on them.

The structuralists (the Radicals and the Feminists) are both of the opinion that society, organized on the principle of the unequal distribution of power, gives certain categories of people, at least, no 'choice' in their destinies. The constraints bearing down on them are such that the notion of 'choice' becomes redundant. Thus, both groups of theorists assert that for people to have 'real' choice - whether it be for women to go out to work or for individuals to choose to work informally - practical reforming steps or full scale revolution in the social and economic structure must be implemented.

For Feminists, women do not have a 'choice' in devoting themselves to domestic work. As a consequence of the capitalist or patriarchal structure of society, women find themselves badly paid on the formal labour market and facing a barrage of social conditioning and pressure to ensure that their primary concerns are for domestic work and childcare. For the Radicals, real choice of how one wants to work will only be possible when the capitalist/industrialist structure has been reformed and/or when the search for profits and growth in traditional terms is no longer the sole motivation for productive activity.

This notion of 'choice' relates to the second question of whether inequality is a feature of society or whether people are merely different in a complementary way. For the Microeconomists and the Free Market Dualists, men and women, or the two populations of the 'dual society' scenario are different but complementary. Since they have 'chosen' different paths, they can live harmomiously with the consequences of their choices. For the Radicals and Feminists, however, these differences are not products of choice. They are inequalities which are the result of an unequal power distribution in society.

On the third question of appraising society as it exists at present, the individualists take a primarily positive view whilst the strucuralists express more negative opinions. The Microeconomists and Free Market Dualists maintain that the system of capitalism is essentially benign and that the market is the best way of regulating inter-human relationships and society. For example, although Sofer deems the constraints which come to bear on women in the labour market to be unfair, this does not lead her to question the market system. Instead, she professes that real liberation for women will come about when the constraints on them are comparable with those affecting men. In similarity, the faith placed in the capitalist market by the Free Market Dualists is expressed in their insistence that international markets must be left to develop freely and that one must not resort to protectionist measures in order to conserve French jobs. It is for this reason that, in their opinion, unemployment will remain a permanent feature of the economy.

Conversely, since both Radicals and Feminists agree that society is based on oppression and the unequal distribution of power, it is not surprising that their appraisal of society is primarily negative. Feminists argue that women's relationship to domestic work is a consequence of the oppression which they face under this social and economic system. The Radicals' negative appraisal of capitalist/industrialist society leads them to search for alternatives to employment in the informal economy. Employment, they contend, is one of the cornerstones of this societal structure and embodies all its problematic aspects.

However, not all the structural theorists describe this social structure in the same way. Indeed, they argue about its precise nature. Some Radicals and Feminists agree on this question, both laying blame at the door of the system that each names as capitalism. Nevertheless, other Radicals develop the more all embracing notion of industrialism to describe a society determined by the technology which it uses, or by its relationship to the natural world. This corresponds with the Radicals' interest in the problems of employment as a prime manifestation of the complex, centralized and highly structured industrial system. Concomitantly, other Feminists argue that patriarchy is the key to understanding the structure of society. This definition too is related to their interest in the position of women in relationship to domestic work.

From this discussion, we can see reflected in the choices of explanation made by the theorists the political and ideological changes of environment detailed in Chapter 3. On the one hand, we have witnessed a reinforcement of the ideal of the free market on the part of the Free Market Dualists and the Microeconomists. On the other hand, we observe a challenge to the centrality of the traditional Marxist categories of capitalist society on the part of both the Radicals and the Feminists.

However, this discussion has only taken account of the disagreements between those theorists who have adopted a universalist methodology, showing that they cannot reach a consensus over basic points of evaluation of the society of which the informal economy is a part - or to which it could be the antedote. It remains to be seen if any of the Empirical studies have resolved these disagreements, or whether the divergences between universalists and empiricists muddy the waters of the 'knowledge' of the informal economy provided by French theorists still further.

Different understandings arising from choice of method

In considering the differences between the universalist theorists - the Microeconomists, Feminists, Free Market Dualists and Radicals - and those researchers who adopt a more Empirical - qualitative or statistical - approach, several points must be borne in mind. First, there is the question of whether the research carried out on the informal economy in the field corroborates the common assumptions of both sets of 'universalist' theorists. Second, one must ask whether such empirical evidence provides information which allows one to decide whether one type of explanation reflects 'the truth' of the matter more closely than another. Finally, in considering the above questions, the proposition will be put forth that these Empirical approaches produce a kind of knowledge which has its own characteristics and is based on assumptions which the universalist approaches do not necessarily share. One of the most relevant of these characteristics is the value placed by many of the 'qualitative' researchers on the testimony of research subjects themselves in explaining their own personal situation. I will begin with the case of the Microeconomists and Feminists.

In their particular case, the common assumptions of the Microeconomists and of the Feminists that much time is devoted to domestic work, and that the majority of this work is performed by women, are given a firm grounding by all the statistical and qualitative Empirical studies. As regards the explanation of this situation, however, the statistical surveys have little in the way of 'proof' to offer for either the explanations of the Microeconomists or the Feminists. The qualitative studies, in contrast, - especially those of Froger & Peyraut (1982) and Glaude & de Singly (1986) - make an important contribution at the causal level. However, far from helping us to decide between the various Microeconomic and Feminist hypotheses concerning women's relationship to domestic work, they tend to offer up explanations of their own which run into a certain amount of conflict with the Microeconomists and/or the Feminists.

First, for example, Glaude & de Singly stress the diversity of women's situations relating to domestic labour. This undermines, to some extent, the efforts of the Feminist theorists to portray women as bearing a common burden. However, the notion of what constitutes similarity of situation and what constitutes difference is a very delicate matter of judgement. Whether one takes differences at their face value, as do Glaude & de Singly, or concentrates on eliciting the common - albeit underlying - thread which links various phenomena, as do the Feminists, is ultimately a product of the argument that one is trying to support.

Second, whilst the Microeconomists explain women's relationship to domestic labour in terms of economic rationality and the Feminists employ the framework of class oppression, these Empirical theorists furnish their own explanations, based to a greater degree, but not exclusively, on the testimony of their interviewees. Froger & Peyraut, for example, indicate that the division of labour which couples practise in their households is correlated with their views concerning morality, politics and the like. Furthermore, Glaude & de Singly describe the division of labour between spouses to be the outcome of a process of 'negotiation'.

At stake here is the degree to which each theorist attempts to apply his or her own general, or 'universal' explanatory framework to the household division of labour, and the extent to which this takes into account individuals' rationalizations of their own lives. The aim of the 'universalist' theories of the Feminists and Microeconomists is to surpass the individual case in order to provide an overall understanding of social and economic processes which may be operating 'below the surface' and thus, without the knowledge of those whom they affect. The Microeconomists, for example, observe the economic 'behaviour' of the couple and mould this into their economic logic of utility maximisation which they believe to be universal. They do not claim that everyone explicitly thinks in that way, but that this is the best framework within which to understand society. Consequently, their 'individualism' must not be confused with an epistemological position which gives priority to the testimony of social actors. Equally, the Feminists recognize that social actors do not always think in terms of oppression but this does not nullify the existence of 'implicit' forces or mechanisms at work of which people themselves cannot be aware.

The explanations offered by Froger & Peyraut and Glaude & de Singly are supposedly grounded more solidly in their interviewees own perceptions of their lives. However, no researcher's final analyses - even those of Froger & Peyraut or Glaude & de Singly - reflect solely the views of their research subjects, avoiding all personal input. The very questions that they pose reflect the correlations between various factors in which they are interested and which they assume to be the most important. The research subject does not have the power to set the agenda of the project.

Just as in the case of deciding whether differences or similarities in women's situation vis à vis domestic work are most salient, there is no right or wrong in deciding the extent to which one should take people's own accounts of their lives as the last word on a particular subject, or search for underlying causes which the individuals concerned cannot formulate themselves. If these various methods produce conflicting results, all must be taken as factors in understanding a given situation. Therefore, it must be concluded that the Empirical theorists do not help in providing a clear picture of the causal variables involved in the household division of labour.

In the case of the Free Market Dualists and Radicals, the common ground between them is of a speculative nature. They concur that unemployment will remain a feature of the economy for the foreseeable future; that the informal economy could play a part in resolving this problem; that the unemployed would be involved in the extension of informal activities; and that changes in attitude have taken place which have made the idea of working informally popular. Furthermore, the Free Market Dualists and Radicals are similar to the extent that both implicitly assume that the informal economy as it is manifested at present - either in the form of black market or domestic work - is to some degree independent of the formal market, and functions according to a different logic. This assertion lies at the heart of their faith in the ability of the informal economy either to help contain the social fall out of mass unemployment (Free Market Dualists) or to constitute the building blocks of a new organization of production (Radicals).

The Empirical studies in this group put some of these assumptions to the test by observing the actual practices of domestic and black market work, for example, by the unemployed, and investigate the reasons why people engage in such work. Indeed, the studies of the informal economy and the unemployed, and the informal economy and small communities, as well as by the studies of the motivations of black market workers, do not bear out the assumption made by the Free Market Dualists and Radicals that the informal sector is relatively independent from the formal sphere. The Empirical studies have shown that black market work or domestic work is dependent on the formal economy for its raw materials; the health of the formal economy determines demand for black market work in a particular region; those who are best placed to find employment - skilled, motivated people - are the most likely to be active in the informal sphere; the social networks needed for informal production reproduce the inequalities of access existing in formal labour markets; and lastly, the prime motivations of independent black market workers do not run contrary to the logic of the 'capitalist' community at large.

Such findings contradict the notion that the informal economy will develop spontaneously. This has especially serious implications for the propositions of the Free Market Dualists since these are based on the ability of the unemployed to become active in the informal sphere without too much aid from the State. As far as the Radicals are concerned, Offe (1985, p. 100) raises an interesting point in suggesting that

> ... advocates of the informal economy have not always made it clear that a blind, laissez-faire process of dualization and a type of consciously designed dual economy which is politically justified and reinforced are diametrically opposed models.

Thus, the findings of the Empirical theorists that working informally is perhaps not as easy and accesible to all as some may have thought, does not nullify the validity of the propositions of the Radicals as such. However, these results reinforce the need to emphasize the distinction outlined by Offe above, namely, that change towards a more diversified pattern of work would have to come about in a planned fashion. This realization is perhaps reflected in Gorz's (1986) and Aznar's (1987) preoccupations in the late

'Eighties with fashioning a guaranteed minimum income which would encourage, as opposed to discourage informal work. Other theorists, such as Roustang (1987) have come to the conclusion that if informal work is not going to prove to be an autonomous panacea to the crisis of the formal economy, then the way in which it works 'with' the formal system should be more fully investigated.

Furthermore, many of the 'Empirical' studies have highlighted the pecuniary and entrepreneurial motivations of the individuals who carry out black market work. This casts doubt on the viability of the scenario envisaged by the Radical theorists. One is led to wonder how this scenario would avoid, in practice, eventually developing into a renewed form of 'capitalism' even if it were possible to bring the scenario into being in the first place. For example, how does one distinguish between the 'small communal enterprise' advocated, for example, by Gorz, and the the creation of small businesses encouraged by the Free Market Dualists and so beloved of free market political parties in the West in general? The Radicals cope with these doubts in two ways. First, they assume that there is a 'natural' fairness to informal exchanges between individuals which does not exist in the capitalist market and second, that people will spontaneously want to cooperate as opposed to compete given the chance. The Free Market Dualists agree that there is a natural fairness in exchange, but believe that it is to be found in the capitalist market as it exists at present, the 'natural' relationship between people being that of constructive competition.

However, the results of these Empirical studies cannot be blindly accepted as confirmation or contrary evidence for any of the scenarios. One must first discuss the limitations of these studies themselves in order to decide on the extent to which their results can in any way be used to evaluate the work of the Radicals or Free Market Dualists. The first point to note - and although rather positivistic in tone is still valid - is that none of the Empirical studies (with the exception of the monetary calculations of Chadeau & Fouquet, 1981) has been carried out on large, nationally representative samples. In fact, the majority of these Empirical studies are of qualitative method. That is, they involve interviews with fairly small samples of people. Moreover, they are in the main carried out in specific regions. Thus, they do not provide statistically significant evidence relevant to the nation as a whole. Be that as it may, it is the information which they provide on the differences between the small, sometimes regionally specific samples with which they deal which is precisely what makes them interesting.

Mendras & Stankiewicz (1986), in an overview of all the Observation du changement social projects which deal with the informal economy, conclude that their significance was to reveal that the aptitudes of individuals and their application to the informal economy are very different; and second, that the nature of the locality in which people live is a determining variable in the potential for development of the informal economy.

Indeed, such specific, localized studies, by their very nature, contradict the Radical and Free Market Dualist approaches. Whilst the former are designed to highlight difference, the latter tend to homogenize French society, implying that all parts of it will evolve in the same direction at the same pace. By concentrating on the experiences of individuals, the Empirical theorists are implicitly saying that life is not as simple as the 'universalist' theorists may like to think. The nuances between individuals' situations as well as those between regions revealed by these studies undermine the assumptions that there are universal trends away from consumerism, or that there is a tendency for the unemployed to undertake black market work. Universalist theories attempt to paper over the cracks of individual difference. Conversely, these Empirical approaches chip away at these cracks.

Defining the relationship of the informal to the formal sector

The question to be addressed here regards the conflicts which arise when theorists attempt to assess how the informal sector - or its various component parts - fits into the overall organization of society and the economy. In other words, the issue arises of whether the informal sector is an integral part of the economy, or independent of it. In the case of it being independent, the question emerges of whether the informal economy is capable of playing a compensatory or challenging role in relation to the formal economy.

The difference here lies neither between individualists and structuralists, nor between the empiricists and universalists, but initially between Microeconomists and Feminists, on the one hand, and Radicals and Free Market Dualists, on the other. Microeconomists and Feminists agree that domestic work is an integral part of the way in which society functions. This means for the Feminists that it is viewed in a negative light because of their negative appraisal of the social structure. Conversely, the Free Market Dualists and Radicals both work on the implicit assumption that the informal economy - black market work, 'l'autoproduction' and the like - functions in a relatively autonomous fashion in comparison with the formal economy. This must be the case if such activities are to compensate for the deficiencies of the formal labour market (Free Market Dualist) or to challenge the centrality of profit, consumerism and productivism (Radical). This means that for the Radicals, the informal economy is generally viewed in a positive light because it runs contrary to the formal organization of the society which they criticize.

This disagreement is expressed most starkly in the rift that ensues between the two structuralist clusters of theorists, namely, the Radicals and the Feminists. Feminists are not interested in encouraging the informal economy at the expense of employment. In fact, there is at least a tacit acceptance amongst the Feminists that the most immediate solution to women's problems is for them to find employment. Many Feminists are highly suspicious of people who argue for the extension of household based services and production because, in their opinion, this would always constitute an extra burden for women. For example, Kartchevsky [2], when asked her opinion of the work of theorists such as Gorz, explained that she equated his work with a discourse which promotes self-help and in consequence a 'disengagement' from the Welfare State. Kartchevsky interpreted such a policy to mean that the State should return more responsibilities to the family - which would inevitably entail women being tied more closely to the home than before. Her reaction to such ideas represents an example of a mode of thought which equates anti-Statist discourse with 'reactionary' discourse.

In contrast, the Radicals base their propositions on the belief that informal activities of all kinds have the potential for challenging the status quo of productivist values and our present organization of employment. Thus, although acknowledging that the present organization of domestic work is constraining for women (they can hardly ignore the whole body of Feminist literature decrying this domestic burden), the Radical theorists reject the Feminist proposition that women will liberate themselves by finding jobs on the formal labour market. This, in their opinion, constitutes an act of throwing the baby out with the bath water.

Therefore, Radical theorists contend that extending wage labour to women is not a blanket solution since it results in the exchange of one kind of oppression for another. In the Radical theorists' opinion, by putting all their eggs in the basket of participation in the formal market as a cure-all for women's oppression, Feminists are putting a misguided emphasis on employment as being liberatory for women. Lalonde & Simmonet (1978, p. 154) explain that women carry out more 'socially useful' work in the home than men do in industry. They emphasize the value of the free work carried out by women but are careful not to confine women to these roles. They suggest that the best solution is to reduce the value of waged work and to encourage men to participate in the household. They assert that there are two choices for the marginalized from male society (including women): either, they can demand their integration into the formal system, with all its faults. Or they can work to dismantle this system.

On this general disagreement between theorists concerning the relationship of the present day informal sector to the formal economy (if not the potential of such activities), the Empirical studies which have concerned themselves with the role of the informal economy in the future of work have emphasized that the informal sector is neither a novel phenomenon nor independent from the formal economy. As no Free Market Dualist or Radical voices appear to have been raised in recent times to contradict these findings, one could put forth the idea that a new consensus has arisen out of the debates. That is, no one any longer appears to deny that the informal sector is closely related to the formal sphere both in the sense that it contributes to the efficiency of the formal economy and that informal production relies on the formal sphere for raw materials. Equally, those best placed to work formally are those best placed to work informally as well. Thus, the appraisal by the theorists of the relationship between the informal and formal sectors has undergone a rapprochement.

Conclusion

In conclusion, one can say that we 'know' that women are responsible for most domestic work. Nevertheless, there is ambiguity concerning first, the degree of similarity of the 'lot' of all women; second, the degree to which economic rationality is at the base of their decisions; and third, the extent to which an oppressive social structure determines women's situations. Furthermore, we 'know' that there is no reason to suppose that the unemployed are massively engaged in black market or domestic work and that informal work seems more rife in small communities.

Moreover, there is a tacit consensus that the informal sector is not independent of the formal market. However, what we do not know is whether, if planned and organized, the Radical scenario could work; whether people would really prefer this scenario to the present day organization of work; or whether its implementation could avoid being ultimately repressive to women. The answers to all these questions constitute choices dependent upon ideology.

From these discussions, we can see that the terms 'Left' and 'Right' are too restrictive to categorize the ideological diversity surrounding the discussion of the informal economy. It is clear that the range of choices pertinent in the field of the informal economy cannot be described in terms of the unidimensional dichotomy between Marxist and non Marxists, or Keynsians and Neoclassicists, or pro- and anti-Statists which the notions of Left and Right traditionally conjure up. This concurs with the conclusion of Rosanvallon (1977, p. 76) that classical terminology dividing Left from Right is no longer generally applicable because this terminology divides between those for or against the proletariat, for or against the State or for or against nationalization. These are not pertinent questions for those theorists who study the informal economy. Whilst the resurgence of economic liberalism reinforces what one might think of as being the political Right - emphasized by the unison between the Microeconomists and the Free Market Dualists - the meaning of what it is to be 'on the Left' is ever more confusing - demonstrated by the different concerns and explanations of the structure of society proposed by the Feminists and Radicals. Furthermore, the dimension of the differences between the empiricist and universalist options cannot be reduced to the difference between Left and Right, a mistake made by some left wing thinkers who are of the opinion that all empirical research is, in some way, 'reactionary', or that it should be classed with neoclassical theories because of its ethnographic emphasis on the testimony of 'individuals'.

Thus, just as important as establishing what 'knowledge' of the informal economy has emerged from these debates is to establish the nature of the ideological disagreements surrounding them. The 'informal economy' as it is defined in this book, is a subject which has grown out of concerns relevant to what one might call the post '68 era. As such, approaches to it must be categorized in terms which are pertinent to this stage of social, economic and political development. It is the inductivist and perspectivist nature of the framework for interpretation used by this book which has allowed this to be revealed.

Notes

1. Even Marxist Feminists, in their analyses, implicitly agree that the most important variable in this calculation is gender. That is why they attempt to align 'women's' oppression to capitalism.
2. Interview conducted in Paris, 1987.

11 The informal economy: birthplace of a new concept of work?

Introduction

The notion of what constitutes 'work' is a facet of the socio-economic and political organization of a certain time and culture. Thus, one could suggest that a change in this definition is likely to occur when this socio-economic and political organization is undergoing change - or, at least, when certain people perceive change to be underway. As Pahl (1984, p. 17) suggests. 'whatever the reason, a society that falters when referring to something apparently so basic to human existence [as work] is likely to be changing in a fundamental way'. The idea that 'work equals employment' has been dominant in the social, political and theoretical arenas for many decades in France and in other industrialized countries. In asserting that 'work' is performed outside the formal structures of employment, or self-employment, the debates on the informal economy - in all their various guises - have reactivated the fundamental question of what work actually is, and in turn, how it should be organized, distributed and remunerated. Thus, as we have seen in Chapter 3, various social, economic, political and ideological changes have influenced the development of the debates on the informal economy, and these debates have given voice to these very changes.

In Chapter 1, I have set out two modes of evaluation and

assessment with which to analyse these French theorists of the informal economy. The aim of the first has been, on the one hand, to decide what 'knowledge' of the informal economy this mass of research and theorizing on the subject has provided and, on the other, to elicit the nature of the principal ideological divisions relevant to this subject area. The second aspect of this process of evaluation has been to reveal the specific ways in which the studies reviewed in this book undermine the 'traditional' concept of 'work' which equates it with employment. Consequently, the function of this chapter is first, to decide what impact these studies of the informal economy have had on this 'traditional' concept. Second, moreover, it is quite evident that not all social activity is 'work'. If it were, 'work' would no longer have an independent meaning. As we will see, in questioning the basic tenets of a conception of work that links it with employment, these theorists are raising problems about how to differentiate 'work' - formal or informal - from other types of activity. This issue, too, therefore will be examined here.

Discussing 'the informal economy' raises questions concerning three of the basic principles upon which the dominant, employment related conception of 'work' is based. The first principle dictates that 'work' is one's public duty to society; the second asserts that 'work' is an activity performed for deferred gratification; whilst the third states that 'work' must be an 'economic' activity. The following discussion will therefore be divided accordingly into three sections. I will begin with the question of 'work as an individual's public duty to society'.

Work as an individual's public duty to society

One of the justificatory stamps which gives an activity the right to be deemed 'work' is that it is registered and taxed by the State (see Chapter 1). This means that the activity is acknowledged in the public sphere as a source of wealth creation. Participation in such activity entitles individuals to protection by the State and to be treated as independent in terms of benefits, pensions and so forth.

However, theorists of the informal economy in general, and of the household division of labour in particular, question this notion that only formally recognized employment constitutes an individual's 'real' contribution to society, to wealth creation and to well-being. The crux of the argument put forward by the Feminists, for example, is that women's major contribution to society is made through their domestic labour and the production of children. Indeed, by acknowledging that one is dealing with a 'division of labour' when one examines the family, all the theorists who tackle this issue are implicitly revoking the notion that useful activity performed within the household is not 'work' simply because it is not directly remunerated. Even though such activity takes place within what one may term the 'private' sphere of the family and is not fully recognized by the State, it is still an individual's contribution to the well-being of society. Rose (1985, p. 139) highlights the fact that the recognition of women's domestic work role has implications for society as a whole because it questions the 'purpose, rewards, organization and standing [of work] as a human act'.

This notion that activities which are part of the private as well as the public sphere constitute 'work' has implications for academic disciplines, theoretizations of societal mechanisms and for practical matters. Taking the question of academic disciplines, the work of the Feminists on domestic labour, first of all, blurs the division between the 'sociology of the family' and the 'sociology of work'. The difference between these two sociological disciplines has traditionally been based on the opposition of the 'sociology of the public' as opposed to the 'sociology of the private' spheres. Indeed, the novelty of the Feminists is to have analyzed the family with concepts used in the sociology (or the political economy) of 'work'. Equally important, but this time for the discipline of economics in France, is the work of the Microeconomists. By using the terminology of the 'public' domain - economics - they are entering and attempting to explain the 'private'. In so doing, they obfuscate the differences between these two spheres. Cot & Lautier (1981, p. 100) explain that

> the new economics dissolves the object of the economic into the social - which then absorbs it into the private. The affirmed universality of economic rationality is believed to be the means of an unmediated unification of the whole of society.

In breaking down the hierarchy of the public over the private, the motivations of the Feminists and the Microeconomists are different. For the Feminists, declaring that 'work' takes place in the private sphere is part of their assertion that the 'private is political'. For the Microeconomists, it is all part of their assertion that the 'public' and 'private' can both be explained in terms of the 'universal' rules of economic rationality.

Furthermore, to consider the family and the work which

takes place within the family as a building block in the structure of society disrupts traditional Marxist theorizations, and in particular, their conceptions of what constitutes 'productive' activity. As Offe (1985, p. 133) explains, 'sociological inquiry into everyday life and the life-world ... represents an obvious break with the idea that the sphere of work has a relatively priviledged power to determine social consciousness and action'. Lastly, stressing the significance of informal activities raises the practical question, for example, of housewives' independent entitlement to pensions and social security payments by virtue of the contribution that their housework has made to society.

Work as an activity for deferred gratification

The notion that work is an activity which is not enjoyable in itself but produces a desired effect (and hence is something that you would prefer someone else to do for you) fits well with the organization of work within the social relations of employment. Indeed, this notion (that we could refer to as that of 'deferred gratification') is the pivot of a society based on employment. That is to say, one enters employment, not for the primary reason of the pleasure of participating in a particular activity, but for the monetary reward that it brings. This income is in turn used to finance consumption. Moreover, one sells one's time for money; for the most part, one does not sell the product of one's labours.

Thus, one can relate the dichotomy of production and consumption to the dichotomy of disagreable and agreable activity. On the one hand, there are activities which are in some way constrained. These are the activities carried out within the relationship of employment and constitute production. On the other hand, there are those activities which are freely chosen and freely undertaken: these activities occur outside employment and are deemed consumption or leisure. The wage is the compensation for the constraint and thus the disagreable activity which is experienced at work. Pleasure is therefore suspended in anticipation of the reward of purchasing market commodities (from which one obtains utility) and having access to 'free time' (on the whole, intended for the consumption of these goods and services). Leisure 'time', therefore, is also an output of production and a source of compensation for the constraint experienced at work.

Despite studies being carried out in such areas as 'the

leisure factor in employment' (see, for example, Parker, 1976), it is still commonly assumed that in 'working hours', whatever activity one is pursuing, it can be deemed 'work'. This is because one is selling one's time for a wage. Therefore, within working hours, one is available to serve the employer. Such a definition is not appropriate, however, to differentiate 'work' from 'leisure' in the informal sphere. The study of the informal economy completely blurs this neat distinction between these two categories of activity which is based on the difference between that time which is sold to an employer and that time which is one's own. Furthermore, the notion that leisure is pleasurable and work unpleasurable activity is also disturbed when one is dealing with the informal sphere because informal work is often 'useful' and 'enjoyable' at the same time.

This notion of informal work, therefore, poses a challenge to the principle that work is an activity carried out in anticipation of some kind of deferred gratification - normally, a wage. However, many theorists have great difficulty in developing a definition of work in the informal economy which differentiates it from leisure without denying, to a very great degree, the element of enjoyment and creativity to be found in such work. This is a specific problem for certain Empirical theorists, and in particular, those who attempt to measure the amount of 'work' carried out in the household. Such theorists require a working definition of domestic productive activity (including D.I.Y., gardening and repair work) in order to be able to evaluate the 'work' component of people's time. Chadeau [1], for example, explained that the criterion that she applies is that 'work is an activity which could be done by somebody else'. However, such a definition, far from undermining, actually reinforces the idea that pleasurable and unpleasurable activity can (and should) be separated, since it implies that if one enjoys the activity - and therefore would rather not have another person carry it out for one - then it is not, on objective grounds, informal work, but leisure.

Some theorists, however, have gone completely to the other extreme deeming all activity 'work'. For example, one of the main shortcomings of Becker's ground breaking Microeconomic theory was that in defining the household as a small production unit, he only allowed for the conception of leisure or the derivation of satisfaction from any activity, even sleeping, in the most abstract of terms. Becker considers all human activity to be 'work' in the sense that it constitutes a continuous input into the production of physical or psychological well-being of the individual.

However, in Becker's definition, work loses all meaning as a separate category of activity. Gronau (1977) revised Becker's model to take into account the leisure factor (this being a revision which has been taken up by Sofer & Lemmenicier). However, in so doing, Gronau was obliged to rely on the criterion of the possibility of the activity being undetaken by an 'employee' to describe work (as outlined above). Lemmenicier [2], for example, contended that 'there are activities which you can get someone else to do for you, and there are activities which you cannot get done by others, and this is the distinction between work and leisure'.

Nevertheless, the Radical theorists (and, to a lesser extent, the Free Market Dualists) are more persistent in trying to overcome the dichotomy of pleasurable and unpleasurable activity in their analyses, not only theoretically speaking, but practically as well (that is, in people's everyday experiences of work). The Radical theorists question the principle of performing stultifying work in return for the deferred gratification of the wage. In their opinion, productive activity should become a field where individuals exert their creative power and in which they can derive direct pleasure from 'work'. The Radical theorists, in their concept of 'autonomous' work, for example, do not attempt to distinguish between the 'leisure' and 'work' component of this type of activity. Aznar (1978, p. 69) goes so far as to develop a new vocabulary which does not distinguish between 'work' and 'leisure', but between creative, enjoyable work (which could also include 'active' leisure) as opposed to constrained activity of any type with which one cannot associate.

In sum, many of the theorists featured in this book proceed on the basis of the principle that 'work' is, in one way or another, a constrained activity which one performs for a reason other than the pleasure of participating in that activity. The novelty of such theorists, however, is to include a wider range of activities in the category of 'work'. In fact, only the Radicals attempt to dismantle this dichotomy.

Work as economic activity

Economics is central to French academic and political life, just as it is in other industrialized countries. This results from economics traditionally being the science of the formal, monetarized economy: in other words, the science of that sector of human activity which occupies a privileged position in society. With the rise of political economy, economics became not so much a methodology resting on a certain model of interaction, but a discipline circumscribed to a specific set of activities linked to production - namely, agriculture, extraction, manufacturing and later, the service sector - which take place within the social relations of employment. As Cornuel & Duriez [3] explained, there is (or was) a tendency for economics to study what could be deemed 'formal' and for sociology to be given the task of taking account of the rest. Thus traditionally, economics, in either its Marxist, neoclassical, or especially Keynsian guises, has not taken into account many of the activities which have been described as 'informal work' in this book.

To describe certain activities which take place outside employment, (and thus outside the spheres commonly recognized as those of the 'economy'), as 'work' or 'production' is to imply that these are 'economic' activities, both in the sense of being part of the 'economy' in practical terms as well as in the sense of being worthy of theoretical economic analysis. Indeed, the rise of the subject of the informal economy in France has not been the outcome of the discovery of a 'new' set of phenomena, but the introduction of subjects into the economic world which have previously lain within the realm of the social world. Perhaps with the exception of 'black market work' (which is a part, albeit undeclared, of the market), the activities discussed under this title by the theorists featured in this book have previously been analyzed using 'non economic' concepts by sociologists and anthropologists. For example, domestic work has been discussed in terms of women's gender role within the family, without mention of its 'economic' aspect, whilst activities which have been termed 'community' work are often examined under the guise of 'sociability'. Duriez [4], an economist, explains that before the early 'Eighties, there was not much research in economics on informal activities, but, he continues, 'in sociology there were a few things, but by definition, not on the economy, but on sociability, on the relationships between neighbours and the like'. Therefore, it is only when such activities become subjects for 'economic' analysis that they are deemed 'work'.

Thus, we have established that in developing the subject area of the informal economy, theorists have not been analysing new forms of activity. Rather, they have been redefining exisiting categories of activities as 'economic', 'productive', and therefore, 'work'. To conclude, then, questions will be asked concerning the significance of transposing the methodologies and concepts of macro- and microeconomics and Marxist political economy onto informal activities. On the one hand, these developments could be taken to be indicative of the strength of economics as a discipline and the symbolic power of money. On the other hand, however, one could interpret the promotion of informal activities in economic terms as constituting an initial assault on the domination of the formal, monetarized sphere in academic and political life.

On the one hand, therefore, the need to deem an activity 'economic' or to speak of it in terms of 'work' or 'production' in order to have it taken seriously is a sign of the strength of economics. The strength of the discipline of economics is most evident amongst the Microeconomist and Feminist theorists. Taking the example of the Feminists, we have seen that it was important for them to ground women's oppression - through the concept of domestic labour - in a material or economic base in order to lever up its theoretical status in a world where the ideological 'Left' is imbued with Marxism. Until recent times, Marxism did not treat 'informal' phenomena with the same degree of seriousness as it afforded to the 'formal' market arena. To render 'domestic labour' a serious issue for socialists, it has had to be brought into the realm of political economy. For example, Moynot [5] explained that in the 'Seventies, certain 'feminists' in the 'CGT' and the 'Pc' were looking for someone to write about women's position in relationship to domestic work. They chose Moynot, although he had no deeper an interest in the subject than many others, because he had a strong reputation as an economist within the socialist movement. Thus, his very interest in the subject in his capacity as a socialist economist would enhance the status of the field of women's work within the movement.

Equally, the macroeconomic work of Chadeau & Fouquet (1981), which, to recap, evaluates domestic work in terms of the G.N.P., bears witness to the strength of economics, and furthermore, the symbolic value of the G.N.P. and monetary representations of the economy in society. Statistics showing the enormous number of hours devoted to domestic labour, especially by women, are liable to surprise many, but in the battle for public and press attention, it is measurements in terms of money which triumph. Thus, the fact that feminists, such as Michel (1978), called for calculations of the G.D.P. of domestic labour to be carried out can only be interpreted as an expression of this power. Furthermore, the Microeconomists make no secret of the fact that their primary objective is to extend the model of rational economic choice to explain all human behaviour and not just that associated with the formal market. Analysing the family as a place of production is a by-product of this overall strategy to strengthen the arm of the discipline of economics.

On the other hand, however, deeming activities which are not undertaken within the social relations of employment to be 'work' can represent a challenge to the place of the economy in society and the validity of the science of economics. This is especially true of the effect of the analyses of the Radical and Free Market Dualist theorists who look outside the formal economic sphere for solutions to the various (economic) crises which they describe. In their analyses is to be found an implicit criticism of the power of the usual economic mechanisms to solve social problems. This engenders a certain degree of doubt as to the centrality of the 'economy' as the driving force of society. Indeed, the emergence of debates on the informal sector has been a source of confusion over what economic activity is and what the realm of economics should be.

In sum, then, the raising of the question of the informal economy is a symptom of a crisis in economics which goes hand in hand with the crisis in the economy. However, at one and the same time, to describe certain activities in economic terminology in order to have them taken seriously is the result of the domination of economics as a discipline and the economy as the driving forces in society.

Conclusions

Although all the theorists featured in this book challenge certain facets of that concept of work which links it solely to employment, on the whole, one cannot argue that a new, general conception of work has emerged from these debates. It appears, rather, that the debates on the informal economy in France have given rise more to confusion than clarity regarding our definition of which activities, in which social relations, constitute 'work' and which do not.

In part, this is a consequence of the disparate motives and methods of, and the diverging problems posed by the various groups of theorists involved in these debates. It is also a consequence of the fact that the currents of thought which have taken up the issue of the informal economy have remained marginal, having failed to introduce themselves into the 'mainstream' of politics or economics. Despite the great deal of discussion concerning the value, organization and distribution of employment between men and women, and between the employed and unemployed which has marked the last two decades, employment retains its position as the pivot of social organization and social theory alike. The informal economy remains, as a field of study, marginal and fragmented. Indeed, the present and future state of the debates concerning the informal economy in France will be the subject for discussion of the following and concluding chapter.

Notes

1. Interview conducted in Paris, April 1988.
2. Interview conducted in Paris, April 1988.
3. Interview conducted in Lille, April 1988.
4. Interview conducted in Lille, April 1988.
5. Interview conducted in Paris, April 1988.

12 Conclusions: the future of the informal economy in France

On reading this book, one could be forgiven for believing that the question of the informal economy has been high on the mainstream political agenda in France. Certainly, in the sense of government campaigns against black market work or demands for the State to provide better childcare facilities to allow women access to the labour market, there has been 'mainstream' interest. However, in the sense of the informal economy being accorded a role in solving unemployment, it has remained a marginal alternative. Gaspard [1] asserted that the subject of informal production had never been anything but a marginal current of thought in France which reached its peak in the early 'Eighties. He maintained that the majority in France never believed that the informal economy could constitute a way out of the crisis. For example, we have seen in Chapter 8 that Jacques Delors was a principal Radical theorist. However, as a leading member of the ruling 'Ps ' he has never managed to translate his personal interest in the 'third sector' and the 'revolution of freely chosen time' into socialist party policies. Instead, he has made these views public through the medium of an independent group - the 'Club Echanges et Projets'.

Indeed, taking the 1988 French presidential election campaign as a convenient concluding date for this study, one must assert that at the end of this period, the informal economy had not made its way into mainstream political discourse. As far as mainstream politics is concerned, the 'traditional' preoccupations which characterize the Left-Right split between political parties in France, and in the Western industrialized countries in general, do not include the informal economy. This, Greffe [2] argues, is for a fundamental reason. Politicians of the Right in France were preoccupied with the market during the 'Eighties, and still are, albeit to a lesser extent. Only private entreprise has been of importance to them. In Left wing party political circles, moreover, the dominant current has always been 'ultra interventionist'. Consequently, the discourse of the Left has not been very favourable to this 'anti-Statist' topic. Greffe explained that 'political debate in France is such that this subject cannot penetrate it'. Furthermore, the currents of political thought into which the issue of the informal economy has infiltrated have themselves remained marginalized from the central political arena. In particular, this is the case of the political ecology movement, despite the recent success in the 1989 European and municipal elections of Waechter's Greens. As Lalonde (1985, p. 87) suggested, in France, in contrast to West Germany, for example, 'there is no political force which sees social problems in terms of the conflicts and choices between industrial society, and, let us say, post industrial society'.

In Britain, in the latter half of the 'Eighties, one has became used to a political discourse informed by the more rapid economic growth which the country experienced in comparison with France. This discourse assumed that the recession was behind us, the free market having triumphed over the Nanny State. There appeared no need for innovations such as the informal economy to solve unemployment. However, far from the discourse being one of economic upturn as it was in Britain, in France, until 1988, at least, the discourse remained one of recession. In a round up of the major policy stances of the candidates in the Evénement du Jeudi magazine [3], it was said of unemployment that the three main candidates, Barre, Chirac and Mitterrand, were persuaded that it was impossible to soak up all the unemployed in new jobs in a matter of a few years. However, their answer to continued high unemployment has been to implement, or support, the provision of a minimum income (similar to Income Support) which precludes the recipient from working at all. In Britain, we have seen the effects of such a sytem in terms of the development of two populations, one, if anything, over employed and prospering, and one idle with no prospect of financial improvement of their position.

Perhaps whilst there was no such minimum income in France,

there was a chance that an innovative solution to the problem of the growing number of those unemployed and not receiving any benefits, which made use of the informal sector, was possible. However, this challenge does not seem to have been taken up. Moreover, after more than a decade of ruminations on 'new' patterns of work, even with a Prime Minister, Michel Rocard, who was motivated by self-mangement ideas, as well as Jacques Delors as part of the ruling party, government policy does not appear to have evolved in this direction. It seems that the ideal of full employment lives on in the national psyche. Indeed, if innovation there has been in the world of work in France, it has taken the form of the extension of 'flexible', contract and agency working known as 'les petits boulots'. However, the flexibility inherent in innovations of this type benefit the employers first and foremost. It has little or nothing to do with a 'revolution of freely chosen time' which would favour the workforce.

This, then, is the position to date of the issue of the informal economy in France. I will now proceed to discuss how the subject has evolved to this point. Such a discussion of the history of the debates will open the door to an exploration of the future of the informal economy debates in France.

To begin this summing up of the development of the debates on the informal economy in France, I will examine the study of domestic work and the household division of labour. First of all, we will discuss the position reached by the Microecononists. These theorists have testified to feeling relatively isolated from other academics working both within this subject area and within their own discipline. This is because the majority of those working on the economy of the family are Feminists whilst within the discipline of economics in general, and even within its Microeconomic wing, the family is viewed as a 'soft' subject and not taken entirely seriously. In fact, both Lemmenicier and Sofer have moved recently into other areas of study. [4] Furthermore, although economic liberalism and neoclassical economics has gained ground on the Right, politically speaking, people such as Lemmenicier have remained marginal. This is because they have taken up currents of thought from abroad before they entered the mainstream in France. In so doing, they have taken these, perhaps in a spirit of avant-garde defiance, to lengths which others perhaps find rather unacceptable. However, all that said, it must be remembered that the Beckerian microeconomic approach (which assumes that the household is a unit of production) is applied to many subjects. Therefore, in all such studies, domestic activity appears as a factor of production as opposed to a factor of consumption.

As has been mentioned above, it is the Feminist theorists who have been dominant in the field of study of the household division of labour in France (in comparison with the Microeconomists). These Feminist debates originally concerned themselves with the theoretical status of domestic labour as the materialist basis of women's oppression. As this highly economistic and functionalist argument began to appear a little circular, certain theorists attempted to transcend its restrictions by returning to a more 'social' and 'empirical' analysis of domestic work. During the past few years, no new research specifically on domestic production has been published. As Kartchevsky [5] pointed out, in the 'Eighties, domestic work as such has not been a major subject for research, but it forms the background to many studies, primarily those which concern themselves with the relationship between professional work life and familial structure. She suggested that the evolution of the subject area has led to domestic work being accepted as a factor to be incorporated in discussing women's relationship to paid work, union activity and to men and power instead of being the object of heated feminist debate in itself.

Thus, it should not be thought that domestic work is no longer of interest at all in France. Instead, the development of the Feminist analysis of domestic work must be examined with reference to the development of feminism as a whole. Over the last twenty years, feminist research has become increasingly acceptable in academic circles. For instance, Ferrand [6] cites the example that the 'Journées de la Société française de sociologie' (conference of the French sociological society) in 1980 were devoted to the subject of familial institutions and women's work. This she interprets as a sign that the variable of gender was becoming an accepted part of sociological research in general. Thus, as the gender variable has become an increasingly universal concern, so has the variable of domestic work become a factor to be included in analyses in an ever wider range of subjects.

Nonetheless, there have been new departures in this area recently. For example, a study on 'Production Domestique' is underway at the moment. This is a new collaborative project between the 'CNRS ' and 'INSEE'. 'INSEE' is carrying out various quantitative studies of the subject whilst the 'CNRS' teams are carrying out more finely targeted qualitative studies. This unprecedented collaboration ensued from a conference organized in 1986 by 'INSEE' and the 'CNRS' on domestic production. This intitiative brings together, for example, Christine Delphy, explicit in her feminist views, with the more descriptive and quantitative research produced by and associated with 'INSEE'. Indeed, the initiative itself is an example of how the study of domestic labour is entering a post polemic, and maybe, a 'post feminist' era.

Furthermore, interest in statistical studies of domestic work no longer comes purely from Feminist sources. Roy [7] explained that latterly, INSEE had received requests for information on domestic work both from the 'Commissariat Général du Plan' and from private market research organizations. Indeed, they wanted statistics concerning the actual volume of domestic production being realized in the country rather than its division of labour since their interest lies in obtaining information on the global pattern of economic activity in the country. Roy [8] added that if you look at the new countries which are carrying out time-budget studies, and examining domestic activity on the basis of them, they often do so at the request of the national accounts offices who want a more overall picture of the economic activity which takes place in their country.

Turning our attention to the question of the role of the informal economy in the future of work, in the early 'Eighties, intellectuals of both Left and Right placed great hope on the informal sector as a solution to the unemployment crisis. For those on the 'Left', these hopes were intensified by the accession to power of the Socialists and Communists in 1981. As Gaudin & Schiray (1982, p. 1) explain, it was in the period of the late 'Seventies and early 'Eighties that 'the subject appeared in its entirety'. Thus, the concept of an 'informal economy', although present in currents of thought before that time, as I have shown, crystallized in France at the beginning of the 'Eighties. Indeed, a series of conferences were held on the subject during this period. These included 'Journées d'études sur l'économie informelle' (study day on the informal economy) at the 'Maison des sciences de l'homme', on 30th May, 1980 and the international conference on 'L'économie cachée, conflits sociaux et l'avenir des sociétés industrielles' (the hidden economy: social conflicts and the future of industrial societies), on 25-28th November 1982. Further still, in July 1983, 'ENA ' ('Ecole Nationale d'Administration': a prestigious higher eduction establishment) took the 'underground economy' as the subject for its annual seminar. [9]

However, several factors intervened to bring about a relative decline in interest in the subject in the last four to five years, this being accompanied by a certain pessimism about the possibilities of the informal economy to deliver what had been expected of it. First, empirical researchers pointed out that the unemployed were not reverting to the informal economy to improve their standard of living. The reasons given for this included lack of income with which to buy access to materials and tools; lack of social networks; and lack of skills. Greffe [10] explained that 'people had invested a lot in the idea of the informal economy' and their disappointment in finding that it was not fulfilling the role which they had hoped for it led them to lose interest. That is, when certain pieces of empirical research revealed that the link between unemployment and informal work was not as straight forward as some had imagined, that the reasons behind people performing, for example, black market work were only ambiguously 'revolutionary' or that the relationship of dependence of the informal on the formal economy is stronger than many wanted to acknowledge, interest waned in some, and changed tack in other quarters.

Second, it was not only the results of empirical studies which led to this pessimism. Evidence of the 'actual' consequences of unemployment was becoming only too apparent on the streets of French cities by the mid 'Eighties. The unemployed have apparently not created for themselves a marginal, or alternative economy in which they may seek refuge from poverty, or even destitution. The 'dual society' of which Michel Houillon, for example, in 1987 spoke, was one which divides between those in employment or receiving unemployment benefit and those who had reached the end of their entitlement to benefit, the latter group representing forty per cent of all those registered as seeking employment in France in 1986. These constitute the class of the 'new poor'. Houillon (1987, p. 33) asks

> is it not the case that post industrial society, object of so many dreams, is threatening to become dominated, in fact, by the coexistence of ostentatious luxury and fragile fortunes and the poverty of an enormous 'social scrapheap': the universe of the jobless, excluded from all forms of social assistance.

Roustang (1987), Aznar (1987) and Gorz (1986) are the last to have published articles suggesting 'informal' activity as a solution to unemployment. However, these latest works do not blithely expect that the unemployed will create their own productive and convivial sector as perhaps some of the earlier works on this topic have done. Foudi [11] explained that

> this type of research has changed in character ... I do

> not pretend that it was our study that brought this about, but afterwards, no one was interested in the development - or lack of it - of the informal economy amongst groups of unemployed ... and if you look at what Gorz is working on now, you will see that it is the minimum income which interests him.

The consequences of these developments seem to be that the informal sector is treated less as a substitute to the formal and more as a adjunct to it. Greffe [12] explained that in his reflections on the subject, he came to the conclusion that the 'informal economy can only progress along with the formal economy' because they are interdependent. Indeed, Roustang (1987) and Stoclet (1983) concern themselves with the 'informal' input into formal production. Roustang (Laboratoire d'Economie de Sociologie du Travail, CNRS report, 1987, p. 117-118) explains

> A systematic study of the changing relations between the market, the non market, the associative and the domestic sectors would be very interesting and is cruelly lacking. The evolution of self assembly, the importance of self build housing or, at least, do-it-yourself finishing or improvements, wood burning stoves and the generalization of self sevice are just a few examples, the consequences of which are very important for employment and the distribution of activities.

Furthermore, Schiray, Passaris & Sachs (all part of the research group of 'CIRED', (see CNRS report, 1986) want to examine this interaction empirically. Passaris is at present, for example, engaged in field studies in Chartres whose aim is to experiment with and refine methods of understanding the urban economy which take into account informal work. He is examining the interdependence of informal work and the public and private formal economies and asking how local policies for development could be improved by recognizing the potential contribution of informal provision. It should also be noted that 'CIRED' is attempting to establish a European Programme on the impacts of new communications technologies on the domestic economy and the articulation between informal and formal sectors. Equally, Gaspard [13] intends to collaborate with Chadeau & Fouquet to use the 1986 time-budget study to calculate the Gross 'Domestic' product once more to allow a comparison with the figures arrived at on the basis of the 1975 time-budget study. He wants to see if there has been 'growth' in this sector, and more specifically, to see if the growth rate in domestic production has been higher than the official growth rate (average 2 to 2½ per cent) of the formal economy over the same period.

In sum, then, we can conclude that the very notion of the informal economy is politically and economically disturbing. This is because mainstream politics concerns itself with the best way to run the 'formal' economy and what to do with the wealth created by it. However, the discussion of the informal economy alone cannot and has not brought about far-reaching change in the way that we work. The acceptance of informal activities as 'work' in various contexts has not bowled over the world of theoretical, political and economic discourse in France because the ideological currents of which it is a part have remained marginal. However, it cannot be denied that the informal economy has become a variable which is increasingly taken into account in a wide range of social and economic equations within the French academic and intellectual community.

Notes

1. Interview conducted in Paris, April 1988. Gaspard was speaking in his role as researcher at the 'Commissariat Général du Plan' who had headed a report in 1983 on Conditions de Vie which took a great interest especially in domestic production.
2. Interview conducted in Paris, April 1987.
3. 21-27th April, 1988, p.62.
4. Interviews were carried out with both Lemmenicier, Paris, April 1988 and Sofer, Orléans, April 1988.
5. Interview conducted in Paris, April 1987.
6. Comments made at a meeting of the 'Cercle Flora Tristan' on the book Le sexe du travail (1984). Reported in the proceedings from this meeting: Cercle Flora Tristan: Le sexe du travail', 1984, p.8.
7. Interview conducted in Paris, April 1988.
8. As above
9. This seminar concerns all the E.N.A. students who are invited to present papers on certain themes which they work on throughout the year. However, this was just after the socialists got into power and Archambault (discussion, 1987) said that since then, the themes have become more classical again.
10. Interview conducted in Paris, April 1987.
11. Interview conducted in Lille, April 1988.
12. Interview conducted in Paris, April 1987.
13. Interview conducted in Paris, April 1988.

Bibliography

ADRET (1977), Travailler deux heures par jour, Seuil, Paris.

Alzon, C. (1973), La femme potiche et la femme bonniche: pouvoir bourgeois et pouvoir mâle, Maspéro, Paris.

Amado, J. & Stoffaes, C. (1980), 'Vers une socio-économie duale' in Danzin, A., Boublil. A. & Lagarde, J. La société française et la technologie, Documentation Française, Paris.

Archambault, E. (1985), 'Associations et bénévolat', Cahiers Français, no. 221.

Aznar, G. (1978), Non aux loisirs, non à la retraite, Galilée, Paris.

Aznar, G. (1981), Tous à mi-temps, ou le scénario bleu, Seuil, Paris.

Aznar, G. (1987), 'La société des trois revenus: scenario prospectif', Futuribles, no. 109.

Bancal,J. (1967), Oeuvres choisies de Proudhon, Gallimard, Paris.

Barthe, M.-A. (1985a), Chomeurs et 'economie non officielle', Plan, construction et habitat, Paris.

Barthe, M.A. (1985b), 'Chomage, travail au noir et entraide familial', Consommation, no. 3.

Barthelemy, P. (1982), 'Travail au noir et économie souterraine: un état de la recherche', Travail et emploi, no. 12.

Becker, G.S. (1965), 'A theory of allocation of time', Economic Journal, no. 75.
Becker, G.S. (1976), The economic approach to human behaviour, University of Chicago Press, Chicago.
Becker, G.S. (1981), A treatise on the family, Harvard University Press, Cambridge, Mass..
Becker, G.S. (1985), 'Human capital, effort and the sexual division of labour', Journal of labour economics, no. 3, vol. 1 (2), pp. 333-58.
Bell, D. (1973), The coming of post-industrial society, Basic Books, New York.
Bosquet, M. (1980), 'Le chemin de la liberté', Le Nouvel Observateur, no. 812 (2/6/80), pp. 40-41.
Bouillaguet-Bernard, P. & Gauvin, A. (1988), 'The effects of the recession on female participation in the labour force', in J. Rubery (ed), Women and the recession, RKP, London.
Bouniol, M. (1980), Le travail au noir, Chambre de commerce et d'industrie de Paris, 14th February.
Bourgeois, F., Brener, J., Chabaud, D., Cot, A., Fougeyrollas, D., Haicault, M. & Kartchevsky, A. (1978), 'Travail domestique et famille du capitalisme', Critiques de l'économie politique, no. 3, pp. 3-23.
Brown, R. (1984), 'Work: past, present and future', in K. Thompson, Work, employment and unemployment, Open University Press, Milton Keynes.
Cahiers francais (1985), 'L'économie sociale: entre étatisation et capitalisme', no. 221.
Cathelat, B. (1981), 'Les styles de vie', Futuribles, no. 43, April.
Centre national de volontariat (1980), Le travail dans les associations: propositions pour une quantification, Paris.
Cercle Flora Tristan (1984), Le sexe du travail, no. 9.
Cercle Flora Tristan (1986), La production d'enfants une production économique essentielle des femmes, no. 18.
Chabaud, D. Fougeyrollas, D. & Sonthonnax, F. (1985), Espace et temps du travail domestique, Méridiens, Paris.
Chadeau, A. & Fouquet, A. (1981), 'Peut-on mesurer le travail domestique?', Economie et statistique, no. 136, pp. 29-42.
Chadeau, A. & Roy, C. (1986), Relating households' final consumption to household activities, Paper given at the annual conference of the International association for research in income and wealth, Noordwijkerhout, Netherlands, 25-31 August.
Chalvon Demersay, S. (1982), 'La répartition des tâches ménagères chez les concubins du XIVe arrondissement', Cahiers de l'OCS, no. 6, CNRS, Paris.

Chambre de commerce et de l'industrie de Paris (1980), 'Enquêtes sur le travail noir', Etudes et documents, no. 12.

Chastand, S. (1982), 'Le travail domestique des femmes mariées selon la catégorie socio-professionnelle', Economie et statistique, no. 142.

Combes, D. & Haicault, M. (1984), 'Production et reproduction, rapports sociaux de sexes et de classes', in Le sexe du travail, Presses Universitaires de Grenoble, Grenoble, pp. 155-174.

Commissariat général du Plan (1983), Comment vivrons-nous demain?, Documentation française, Paris.

Conseil Economique et Social (1983), Le travail clandestin, Journal officiel de la République française, February.

Conti, L. (1978), Qu'est-ce que l'écologie?', Maspéro, Paris.

Cornuel, D. & Duriez, ,B. (1985), 'Local exchange and State intervention', in Redclift & Mingione (eds) Beyond employment, Basil Blackwell, Oxford.

Cot, A. & Lautier, B. (1981), 'La frontière du capital', Non! Repères pour le socialisme, no. 9. (Sept. - Oct).

Dalla Costa, M. & James, S. (1972), The power of women and the subversion of the community, Falling Wall, Bristol.

Debout, S. (1978), L'utopie de Charles Fourier, Payot, Paris.

Delorozoy, R. (1980), Le travail clandestin, Report from the 'Assemblée permanente des Chambres de commerce d'industrie de Paris', February.

Delors, J. (1979), 'Le troisième secteur: le travail au-delà de l'emploi', Autremement, no. 20, pp. 147-152.

Delors, J. & Echanges et projets (1980), La révolution du temps choisi, Albin Michel, Paris.

Delors, J. & Foucauld, J-B., (1980), 'Contre la société duale: la maîtrise de son temps', Le Monde, 26th October.

Delors, J. & Gaudin, J. (1979), 'Pour la création d'un troisième secteur', Echanges et projets, no. 17.

Delphy, C. (1978), 'Travail ménager ou travail domestique?', in Michel, A. La femme dans la société marchande, Presses Universitaires de France, Paris, pp. 39-54.

Delphy, C. (1984), Close to home, Hutchinson, London.

Des Femmes en Mouvement Hebdo (1981), 'A la maison, les femmes travaillent de 28-73 heures par semaine', no. 68, 27th November.

Drevet, D. (1977), 'Quel travail, quel salaire', Revue d'en face, no. 2.

Dubost, F. (1981), 'Les nouveaux usages du jardin', in J-D Reynaud, Français, qui êtes vous?, Documentation Française, Paris.

Duchen, C. (1986), Feminism in France from May '68 to Mitterrand, Routledge, London.
Dupont, C. (1970), 'L'ennemi principal', Partisans, no. 54-55.
Duverger, M. (1980), 'Les chemins de l'illusion', Le Monde, 27th March, p. 2.
Elles Voient Rouge (1981), Féminisme et marxisme, Tierce, Paris.
Engels, F. (1972), The origin of the family, private property and the State, Lawrence & Wishart, London.
Eurostat (1984), Working time statistics: methods and measurements in the European community, Brussels.
Faugere, J-P., (1980), 'L'allocation du temps entre travail domestique et travail marchand: discussion autour d'un modèle', Revue économique, vol. 31, no. 2.
Feige, L. (1982), 'Le malaise de la macroéconomie et l'économie invisible', Consommation, no. 2.
Forse, M. (1984), 'Les créations d'associations: un indicateur de changement social', Observations et diagnostiques économiques, no. 6.
Foudi, R., Stankiewicz, F. & Vanecloo, N. (1982), 'Chomeurs et économie informelle', Cahiers de l'observation du changement social et culturel, vol. 17, Ed. du CNRS, Paris.
Fourastie, J. (1979), Les trente glorieuses, Fayard, Paris.
Fournier, G., Glaude, M. & Raynaud, E. (1984), 'Familles ouvrières et chômage: des budgets difficilement compressibles', Economie et statistique, no. 170.
Frankel, B. (1987), Post-industrial utopians, Methuen, London.
Friedman, G. (1966), Sept études sur l'homme et la technique; le pourquoi et le pour quoi de notre civilisation technique, Denoel/Gonthier, Paris.
Friedman, Y. (1978), 'Le secteur 'D' de l'économie, Futuribles, no. 15, p. 331.
Friedman, Y. (1982), 'L'art de la survie', Autogestions, no. 8-9, pp. 89-95.
Froger, J. & Peyraut, J. (1982), Le couple et la répartition des tâches, Paper given at conference 'Femmes, féminisme, recherche', Toulouse.
Gaudin, J. & Schiray, M. (1982), L'économie cachée: taxinomie, CIRED working paper, Paris.
Gaudin, J. & Schiray, M. (1984), 'L'économie cachée en France: état du débat et bilan des travaux', Revue économique, no. 4.

Gaudin, J. & Greffe, X. (1980), 'Partage du travail et nouveau mode de développement, Droit social, no. 1, pp. 86-99.
Geoghan, V. (1987), Utopianism and Marxism, Methuen, London.
Girard, A. & Bastide, H. (1959), 'Le budget-temps de la femme mariée à la campagne', Population, Oct.-Dec.
Glaude, M. & de Singly, F. (1986), 'L'organisation domestique: pouvoir et négociation', Economie et statistique, no. 187, pp. 3-30.
Godard, F. (1985), 'How do ways of life change?', in N.Redclift & E.Mingione, Beyond employment, Basil Blackwell, Oxford.
Godchau, J-F. (1970), 'La lutte de sexes ou lutte de classes', Partisans, no. 54-55.
Gorz, A. (1978), Ecologie et politique, Seuil, Paris.
Gorz, A. (1982a), A farewell to the working class, Pluto, London.
Gorz, A. (1982b), 'La conquête de l'autonomie', Autogestions, no. 8-9. pp. 187-203.
Gorz, A. (1985), Paths to paradise: on the liberation from work, Pluto, London.
Gorz, A. (1986), 'Qui ne travaille mangera quand-même', Futuribles, no. 101, pp. 56-73.
Granstedt, I. (1980), L'impasse industrielle, Seuil, Paris.
Greffe, X. (1981), 'L'économie non officielle', Consommation, no. 3.
Grimler, G. & Roy, C. (1987), 'Les emplois du temps en France en 1985-6', Premiers résultats, no. 100, Collections de l'INSEE.
Gronau, R. (1977), 'Leisure, home production and work: the theory of the allocation of time revisited', Journal of political economy, no. 85.
Grossin, W (1984), 'Temps de travail et temps libres', Revue française des affaires sociales', no. 2, pp. 9-20.
Guilbert, M., Lowit, N. & Creusen, J. (1967), 'Les budgets-temps et l'étude de la vie quotidienne', Revue française de sociologie, April-June.
Guillaumin, C. (1978), 'Pratique du pouvoir et idée de nature', Questions féministes, no. 2.
Gutmann, P.M. (1977), 'The subterranean economy', Financial analysts' journal, Nov-Dec.
Haicault, M. (1980), 'Sexe, salaire, famille", Annales de l'université de Toulouse - Le Mirail, vol. 16, no. 4.
Haicault, M. (1984), 'La gestion ordinaire de la vie en deux', Sociologie du travail, no. 3.
Heerjte, A. & Barthelemy, P. (1984), L'économie souterraine, Economica, Paris.

Heran, F. (1987), 'Comment les Français voisinent', Economie et statistique, January, pp. 43-59.
Houillon, M. (1987), 'Le retour des misérables. La société duale en question', Futuribles, no. 107, pp. 33-40.
Insoumise collective (1977), Le foyer de l'insurrection, Geneva.
Interfuturs (1979), Face aux futurs, OECD, Paris.
Jouvenel, H. de (1980), 'Sur l'évolution des mentalités', Futuribles, no. 37, pp. 3-14.
Kartchevsky, A. & Bourgeois, F. (1983), Famille: object économique, sujet social, Doctoral thesis, Univ. Paris X.
Kende, P. (1975), 'Vers une évaluation de la consommation réelle des ménages', Consommation, no. 2.
Kende, P. (1978), 'Les biens et les services autoproduits dans la consommation des ménages français', in Michel, A. (ed.) La femme dans la société marchande, Presses Universitaires de France, Paris, pp. 225-244.
Klatzmann, R. (1979), 'Le travail noir', Futuribles, no. 26, pp. 43-59.
Lae, J. (1987), Travailler au noir, Research report, Commissariat général du plan, Paris.
Lalonde, B. (1985), 'Le mouvement écologique. Entre la tentation politique et le modernisme', Futuribles, no. 89, pp. 87-90.
Lalonde, B. & Simmonet, D. (1978), Quand vous voudrez, Pauvert, Paris.
Landier, H. (1981), Demain: quels syndicats?, Livre de poche, Paris.
Lautier, B. (1977), 'Formes de production capitaliste et procès de travail domestique', Critiques de l'économie politique, no. 1
Lebars, J-J., Camus, G., Cosset, A. & Nottola, Y. (1980), Essai d'analyse des causes socio-économiques du développement du travail au noir dans les métiers bâtiment, SEDES-CORDES, Paris.
Lebreton, P. (1978), L'Ex-croissance: les chemins de l'écologisme, Denoel, Paris.
Lecaillon, J. & Vernieres, M. (1974), Théorie du salaire, Cujas, Paris.
Legrain, C. (1982), 'L'économie informelle à Grand Failly', Cahiers de l'OCS, no. 7, CNRS, Paris.
Lemarche, S. Rogers ,C. & Karnoouh, C. (1970), Paysans, femmes et citoyens.
Lemel, Y. (1984), 'Le sociologue des pratiques du quotidien entre l'approche ethnographique et l'enquête statistique', Economie et statistique, July-Aug.

Lemmenicier, B. (1980), 'La spécialisation des rôles conjugaux. Les gains du mariage et la perspective du divorce', Consommation, no. 1, pp. 27-72.
Lemmenicier, B. (1988), Le marché du mariage et de la famille, Presses Universitaires de France, Paris.
Lemmenicier, B. & Levy-Garboua, L. (1981), 'L'arbitrage autarcie-marché: une explication du travail féminin', Consommation, no. 2.
Le Net, M. & Werquin, J. (1985), Le volontariat: aspects sociaux, économiques et politiques en France et dans le monde, Notes et Etudes Documentaires, no. 4780, Documentation française, Paris.
Llemann, A. (1985), 'Le travail à temps partiel de 1978 à 1983', Travail et emploi, no. 26, December.
Lukes, S. (1982), 'Relativism in its place', in M. Hollis & S. Lukes (eds.), Rationality and relativism, Basil Blackwell, Oxford.
Mallet, S. (1969), La nouvelle classe ouvrière, Seuil, Paris.
Marks, E. & Courtivron, I.de (eds.) (1980), New French feminisms: an anthology, Harvester, Brighton.
Mauss, M. (1973), 'Essai sur le don: forme et raison de l'échange dans les sociétés archaïques', Sociologie et anthropologie, Presses Universitaires de France, Paris.
Meadows, D.H., Meadows, D.L., Randers, J. & Behrens, W.W. (1972), Limits to growth, Pan, London.
Meillassoux, C. (1981), Maidens, meal and money: capitalism and the domestic economy, Cambridge University Press, Cambridge.
Mendras, H. & Stankiewicz, F. (1986), 'Diversités locales de l'économie non comptabilisée', L'esprit des lieux, Ed. du CNRS, Paris.
Metton, J. (1979), Les moyens à mettre en oeuvre pour lutter contre le travail clandestin, Federation du Batiment.
Michel, A. (ed.) (1978), La femme dans la société marchande, Presses Universitaires de France, Paris.
Minc, A. (1980), 'Le chômage et l'économie souterraine', Le débat, no. 2, pp. 3-14.
Minc, A. (1982), L'après-crise a commencé, Gallimard, Paris.
Moi, T. (ed) (1987), French feminist thought: politics, patriarchy and sexual difference,Basil Blackwell, Oxford.
Moynot, J-L. (1978), 'La force de travail féminine dans la production et la société', in Centre d'études et de la recherche marxistes, La condition féminine, Ed. Sociales, pp. 131-184.
Offe, C. (1985), 'New social movements: challenging the boundaries of institutional politics', Social research, vol. 52, no. 4, pp. 830-880.

Pahl ,R. (1984), Divisions of labour, Basil Blackwell, Oxford.

Parker, S. (1976), The sociology of leisure, Allen & Unwin, London.

Rabier, J. (1978), Les attitudes de la population active à l'égard des perspectives de la retraite, EEC, Brussels.

Rosanvallon, P., (1977) 'Ecologie et liberté', Le nouvel observateur, 13th June, pp. 76-7.

Rosanvallon, P., (1980) 'Le développement de l'économie souterraine et l'avenir des sociétés indutrielles', Le débat, no. 2.

Rose, M. (1979), Servants of post-industrial power? Sociologie du travail in modern France, Macmillan, Basingstoke.

Rose, M. (1985), Re-working the work ethic, Batsford, London.

Rousse, H. & Roy, C. (1981), 'Activités ménagères et cycle de vie', Economie et statistique, no. 131.

Roustang, G. (1982), Le travail autrement, travail et mode de vie, Dunod, Paris.

Roustang, G. (1987), L'emploi: un choix de société, Syros, Paris.

Roy, C. (1981), 'Les activités quotidiennes des Français: différences entre catégories sociales', Données sociales.

Sachs, I (1980), 'La crise actuelle et les structures de consommation', Futuribles, no. 32, pp. 59-64.

Sachs, I. (1983), La crise, le progrès technique et l'économie cachée, CIRED working paper.

Sahlins, M. (1976), Age de pierre, age d'abondance, Gallimard, Paris.

Sauvy, A. (1984), Le travail noir et l'économie de demain, Calmann-Levy, Paris.

Scardigli, V. (1981), 'La durée du travail: quelques comparaisons', Futuribles, no. 48, pp. 19-25.

Schiray, M. & Vinaver, K. (1980), 'Consommation, usages du temps et styles de vie', Futuribles, no. 32, pp. 65-70.

Sofer, C. (1985), La division du travail entre hommes et femmes, Economica, Paris.

SOFRES (1980), 'Economie et perception du temps de travail', Temps et emploi, January.

Soupa, J. (1971), Le travail clandestin, Conseil Economique et Social, May.

Stoclet, D. (1983), 'Les transferts entre marchand et domestique. Travail des femmes - loisirs des hommes', Observations et diagnostics économiques, February.

Stoléru, L. (1979), 'Le travail au noir hors-la-loi', Futuribles, no. 26.

Stoléru, L. (1982), La France à deux vitesses, Flammarion, Paris.

Stoetzel, J. (1948), 'Une étude des budgets-temps des femmes dans les agglomérations urbaines', Populations, Jan.-March.

Tanzi, V. (1982),The underground economy in the United States and abroad, Lexington Books.

Testard, A. (1982), 'Le travail domestique, la force de travail et les femmes', Les temps modernes, no. 426, pp. 1139-1185.

Tievant, S. (1982), 'Vivre autrement: échanges et sociabilité en ville nouvelle', Cahiers de l'OCS, vol 6.

Touraine, A. (1987), The workers' movement, Cambridge University Press, Cambridge.

Troimphe, A. & Caye,C. (1982), 'L'action sociale volontaire en France', Revue des affaires sociales, no. 2.

Vitek, J. (1977), Le travail noir ... un frein à l'emploi, Bureau International du Travail, Geneva.

Williams, C.C. (1988), Examining the nature of domestic labour, Avebury, Aldershot.

Les écologistes présentés par eux-mêmes, Verviers, Marabout. (1977).

Le sexe du travail, (1984), Presses Universitaires de Grenoble, Grenoble.